INSIGHT GUIDES

The world's largest collection of visual travel guides

BaRBaDOS

Edited by Rachel Wilder
Photography by Tony Arruza
Editorial Director: Brian Bell

APA PUBLICATIONS
Part of the Langenscheidt Publishing Group

Everyone, it seems, knows about the glorious sun, clean sand and spectacular sea that mark Barbados. But what about the people of this island in the Caribbean Sea? Their history, their music, their language?

Such a destination lends itself perfectly to the approach taken by the *Insight Guides* series, created in 1970 by **Hans Höfer**, founder of Apa Publications. In the series with almost 200 titles each book encourages readers to celebrate the essence of a place rather than try to tailor it to their expectations and is edited in the belief that, without insight into a people's character and culture, travel narrows rather than broadens the mind.

Insight Guide: Barbados is carefully structured: the first section covers the island's history, and people. A section of essays then provides background on aspects of the island's culture. The main Places section provides a comprehensive run-down on the things worth seeing and doing. Finally, a comprehensive listings section contains useful addresses, telephone numbers and opening times.

For the original volume, New York-based writer-editor **Rachel Wilder**, who visited Barbados regularly for more than 20 years, assembled the best local writers to explain the "Bajan" culture to the uninitiated. She found, with the help of the Barbados Board of Tourism in New York, one of the world's most talented travel photographers: Cuban-born **Tony Arruza**. Florida-based Arruza is an avid surfer and surfing photographer with a natural talent for documenting people in their surroundings. He also wrote the feature "A Day in the Life of a Fisherman".

Included on the expert team of local writers was prominent historian **Trevor G. Marshall**, a research officer at the National Cultural Foundation in Barbados and a lecturer on the history of the Caribbean at the island's

Wilder & Arruza

Community College. Marshall contributed regularly to *The Bajan* magazine, the *Advocate News*, and also for *Contact*, a regional newspaper. He is also the co-author of the book *Folk Songs of Barbados*.

Marshall was educated at the University of the West Indies and at the University of Waterloo, Ontario, Canada. His articles in this guide include *After Emancipation; All O' We Is Bajan*; *A Ship on Land?*, which looks at the ethnic mix on the island; *Bajans, Come Back to Calypso!* about the roots of Bajan music; and, *A Very Sweet Thing: The Story of Rum*.

Mark DaCosta Alleyne was a Rhodes Scholar in International Relations at Oxford University and he holds a BA in journalism from Howard University, Washington DC. Now based in Chicago, Alleyne worked as a radio broadcaster, newspaper writer and reporter and was the features editor for *The Bajan* magazine. He wrote *The South* and *The North and East*.

Annette L. Trotman, is a former secondary school English, Foreign Languages and drama teacher. She was the cultural officer responsible for Theatre Arts at the National Cultural Foundation when first involved with the project. Trotman is a freelance film and theater consultant and journalist, who wrote the weekly feature, *Bajan Folkways* for the *Nation* newspaper. Her chapter is *Dance and Drama: Street Beats, Stage Treats*.

Addinton Forde, a former English teacher who holds a BA from the University of the West Indies, was also a cultural officer at the National Cultural Foundation. He specializes in Bajan folk traditions. He was also a calypso singer and a writer for the *Nation*. He wrote *A Religious Mosaic* and *The Standpipe*; and provided hundreds of traditional Bajan sayings and their translations from which we culled *40 Bajan Proverbs*.

Tony Cozier is one of the island's

Marshall

Alleyne

Forde

Cozier

foremost sportswriters. While writing his feature he was also working as the sports editor of the *Sunday Sun*, and as the Barbados correspondent for the London *Financial Times*. He has been a radio and TV commentator for cricket since 1963 and has worked for radio stations in England, Australia, New Zealand and India. Cozier was educated at Carleton University in Ottawa, Canada, and is author of the book *The West Indies: 50 Years of Test Cricket*. Appropriately, Cozier contributed the feature, *Cricket: The National Religion*.

John Wickham, a noted fiction writer, was the editor of the respected literary magazine *Bim*, first published in Barbados in 1942 and is on the staff of the *Nation*. He provided the introduction for this guidebook.

Christine Barrow was a lecturer in sociology at the University of the West Indies. Born in England, she moved to Barbados in 1969. Barrow holds a PhD in social anthropology from the University of Sussex. Her contributions to the book are based on several periods of anthropological field work in Barbadian villages. Her piece on family life is *Like Family To Me: The Bajan Household*. She also created and co-authored with Averille White, her research associate, an unusual feature that provides an intimate look into the everyday life of a rural Barbadian village. It is a letter – in dialect – from a mother to her daughter, entitled *A Letter from 'The Rock'*.

Barrow

Averille White, a former secondary school teacher was a research assistant at the Institute of Social and Economic at the University of the West Indies when she worked on this book.

The late **Timothy Callender** was a multifaceted and talented fiction writer, journalist, painter, sculptor and teacher, with a BA in English and an MA in painting and sculpture from the University of the West Indies. His contributions to this book include *A Living Art; From Legends to Literature: A*

White

Story-telling Tradition; and *The Boyfriends*, a delightful short story.

Elizabeth Best, was working as a rewrite editor at the *Advocate News* and as a lecturer at the University of the West Indies. She has an MA in English Language and Linguistics from the University of York, England. She wrote the chapter on language – *Bajan Dialect: A Good Cook-Up* and provided editing assistance on a number of other pieces.

Rita Springer, a food writer and author of *Caribbean Cookbook*, wrote *Land of Cou-Cou and Flying Fish*.

Peggy McGeary has been a secondary school teacher for many years. She is interested in Bajan folk culture, bush medicine and home cures. She is the co-author of the book, *Folk Songs Barbados*. Her article is *Herbal Cures* and *Itals*.

Angela Carter, a features writer for the *Nation*, specializing in tourism and business. Her articles have been published in *The New York Times* and the *Richmond Times Dispatch*. She wrote the travel sections *The West* and *Central Bridgetown*.

Divya Symmers is a freelance travel writer who has worked on *Insight Guide*, *Pocket Guide* and *Compact Guide: New York City*. She also has an in-depth knowledge of Barbados which she used to research and write the original *Travel Tips*.

T hree talented Barbadian photographers – **Ronnie Carrington, Stephen Smith** and **Willie Alleyne** – contributed some striking pictures. Barbados resident and publisher, **Keith Miller**, updated this edition of *Insight Guide: Barbados*, which was edited in Apa's London editorial office by **Lesley Gordon**.

Thanks go to Robert "Goggie" Ilfill who helped shaped the original book, the Cobblers Cove Hotel and to the Barbados Tourism Authority in London and Barbados.

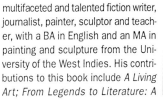

Best

Symmers

CONTENTS

TRAVEL TIPS

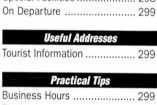

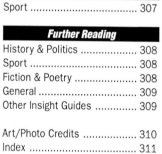

WELCOME

"To confess truly, of all the islands that I have seen unto this day, not any pleaseth me so well," said one of the first visitors to Barbados, the Englishman Sir Henry Colt, who arrived in 1631.

For well over three centuries, visitors to its glittering shores have been impressed by this "gem of the Caribbean Sea." Barbados "has an air of neatness, politeness and opulence which one does not find in other islands," wrote a French missionary back in 1700, and it is still true today. Barbados is the only place outside the United States that George Washington ever visited: in 1751, he was "perfectly ravished by the beautiful prospects on every side" of the island.

Barbados is called the "singular island," perhaps because it's a bit off the beaten track, 100 miles (160 km) to the east of the Caribbean chain, somewhat separated from its neighbors. During the days of sailing conquerers and Caribbean settlement, this isolation provided Barbados with an unwitting defense: it is difficult to sail to Barbados from the other islands because of the prevailing easterly winds.

The island is coral rather than volcanic, and relatively flat, though this doesn't seem so when you're trying to maneuver your car up a steep road in the hilly "Scotland District." The highest point, Mount Hillaby, is only 1,100 feet (335 meters) above sea level – perhaps that's why Columbus never spotted it on any of his trips to the West Indies.

Barbados confirms the theory that the character of a people is molded by the landscape they inhabit. Ever since the English landed on its shores in the 1600s, the entire island has been intensely cultivated, even to the tops of its modest hills. The patchwork of flat, tidy fields which stretches to the sea has produced a hardy, down-to-earth people with a reputation for seriousness, self-assurance and frugality. In the small, crowded space of the Barbadian environment, order and discipline have always been essential. Perhaps that's why Barbados has supplied so many teachers, preachers and policemen to neighboring islands.

Barbadians are not slow to trumpet their own virtues. They firmly believe, as a piece of doggerel from more than 50 years ago says, that "when the great trump shall blow, all other nations will please stan' back and Buhbadians march up first."

Despite the island's dense population – almost 260,000 people live in a space just 14 miles (23 km) wide and 21 miles (34 km) long – Barbadians have one of the highest per capita incomes in the Caribbean and a proud tradition of stable, democratic government. Most houses have running water (pure and drinkable anywhere on the island) and electricity. Inside some of the most modest of the traditional "chattel houses," you're likely to find all the modern conveniences, such as stereos, TVs and video recorders.

Barbados is a land where the old and the new coexist. The offices

Preceding pages: fishing, a Barbadian motif; bougainvillea, Flower Forest; bikes for two, St James; the bar at the Atlantis Hotel, St Joseph; St Lucy coastline; St Philip beach; chattel house; at the beach in St Michael. **Left**, a welcoming smile from a St George boy in front of his parent's store – a flying fish emblazons his shirt.

of international accounting firms sit beside ramshackle "rum shops," a flock of black belly sheep scampers through Bridgetown traffic, a "tuk band" parades through a village where people are watching *Roseanne*, *Ricki Lake* or the *Oprah Winfrey Show*.

Unlike many of the other islands, Barbados was colonized by just one nation – England. Once called "more English sheself," this singular connection is reflected throughout the island still, in its "very British" traditions, in its nickname "Bimshire," and in many of its place names: Worthing, Hastings, Cheapside and Trafalgar Square, for example.

And little wonder, for when the first English settlers landed in 1627, the only welcome they received was from a multitude of wild hogs; the island was barren of inhabitants and ripe for the imposition of British culture, tropical-style. Quickly, English traditions were to coexist with the African heritage of the many slaves brought to work the island's sugar fields. The island remained resolutely British, until 1966, when it became an independent state within the British Commonwealth.

Today's Barbados is a blend of English, African and North American cultures. One local poet has characterized it as "a land of pastel tints and compromise." Since independence, Barbadians have gained a deep appreciation of their unique cultural heritage. This has encouraged the exploration and celebration of some of the African-inspired aspects of the island's music, dance, art, religion, food, language and family structure.

It is truly a singular island, as Barbadians know and visitors quickly discover. Barbados may have glorious sunny days, a glistening azure sea and spectacular scenery, but it is a fascinating cultural vantage point as well – an example in miniature of the way history and geography can shape both a people and a place.

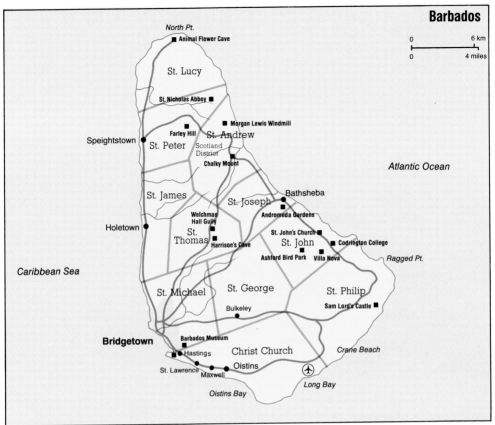

Barbados

| 0 | | 6 km |
| 0 | | 4 miles |

North Pt.

■ Animal Flower Cave

St. Lucy

■ St. Nicholas Abbey ■

■ Morgan Lewis Windmill

■ Farley Hill

St. Andrew

Speightstown ●   St. Peter

Scotland
District

■ Chalky Mount

Atlantic Ocean

St. James

St. Joseph   ■ Bathsheba
■

■ Andromeda Gardens

Welchman
Hall Gully ■   ■ St. John's Church
St.   St. John   ■ Codrington College

Holetown ●   Thomas
■ Harrison's Cave   ■   ■ Villa Nova

Ashford Bird Park

Ragged Pt.

Caribbean Sea

St. Michael   St. George   St. Philip

● Bulkeley   ■ Sam Lord's Castle ■

Bridgetown   ■ Barbados Museum
■ ● Hastings   Christ Church   Crane Beach
St. Lawrence ● ● Maxwell   ● Oistins
Oistins   ✈
Long Bay

Oistins Bay

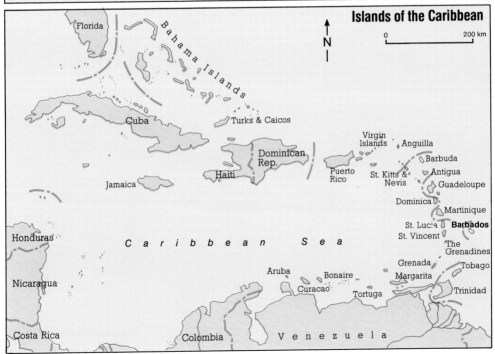

Islands of the Caribbean

↑
N

| 0 | | 200 km |

Florida

B a h a m a   I s l a n d s

Cuba

Turks & Caicos

Virgin
Islands   Anguilla

Dominican
Rep.   Barbuda

Jamaica   Haiti   Puerto
Rico   St. Kitts &   Antigua
Nevis   Guadeloupe

Dominica

Honduras   Martinique

C a r i b b e a n   S e a   St. Lucia   **Barbados**
St. Vincent
The
Grenadines
Nicaragua   Grenada   Tobago
Aruba   Bonaire   Margarita
Curacao   Tortuga   Trinidad

Costa Rica   Colombia   V e n e z u e l a

A PROSPECT OF BRIDGE TOWN

BARBADOS. 1695 By Samuel Copen

THE FIRST BAJANS

Cannibals and convicts, pirates and planters, slaves and social reformers… A fascinating cast of characters has shaped the destiny of the tiny coral island of Barbados. Though Columbus missed it completely on all four of his trips to the West Indies, Caribbean Indians, Africans and Europeans have all left their mark on this 166-square-mile (432-sq.-km) spot of ground.

The story began 5,000 years ago, when Amerindians were "island hopping" in the Caribbean, and probably visited Barbados. Recently, major archaeological discoveries have been made at Heywoods, the site of the new Port St Charles Marina Development. Radiocarbon dating of Amerindian shell tools unearthed here have obtained a date of 1630 BC, making Heywoods a site of continued human occupation for almost 4,000 years. This has pushed back the date of the first settlement of Barbados by some 2,000 years and literally re-written the history books.

The Barbados Museum and Historical Society has worked closely with the Port St Charles developers and a team of overseas archaeologists to ensure that the site benefits from a carefully planned, ongoing excavation. This project was awarded the prestigious 1996 American Express Caribbean Preservation Award. There is a permanent Amerindian exhibition at the museum.

The Arawaks were the first Indians to set up villages in Barbados, about 400 BC. They came from the area that is now Venezuela, crossing the sea in canoes up to 90 feet (27 meters) long, carrying women, children, animals, water, plants, religious objects, navigational devices and weapons. The Arawaks farmed and fished; they also brought with them a calendar system and a unique tradition of pottery-making. Archaeologists have found remains of their villages in Chancery Lane, Silver Sands and Pie Corner.

The Arawak population declined dramatically around AD 1200, probably because they were wiped out by the aggressive Caribs, a

Preceding pages: Samuel Copen print of the Careenage, one of the most accurate views of a 17th-century port. **Left,** portrait of a Carib family by Agostino Brunias.

somewhat less sophisticated tribe of hunters and fishermen. The Caribs dominated Barbados for about 300 years.

Many Europeans who visited the West Indies in the 16th and 17th centuries told tales of Carib cannibalism. Were they true? Anthropologists now say these Indians probably never depended on human flesh for nutrition, but occasionally did share an enemy's flesh as part of a ritual to promote courage in battle. In fact, the Caribs may have sampled European flesh often enough to have concluded, as one English historian recounts, that "Spanish flesh caused indigestion, the French were delicate in taste, while the English were too tough."

Mysterious disappearance: Based on claims

Indians from Guyana to move to Barbados and taught them to grow Caribbean crops.

Traces of Carib and Arawak culture are still evident in modern Barbados. Whether you are handling a piece of prehistoric pottery, sipping soursop punch or ladling out a peppered stew, you may have the momentary sensation of taking a journey back in time. You'll even be uttering the sounds of an ancient Indian language as you use these familiar words:

huracan	hurricane
maiz	maize or corn
canaua	canoe
tobaco	tobacco
hamaca	hammock
sabana	savannah

of "unhumanly" cannibalism, Spanish law justified Indian enslavement until 1542. According to early Spanish documents, many Indians were abducted from the small Caribbean islands like Barbados and taken to work in the fields and mines on the larger Spanish colonial islands. Perhaps it was the Spanish enslavement or famine or disease, but no one knows for sure why the Indians had vanished from Barbados when the English arrived in 1627. All they found was a flourishing population of wild hogs, left by Portuguese explorers who had anchored briefly there in 1536.

Soon after the English adventurers landed, however, they persuaded about 40 Arawak

guayaba	guava

Other Caribbean Indian terms, literally translated, are jewels of creativity:

father of the fingers	thumb
soul of the hand	pulse
my heart	wife
he who makes me little children	son-in-law
God's plume of feathers	rainbow
the pot is boiling	earthquake

A European was called a "misshapen enemy" because of his clothing and armour.

Near miss: The voyage from Europe to Barbados is made easy by the currents and trade winds. Even today, it is possible to float on a raft from the Canary Islands to Barbados. Still, the Spanish explorers bypassed Barbados, settled down in Cuba, Hispaniola and Puerto Rico instead. It's possible they missed Barbados, which is relatively flat and isolated. But it's more likely that the fortune-hunting Spanish were not intrigued by this small island's charms. Its armadas were not interested in settling and cultivating islands, but in wresting precious metals and minerals from existing civilizations, like the riches of the Mexican court of Montezuma and Peru's silver mines. Benign Barbados, its wealth in fertile soil, was no lure to Spanish fleets.

Barbados's name is Portuguese. At some point during the Caribbean exploration, the

The first English settlement began in earnest two years later. On February 17, 1627, 80 English settlers and 10 black slaves (captured from trading vessels) landed on the west coast, or Caribbean side of the island.

Skewed sex ratio: The first settlers were intrepid, willing to risk their lives for the promise of wealth and power. Nearly all were men: 94 percent of 1,408 migrants from London in 1635 were male, for example. Most were in their teens or twenties: during the 1600s in England, life expectancy was 35. It would prove shorter still on Barbados.

Black slaves – introduced sporadically during Barbados's earliest years by Dutch and Portuguese traders – were predominantly male,

Portuguese referred to the island as Los Barbados, meaning "the bearded ones." It's possible the reference is to Barbados's bearded fig trees. Other theories are that Arawaks, bearded men, were inhabiting the island, or that bearded Africans were among the pre-European "citizens" of the island.

It fell to English explorers in 1625 to land near today's Holetown and claim Barbados in the name of James I, King of England. Captain John Powell led the adventurers.

Left, carved stone used by Arawak men for body painting. **Right**, sacred object portraying the deity "Giver of Cassava."

too. In fact, during the first 50 years of settlement, a severe imbalance of the sexes, black and white, tempered population growth. However, if the white settlers did not increase and multiply, the slave population fared worse still. "Negroes imported to the sugar islands died much faster than they were born," writes historian Richard S. Dunn. "West Indian slave masters soon gave up trying to keep their Negroes alive long enough to breed up a new generation and instead routinely bought replacement slaves year in and year out."

The grim quality of life during the first years of settlement contrasted with the glory of the island. Remarked one early observer:

"The Land lyeth high much resembling England more healthfull than any of hir Neighbors; and better agreeing with the temper of the English nation." Governor James Kendall, in 1690, declared Barbados "the beautyfulls't spott of ground I ever saw."

Anything goes: Beautiful as it was to the English, Barbados was miles from home, on the map and in spirit. Life on the island took on an anything-goes quality described as being "beyond the line," that is, outside territorial limits of European treaties. Barbados became a stage for gamblers, fighters, fortune hunters, for political refugees and outcasts, for kidnappers and their bounties.

Many of Barbados's first English settlers

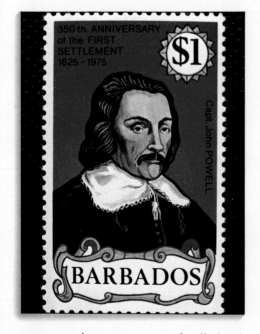

350 th ANNIVERSARY
of the FIRST
SETTLEMENT
1625 - 1975

$1

Capt. John POWELL

BARBADOS

were second or younger sons of well-placed Englishmen. These younger siblings would receive none of the inheritance earmarked for first-born sons: they faced financially dubious futures – and Barbados was rumored to be the new frontier. Subsequent migrations included political outcasts such as Royalists and Roundheads who had backed losing factions at home, and lower class laborers from England, Ireland, Scotland and Holland without money to buy land. Many agreed to serve as indentured servants on the island for two to 10 years, after which they would be given a small parcel of land or start-up sum by their employers. Unfortunately, few planters kept their

promises to indentured servants. Many of them, recognizing their fate, left Barbados for other islands or for North America, especially Virginia and the Carolinas.

"The Caribee Islands": From the start, the colonizing of Barbados was motivated by economics. The initial settlement was funded, to the tune of £10,000, by a London merchant, Sir William Courteen. He had obtained a deed to Barbados and other "Caribee islands" not already held by any "Christian prince." The first settlers did not own land or stock, but acted as freeholders or tenants, often keeping a small plot of land and two or three indentured servants or slaves. Profits from tobacco, cotton, ginger and indigo, the original crops, went to William Courteen and Associates.

During Barbados's first "English" decade, indentured servants from Europe did most of the servile and agricultural work. Slaves were a minority. According to historian Hilary Beckles, the number of blacks on Barbados didn't exceed 800 through the 1630s. Even in 1643, the population numbered roughly 37,000 whites to only 6,000 blacks.

If the island were "owned" by one man, at least Courteen was a sympathetic and able administrator. His successor, the Earl of Carlisle (a Scot and a favorite of the English crown whose name is given to Carlisle Bay) was less of a humanitarian. Recognizing colonization as profitable, he convinced King Charles I to grant him rights to the Caribbean islands, including Barbados. Although in direct conflict with Sir William Courteen's deed, it didn't prevent Carlisle from sending his own band of settlers to Barbados – to a southwestern bay which became Bridgetown.

Dumbfounded by the turn of events, Courteen enlisted the help of the Earl of Pembroke in restoring his rights to the island. King Charles I granted him his petition for proprietary rights. In a turnabout, however, the king then re-granted ownership rights to Carlisle, whose will prevailed. The dispute, and especially its outcome, would later be dubbed the "Great Barbados Robbery."

With Carlisle as overlord, Barbados's star temporarily dimmed. Political dueling between Carlisle and Courteen factions sapped

Left, the first Englishman to land here. Right, the Portuguese who visited in the 1500s named the island *Los Barbados*, "the bearded ones," perhaps after the bearded fig trees.

Nth Point

SCOPLAND

Strecl head

Mr Arnills
Becocks bay
Humphreys bay

Abbots
Spout
Louis hole
Land Lock
Mr Maurich
Peins Mt
Abelijay
Rock
Coll Bayleys

Seemen Bay
D.r Painter
Spikes Towne
Coll Baylys well
Chalky Mt.
Joseph R.

Reeds bay

Indian Corne

A Cabage tree

Fosters pot house
Hill

Smith shop

Coll Arrandells

Nole Towne

Sugar Cane

Suggar tree

Bannano tree

Foshtabell
Indian R.
Humphreus Forts
Brids
St Michels Towne
Willowbies Fort
Carlile Bay
Coll Maly
Nethams Forte

Pellicans

Nethams Pt.

Austinian
Speck bands

Scala Milliarum Anglicorum

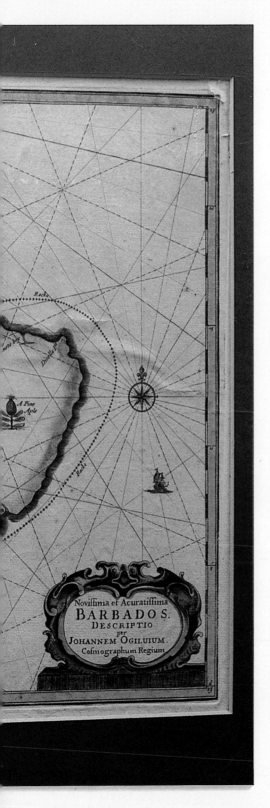

the island's economic momentum. Infighting was compounded by drought and a drop in food production that shook optimism. Carlisle saw to it that his personal profit margin from Barbados exports also increased substantially. Islanders called the mid-1630s were christened "the starving time".

Restless and scheming: Carlisle appointed as governor Henry Hawley, whose name remains notorious. Hawley, says one account, was "a restless and a scheming soul." To appease powerful planter opposition to his appointment, Hawley set up, in 1639, a House of Assembly, a "representative" body of citizens added to the island's system of government. Many of the first representatives of the Assembly – all white male landowners – became big planters and heads of influential families. In the 1630s, a Captain Futter commented to the island's Judge Read about the character of Barbados's appointed officials, "If all whore-masters were taken off the Bench," he inquired, "what would the Governor do for a council?"

Reaping the sweets: The 1640s were a pivotal decade for Barbados. These were the years in which the colonists "retooled" to produce sugar, making Barbados the first British colony to plant sugar on a large scale.

The first man to bring sugarcane to the island was a Dutchman, Pieter Blower, in 1637; he had learned how to grow and process it in Brazil. At first, canes were used to produce rum, but by 1642 sugar would be producing sweet profits. Sugar bred success – immediate success, "There is a greater change on this island of late, from worse to better, praise be God," wrote one Barbadian in 1646. That change was the crystallized and refined juice of the sugarcane.

Everything grew – canes, population and land values. In 1646, one plantation was sold for £16,000 – which, according to historian Dunn, was more than the Earl of Carlisle had been offered for the proprietary rights to the whole of the island a few years before.

Barbados's success story was partially underwritten by the Dutch. In the late 1600s, the Dutch dominated European and Caribbean trade. They brought slaves from Africa, and offered high prices for Barbados sugar, cash

Left, map from a 1671 atlas, *America*, by Englishman John Ogilby, a royal cartographer and inventor of the road map.

on the barrelhead. Producing sugar was costly too, and they came forward with financial backing and sugar-making expertise – a double-barreled enticement.

Of course, England frowned upon its colony's close ties with Amsterdam. Once Britain's own house was in order, following the civil war which resulted in the formation of the British Commonwealth, Parliament passed several Navigation Acts to limit foreign imports to English-owned colonies. In Barbados, the Dutch had been enjoying brisk business selling food, provisions and luxury items to rich planters – a seller's market of which Britain was jealous. In fact, producing sugar on Barbados was so profitable that planters

change is that it favored the big planters, or those with investment connections in London, over small planters without access to capital. The reason: sugar-producing required a sizable initial outlay. And while one acre of land yielded a generous one ton of sugar each year, the initial outlay in sugar-making made it difficult for small planters.

The population shift during Barbados's boom sugar years – roughly 1643 to 1660 – was dramatic. The number of whites on the island decreased as small planters were squeezed out by the giants, who now owned hundreds of acres and slaves. And the black population of the island increased quickly as slaves were brought in from Africa, a practice

were reluctant to "waste" land to grow food. As one observer wrote in the 1640s, Barbadians were "so intent upon planting sugar that they had rather buy foods at very dear rates than produce it by labour, so infinite is the profit of sugar workes after once accomplished." In Barbados, the Dutch and English had a captive market with money burning in its pocket.

The big get bigger: Along with sudden wealth, sugar-making dictated two other sweeping social changes on the island. The more far-reaching was the large numbers of slaves brought in to work the sugar fields, mills, boiling houses and distilleries. The other

which would continue for 150 years.

By the 1650s, the plantation system was established. The island probably looked then much as it does today, heavily cultivated, with little forest left. For the white upper class, a period of unparalleled prosperity was under way – at a price. When historian Richard Ligon arrived in 1647, an epidemic of yellow fever was sweeping the island. Planters who had begun "sugar workes" were "laid in their dust, and their estates left to strangers."

Price of prosperity: Sugar meant wealth on one hand but also abject poverty for slaves. The notes of Henry Whistler, written during a 1655 visit to Barbados, are even more specific and revealing: "This island is the dunghill whereon England doth cast forth its rubbish. Rogues and whores and such like people are those which are generally brought here."

Without slaves, plantations could not have existed. The slaves brought from West Africa to the West Indies by the Portuguese and Dutch, were from areas which are now Sierra Leone, Guinea, Ghana, the Ivory Coast, Nigeria and the Cameroons. According to historian F.A. Hoyos, they included such peoples as the Eboa, Pawpaw, Whydah, Moco, Nago, Angola, Kongo and Mandingo. They came from the Fanti-Ashanti peoples of the Gold Coast, from the Dahomey and the Yoruba and Bini peoples of areas in western Nigeria.

always the case. The whites suppressed any display of pride or solidarity that might erupt into resistance, enforcing the British view of the superiority of European ways.

During the sugar boom, the number of slaves increased from 5,680 in 1645 to 60,000 in 1684. Slaves outnumbered whites by three to one – a threat to their masters which resulted in severe measures of control. Slaves were purposely kept in awe and not discouraged from believing, for instance, that Anglican church services were sessions of witchcraft directed against them.

Police action, usually brutal, was a major tactic against uprisings. Slave laws, reports historian Karl Watson, "tried to limit mobil-

The Schedule contin...

Country	Employ. Labourer	Sex Males	Females	Names	Age	Colour	Country	Employ. Labourer	Sex Males	Females	Names	Age	Colour	Country
Barbadian	L		1	Ruthy	12½	Black	Barbadian	L	1		Mingo	40	Black	Barbad.
"	L		1	Peggy Ann	12½	"	"	L	1		Scipio	37	"	"
"	L		1	Nancy Molly	12	"	"	L	1		Cato	35	"	"
"	L		1	Pamelia	11½	"	"	L	1		Cyphax	34	"	"
"	L		1	Eve	11½	"	"	L	1		Apphia	34	"	"
"	L		1	Sally Ann	11	"	"	L	1		Will John	30	"	"
"	L		1	Molly Quash	10	"	"	L	1		Jeffrey	26	"	"
"	L		1	Eliza	11½	Coloured	"	L	1		Billy	25	"	"

From different ethnic groups and places, and speaking different languages, the Africans brought to Barbados were extremely diverse. However, they also shared a number of expectations, attitudes, and everyday practices. From these they rebuilt workable communication patterns, as well as innovated and reconstituted their own folk traditions. While these African traditions are being recalled today with pride and relish, this was not

ity. A pass system was devised to prevent slaves from moving about freely. Rigid laws were enacted for the capture and punishment of runaway slaves... Efforts also were made to reduce the risk of rebellion by the prohibition of drumming, blowing of horns... assemblies."

Barbadian slaves were the property of their owners – a kind of property seen partially as chattel and partially as real estate. Slaves could be sold, or traded against debts.

How slaves lived: Living conditions were abysmal. Slaves were housed in floorless huts, sustained on meager food supplies, and worked six days a week, 12 hours a day. About three-quarters of Barbados's slaves were plantation

Left, aspects of plantation life: main house, mill, slaves, owner, slave huts. Right, a register listing slaves, with age and race. ("Colored" means mulatto or mixed race.)

A. Brunias pinxt. et sculp.t

The Barbadoes Mulatto Girl.

workers. "The day began at half-past five, when the plantation bell summoned them to the main estate yard to receive instructions," writes historian Watson. After an issue of hot ginger tea, they were divided into three groups. The able men and women were sent out to dig cane holes, to manure, or to cut and crop mature cane. Less able adults, children and nursing mothers performed less arduous tasks.

Slaves were given food weekly. A typical weekly ration consisted of 28 lbs (13 kg) of yams or potatoes, 10 pints (5 liters) of corn, ½ lb (¼ kg) of fish, and 1½ pints (1 liter) of molasses. The yearly ration of men's clothing might be a flannel jacket, a shirt, a pair of trousers and a cap. Women might get a flannel jacket, a gown, petticoat and a cap.

Slaves in skilled positions fared better. Barbadian blacks and the continuing influx of African blacks used skills mandated by plantation life. Slaves became overseers of other slaves, boilers, distillers, cattle keepers, drivers, carpenters, and tailors. Women worked as stock-tenders and child-minders. Domestic slaves were more trusted, and better treated, than field workers. A visitor to one household wrote: "It surprised me on first going to the West Indies to observe the unchecked and even disputatious familiarity of the house Negroes and servants; and at dinners, where much company was present, I have frequently observed them wholly occupied in listening to any good stories and laughing at them much louder than any of the Company."

The rare planter freed his slaves, sometimes upon his own death, according to his will, or as an act of compassion, after the slaves had reached a certain age. Economics as well as compassion were at work – aging slaves were plantation liabilities. Free blacks tended to migrate to the city of Bridgetown, if they did not leave the island.

During Barbados's growing years, intermarriages were few, according to church records, or perhaps just kept secret. However, interracial liaisons were many, especially between white planters and black slaves. A mulatto population grew up in Barbados, creating a new class of "coloreds" generally treated better than blacks. It was not uncommon for a planter who had fathered a mulatto

child to baptize the child into the Church of England and free the child from slavery.

Home rule: By the 1650s, "the prevailing view in the mother country," wrote historian Gary A. Puckrein, "was that England alone should enjoy the market of her colonies."

Accustomed to local rule, the colonists trembled at the notion of home (English) rule. In 1651, the Barbados General Assembly declared that "being bound to the government and lordship of Parliament in which we have no representatives, or persons chosen by us... would be slavery far exceeding all that the English national hath yet suffered."

But home rule was inevitable. Barbados lacked the political sway and military strength

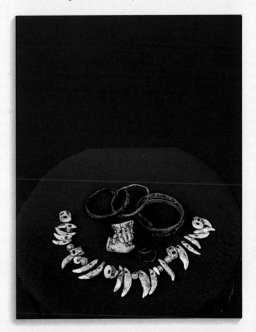

to declare itself a free state. It depended upon its colonial relationship. A blow came in 1663, when the governor, Lord Willoughby persuaded the Barbados Assembly to grant England a 4½ percent duty on all exports – a duty that symbolized Britain's ascendancy. The plantation system received another shock. Unable to tolerate dismal living conditions, a group of white servants plotted a revolt. The conspiracy was crushed and 18 servants were executed. But open resistance to the planters was a harbinger of changes to come.

Soon, England's Lord Protector Oliver Cromwell would launch his "Western Design," a campaign to seize further Caribbean

Left, print by Brunias (c. 1790) shows what house slaves wore for special occasions. **Right**, jewelry found by archaeologists in slave graves.

territories and annex them to the British Empire. During this period, Jamaica would come under British rule, cultivate sugarcane, and force down the world market value of Barbados's sugar. It was a new era for Barbados, one characterized by increasing restrictions.

Volatile time: The late 1600s proved an especially volatile time for slave relations. The British Parliament had granted planters in the West Indies the right to "fight, kill, slay, repress and subdue all such as shall in a hostile or mutinous manner...disturb the peace." A trained militia on Barbados was the chief weapon against slave rebellion.

Even so, a 1675 plot by blacks from the Gold Coast of Africa, one that was painstakingly planned for three years, escaped notice and might have succeeded. But just eight days before the insurrection "cunningly and clandestinely carried and kept secret," a few whispered words were overheard by a house servant, who reported the planned revolt to her white master. The result was 100 arrests and the execution of many of those held.

Scares and plots for rebellion occurred in 1683, 1686, 1692 and 1702. Still, black rebellion was more subdued in Barbados than in Jamaica where there were more slaves and where dense woods provided asylum for hunted blacks. Barbados, small and highly cultivated, was too open for successful hiding. In both Barbados and Jamaica, however, the irony of failed revolts was that carefully constructed plans were thwarted when some slaves reported the conspiracies to their masters. Blacks undermined black resolve.

The nature of black protest changed in the 1700s. Certainly, a strong militia – aided by English ships in the West Indies fighting trade wars – helped squelch uprisings, but black status was changing too. Over generations, Africans became native-born or "creolized" blacks. As such, they were favored over newcomers form Africa, and considered more "capable of instruction." Planters began to grant creole slaves more liberties. At least in appearance, the slaves generally seemed less aggressive and more loyal than in earlier years. In fact, Barbados was known for granting more concessions to slaves than any of the other sugar islands.

In 1807, the slave trade was officially abolished by the British Parliament, but humanitarians in England feared it was still going on. To hedge against this possibility, in 1815 the British passed a bill which declared that all slaves in the West Indian colonies had to be registered. This caused a furor among Barbadian planters, who saw it as a threat to their right of self-government.

The slaves got wind of the controversy, too, but misunderstood it. They thought that the bill everyone was talking about was not to register them, but to *free* them. Resentment grew as they wondered, "Why Bacchra (white man) no do that the King bid him?"

The ensuing 1816 slave revolt, nicknamed "Bussa's Rebellion," came at a time when food was plentiful and the slaves' working conditions better than they had ever been. It was the unfulfilled expectation of freedom that caused the insurrection. Free mulattos and slaves, including one named Bussa, met at weekend dances over a period of months to plan the revolt. Then, on the night of April 14, 1816, cane fields were set on fire on a plantation in St Philip. The revolt spread, and was eventually suppressed by the British militia only after one-fifth of the island's sugar crop had been destroyed.

"What I have for some months been dreading has... come to pass," wrote one white planter to a friend. Only one white man was killed, but 176 slaves died in the upheaval and 214 more were executed.

Because of the rebellion, the British government decided to let Barbados pass its own slave registry bill – a triumph for the colony. The 1816 uprising also gave the impetus for further reforms, and was another step on the road to emancipation. The humanitarian and abolitionist movements were now irrevocably underway. But it would not be until 1834 that slavery was abolished.

In the end, it was a quiet reform. As William Hart Coleridge, an influential abolitionist and Anglican Bishop on Barbados reported: "800,000 human beings lay down last night as slaves, and rose in the morning as free as ourselves... It was my peculiar happiness on that ever memorable day to address a congregation of nearly 4,000 people, of whom more than 3,000 were Negroes just emancipated. And such was the order, the deep attention, and perfect silence, that you might have heard a pin drop."

Right, planters had a busy social life, with much feasting and copious drinking of rum concoctions such as falernum.

Lick an' lock-up done wid,
Hurrah fuh Jin-Jin!
Lick an' lock-up done wid,
Hurrah fuh Jin-Jin!

De Queen come from England
To set we free;
Now lick an' lock-up done wid,
Hurrah fuh Jin-Jin!

–Barbadian Folk Song, c. 1838

With these joyous lyrics, 70,000 laborers of African descent celebrated their freedom on

But after years of transatlantic debate between island planters and British abolitionists, a compromise was reached.

On August 1, 1834 the slaves became "apprentices." For the next four to six years, the ex-slaves continued to work for their particular plantation, while masters continued to provide food, clothing and shelter. According to the law, masters could expect 45 hours of work each week without pay. In exchange, the apprentices could remain in their meager huts, eating with what utensils

August 1, 1838. The apprenticeship system, which followed the abolition of slavery in 1834, ended on that day. The Barbadian apprentices could now hope that "licks" (whippings) and "lock-up" (jailings) were "done wid" and that "Jin-Jin" (the young Queen Victoria) had come to the rescue. Unfortunately, the descendants of these former slaves would not see true, harmonious emancipation for more than a century.

British humanitarians campaigned zealously for 40 years to bring about the official abolition of slavery. The white Barbadian planters were, of course, opposed to the plan. Economically, they depended on their slaves.

they had and sleeping on boards of dried foliage, covering themselves with crocus bag blankets. Planters were not pleased with the idea of apprenticeship and were severe in their interpretation of this first phase of emancipation. During slavery, for example, children began working at the age of four or five, collecting grass for the livestock. Under the apprenticeship system children under the age of six were no longer required to work, and the planters responded to this by refusing to support young children.

Even the state-supported Anglican Church was sluggish in its efforts to support emancipation. Although William Hart Coleridge, first Bishop of Barbados, tried to promote peace and reconciliation and to help keep the transition bloodless, his speech to the slaves on the day they become apprentices offered a mixed message: "Your masters are good men who will continue to look after you when the day of freedom comes. You owe it to them as God's deputies to obey their orders even though you are no longer slaves. Your masters are your fathers on earth even as God is your father in Heaven."

Coleridge was asking the newly freed slaves, to remain subservient. Essentially, that was the nature of the apprenticeship system: a trial period in which planters, laborers and the government could adjust.

Police protection: The planters were worried that their slaves would emigrate, and the sugar industry would collapse. To guard against this and to keep in check any unruliness resulting from the slaves' first taste of freedom, the legislature created one of the first police forces in the British West Indies. The transition period was peaceful, and emigration was minimal. For other islands in the British West Indies, this system of apprenticeship may have been necessary, but not in Barbados. The slave population didn't really need a transition period. Planters didn't have to worry about losing their laborers because they owned almost all the island's arable land and, at the time, there was no wage competition. Finally, some planters came to believe that they could cultivate their land more cheaply with a freed labor force than with apprenticed help for whom they had to provide.

Thus, in early 1838, four years after the apprenticeship system was installed, the Legislative Assembly quickly and with little opposition called for complete emancipation on August 1, 1838. The transition itself was simple and bloodless. The problems of reconciling a large black labor force and a small, wealthy leadership class, however would take more than a century to solve.

Legal shackles: In the first years of emancipation, lawmakers concentrated on ensuring that the sugar industry remained active and

profitable, keeping the ex-slaves under control and maintaining the island's reputation for order, good government and loyalty to the British imperial system.

Meanwhile, laborers moved from one plantation to another, looking for the highest wages. The planters responded by binding the ex-slaves firmly to the plantations with legal shackles, namely the Masters and Servants Act of January 7, 1840, which established the "Located Labor" system. By this measure, all laborers became tenants on their masters' land. Here, they could live on tiny "house-spots" at the discretion and whims of the master – and for a weekly rent – as long as they provided the kinds of labor they and

their ancestors had during the previous 200 years of slavery. This system was meant to protect planters from losing their labor force to neighboring plantations and islands, but in doing so, it stripped workers of most of their rights. The master was legally the sole judge of the rights of his workers when any disputes arose over services required. Any worker who resisted was kicked off his bit of land with four weeks' notice and his crops were taken over and appraised at a value usually below the real one. And if a tenant quit, he lost his house and land and had no claim to the value of his crops.

Because this system was so effective economically, there seemed no pressing reason to change it. Barbados recorded steady economic growth between 1838 and the 1870s. Consequently, there was no "fall of the planter class" as had occurred in Jamaica and other colonies where the laboring classes had more freedom of movement.

The people's tribune: One man who would not allow this virtual return to slavery to destroy the hope of true emancipation was Samuel Jackman Prescod, the son of a slave mother and white father. He became a powerful speaker and writer, championing the cause of justice, freedom and equality. In 1843, when the constitution was amended to give Bridgetown two seats in the House of As-

stalwart "tribune of the people" from the society at a time when such gifted individuals were sorely needed. Prescod's demise signaled the end of an era in Barbados, an era in which a man with roots in slavery could provide a strong voice in government. Five years later, the island was in the middle of yet another governmental shake-up, one that pitted whites against blacks, poor against rich. And this time, no strong voice spoke out for the powerless and disinherited.

United colonies: In 1878, the island was confronted with the "Confederacy Question." The British government proposed linking Barbados with the Windward Islands in a loose association of British colonies. The

sembly, Prescod won the election for the city, becoming Barbados's first non-white member of Parliament in 204 years.

In the House of Assembly, Prescod fought against open hostility to his ideas and gained some measure of advancement for the new citizens. He helped found the Liberal Party, whose adherents included small landowners, businessmen, and mulatto and black clerks, and was their leader for over 20 years.

As a journalist and a parliamentarian, he highlighted the plight of the masses, both white and black, and agitated for redress of their grievances. His retirement from Parliament in 1862 and death in 1871 removed a

Governor, John Pope Hennessy, tried to persuade the Barbadians to accept this scheme, but the island's decision-makers couldn't agree to the idea of becoming a Crown Colony; after all, they reasoned, Barbados had enjoyed self-rule for more than 230 years. The planters also feared they would lose control over cheap labor, and the legislators worried that non-whites would gain more political influence under the new association.

The fear of emigration again swayed public opinion. The whites opposed confederation because it would provide the masses with an outlet to seek fair wages and gainful employment in other, less densely populated colonies. For the same reason, blacks were in favor of confederation. This conflict was not to be resolved without bloodshed.

Riots erupted in April 1876 as the black Bajan masses reacted violently to the attempts of the white plantocracy to continue repression through the old system. After three days, eight blacks had been killed, 30 people (mainly blacks) injured and 400 rioters jailed. In response, the president of the Legislative Council wrote to the Colonial Office in England to complain that the governor had "spread alarm" throughout the island by "exciting that peculiar element in the character of the Negro, which varies

The problems spotlighted by the Confederacy Question continued to rage. The non-representational government ignored the needs of the masses, and only 1,300 of the island's 160,000 inhabitants were eligible to vote. In time, however, the oligarchs began to make attempts at improvement. In 1884, the constitution was amended to include the Franchise Act, making it possible for people with less land to vote. The new act was supposed to remedy the island's gross disenfranchisement of non-whites. But the lower earning and landholding requirements were not low enough to include the working class.

The black knight: Yet these changes were considered epoch-making in Barbados, a step

according to circumstances from the docility of a child to the ferocity of a Savage." When news of the riots reached England, Pope Hennessy was transferred to Hong Kong.

Nonetheless, the people continued to regard Pope Hennessy as a hero; months after his departure, observers reported that many blacks believed he would someday return to free them from their lives of oppression.

Left, manumission certificate freeing slaves upon a plantation owner's death. **Above**, newspaper editor and statesman Samuel Jackman Prescod. **Right**, John Pope Hennessy, governor of Barbados 1875–76.

towards true democracy. And William Conrad Reeves, a mulatto politician who designed these measures, was praised not only for "saving" Barbados from Crown Colony government but also from "mob rule". He was even knighted – the first black Barbadian to receive such an accolade – and was elevated to be Chief Justice of Barbados from 1886 to 1902 – the first black man in the entire British Empire to hold such a position.

By the end of the century, despite some democratic reform, the white planter class had regained control of the local Parliament. The Franchise Act of 1884 meant little on an island where whites still owned 90 percent of the land and there were few villages and no substantial property-holding peasantry. The plantation system with its dependence on cheap labor still dominated the social and economic life of the island.

This time, however, blacks took the course of action so feared by the power-brokers: emigration. Between 1850 and 1914, several thousands laborers left for Panama to help build the canal. Others left for Brazil, British Guiana, Trinidad and Curacao – anywhere that promised employment and relief from the discrimination that kept them on the lowest rung of the socio-economic ladder.

At the time, Barbados's economy was severely depressed. The sugar industry, which

Barbados with nothing – much to the chagrin of their girlfriends or families. One such case was related in the folk song "Panama Man":

Oh de Panama man 'ent got no money
Still de Panama man want love...
But 'e cahn get me wid-out de money
To buy me a taffeta dress!
If de Panama man gwine court wid me,
He gwine treat me like a queen...

Nevertheless, many men *did* increase their families' wealth by going to Panama. The money was used to educate their children, raise their standard of living on the island and, above all, to buy land on which they could provide for their own livelihood.

For the first time, laborers were able to buy

had withstood many threats and alarms in the preceding 50 years, was being hurt by stiff competition from Europe and by disease. To cut costs, Barbadian planters were forced to fire laborers. This brought greater hardship to the already troubled masses and inspired many more Barbadians to leave the island.

Panama money: Between 1850 and 1914, 20,000 men emigrated to Panama, where they toiled industriously to build the canal and sent home money to their families. Most of the men who worked in Panama came back wearing flashy clothes, their pockets stuffed with US currency. But there were a few who talked big and then returned to

land from planters, who were sorely in debt, because of the fall in sugar prices. Between 1900 and 1920, the number of estates fell from 437 to 305, and the major portions of more than 60 estates were converted into free villages. While laborers' families battled starvation with remittances from Barbadians abroad, the planters scrambled to modernize their troubled industry. The keys to the salvation of the Barbadian sugar industry and economy were the development of fertilizers, the introduction of a new kind of sugarcane and the discovery of new markets.

In 1859, J.R. Bovell, a botanist, and J.B. Harrison, a chemist, experimented with sugarcane germination techniques, dabbled with new cane varieties and studied the incidence of cane diseases in Barbados. Their experiments had profitable results.

Growers began using manures as fertilizers, producing record crops in the 1890s and offseting the low price of sugar. By 1900, the old "Bourbon" type cane was successfully replaced by the "white transparent" variety. And the problem of finding a ready market for the product was eased by trade with the United States which began in the 1890s.

Meanwhile, the British government recognized the possibility of an economic collapse in her West Indian islands and, in 1897, set

Although the island's economy was in better standing, the Barbadian masses were still in trouble, plagued by the unkind forces of nature. The hurricane of 1898 killed 80 people, blew down 18,000 ramshackle houses and increased the incidence of dysentery and typhoid already common among the poor. Then, in 1902, an epidemic of smallpox struck, followed by yellow fever in 1908 – all of which greatly increased the death rate.

Yet the government did not improve health or sanitation or pay workers enough to help them improve their standard of living. There were not even the meanest social welfare programs for the majority of Barbadians. Children went to "ragged" schools until they

up a Royal Commission under Sir Henry Norman to look into the problems of the Caribbean sugar industry. Upon the recommendations of the Commission, the British government invested large sums of money in the sugar industry. With its £80,000 share, Barbados set up the Sugar Industry Agricultural Bank, a move which made the difference between solvency and bankruptcy for the next 50 years. Bounties on sugar beet were removed, and Barbados began to benefit from easy access to the British market.

Left, young Bajan women ginning cotton. Right, photo of members of the House of Assembly.

were old enough to work. Meanwhile, higher-class children attended such exclusive schools as Harrison College, Queens College and Codrington High.

Workers' rights: In 1914, the construction of the Panama Canal was finished, shutting off a dependable outlet for industrious workers. And by the 1930s, workers could only go to Trinidad, British Guiana, Brazil, Cuba or Costa Rica in small numbers.

With few ways to better one's lot, those Barbadian laborers who remained emerged as a peasantry of sorts between 1900 and 1920. The large majority lived in tenantries that were part of the plantations where they worked. And when the depression shook the American, Canadian and British economies in the 1930s, these workers were hit hardest.

New political movements developed in response to these harsh social and economic realities. Dr. Charles Duncan O'Neale, a doctor, rose to the cause and devoted his life to fighting for the improvement of the masses in the same way that Prescod had done 60 years earlier. In 1924, O'Neale founded the Democratic League, the first mass-based, radical, political force to be launched on the island in the 20th century.

The league attracted many non-white, middle-class professionals and sent several candidates to the House of Assembly. O'Neale

won a seat in 1932, and though his health was failing, he left behind the twin legacy of the early trade union, the Workingmen's Association (founded in 1925), and the League itself. Both organizations influenced the formation of the Barbados Labour Party in 1938 and the Barbados Workers' Union in 1941, which fought for workers' rights.

Equally significant to the workers' cause was the emergence of the Garveyite movement in the 1920s and 1930s. Marcus Garvey was a black Jamaican who fought the oppression of blacks and wanted to see an exodus from the Americas back to Africa, toward the creation of a black nationality.

Garvey spoke to the growing dissatisfaction of the Bajans. Emancipation had occurred 100 years earlier, but equality did not follow. Barbadians took their frustration to the streets in the riots of 1937, inspired by Prescod and O'Neale, who made inroads in government, and Garvey, who offered strong black leadership. In fear of famine and disease, with little hope for education or land to cultivate, and an ever-increasing population threatening to strangle the island with competition for jobs and resources, their anger exploded.

Riots in the streets: Clement Payne was the spark that ignited the social disturbances. Payne was Trinidadian by birth, but both his parents and his brothers and sisters were born on Barbados. He began advocating the formation of trade unions at public meetings in Bridgetown and incited such a fever among the people that on the night of July 26, 1937, the authorities deported him.

Crowds gathered on town squares to protest his deportation. And as the number of people grew, so did the sense of outrage, which suddenly exploded. The crowds began smashing windowpanes, street lamps and anything else that beckoned their stones and anger. The rioting lasted three days and spread quickly to the isolated rural areas. Cars were broken into, shops were looted and fields were raided. These responses were prompted less by the deportation of Payne than by hunger and the fear of hunger.

The fervor of these days produced the kind of myths and folksongs that sprang forth out of the excitement of emancipation. One such song is "The Riot Song," a personal and tangible look at the events of this time:

Listen friends to what was composed
De twenty-seventh of July I couldn't
  show much nose.
Civilian wid rocks, policemen wid guns
Doan doubt me friends it wasn't no fun
For everything dat yuh hear a sound
Somebody dead and somebody wound.

The most colorful account of the riot is found in W.A. Beckles's *The Barbados Disturbances,* a report summarizing the findings of a commission appointed to pinpoint the causes of the 1937 riot. Beckles likens the violent riots to a volcanic eruption: "While the rumblings revealed the presence of a "volcano," it gave no indication whatever of the gigantic crash that was to take place shortly after... In two days the hot lava that belched forth from the crater had spread its ravages to practically all parishes of the Island… Reviewing the situation dispassionately… It is manifest that circumstances, and not the qualities of a leader, made Payne, a slim, slight unimpressive stranger, a Moses in our midst."

For the first time, Bajan masses had come to the center of the political stage. Unlike in 1816 and 1876, they challenged the fact that 70 percent of the population was still disenfranchised on an island that called itself a democracy and touted its "long and proud tradition of Parliamentary government."

Little England: In 1946, Barbados was the most crowded area in the Caribbean, with a

The island's social and economic life was fully bound up with sugar cultivation. The plantation system was more completely preserved than in any other Caribbean colony, which resulted in inequities. The top layer of Barbados society, about two percent of the population, received about 30 percent of national income and controlled the economic institutions. Moreover, the only commercial banks were run by Britain and Canada, further protecting the island's finances from the laboring masses. And for almost 300 years this ruling economic group had dominated the government under a franchise system that limited voting rights to less than four percent of the country's entire population.

population density of over 1,200 people per square mile. It was the most British colony in the New World, never having existed under any other flag. Nicknamed "Little England," Barbados sometimes seemed "more English than England sheself," as one Bajan put it. Its church was more distinctly medieval in cultural and religious matters than any other Anglican church and all other conventional Christian sects established in the New World.

Left, Clement Payne, Trinidadian-born trade unionist whose agitation helped start the labor movement in Barbados. **Right,** farm workers on strike in the 1940s.

The fervor, anger and sentiment unleashed by the 1937 riots had led to change. The first lasting labor parties were formed. The nature of the constitution, Barbados's relationship to other British Caribbean colonies and the problems of poverty were questioned. And in the next 40 years, the political and social character of the island altered dramatically.

Democratic vistas: Grantley H. Adams was the primary catalyst for these changes. Between 1938 and 1945, Adams became the acknowledged leader of and spokesman for an emerging mass movement that coalesced around a political party and a labor union. Adams firmly believed in the British monarchy and the sanctity of the British parliamentary institutions. But he was determined to modernize the Barbadian political system by narrowing the traditional boundaries between the planters and the laboring masses.

In 1938, Adams, along with C.A. Braithwaite and several others, formed the Barbados Progressive League, also known as the Barbados Labour Party. Adams headed this coalition and vowed to work for greater equality until the island's wealth and resources would be controlled by the government on behalf of the people. Adams demanded fair labor laws, including workers' compensation in case of injury on the job, and formation of tribunes to monitor wage fairness and factory condi-

tions. It also advocated a slum clearance and housing plan.

The party gained its first political victory in 1940 when it won five seats in the House of Assembly and Adams was able to push through legislature requiring an old age pension and a Minimum Wage Act. But his most pressing task – modernizing the political system – met with strong opposition. A bill to provide for adult franchise was consistently voted down. In 1942, however, the members of the Assembly recognized the mood of the times and agreed to a compromise. The bill passed reduced the income qualification of voters to £20 and permitted women

to vote and to be eligible for membership to the Assembly on the same terms as men.

Most important during this time of remarkable change, however, was the realization by Governor Bushe that the constitutionally mandated system of government was, in his own words, "incapable of coping with modern conditions." Bushe adopted a constitutional change, dubbed the "Bushe Experiment," whereby the governor transferred the res-ponsibility of choosing an executive committee from himself to a spokesman for the majority in the Assembly. (Adams was the first majority leader.) The Executive Committee thereafter was privy to and accountable for decisions made in the House.

Working out the kinks: These changes – though conceptually sound and well-intentioned – did not make any significant impact because the Legislature was still controlled by white planters. When reforms such as the nationalization of public utilities, paid holidays for workers and adult franchise came up, the two bodies inevitably clashed. By 1949, however, this kink was worked out by limiting the powers of the Legislature to the functions of revision and delay, thereby leaving the ultimate say in the enactment of legislature to the House.

The constitution endured further changes in the next few years, including the formation of ministries for formulating specific governmental policies. In addition, the leader of the Barbados government would become premier of Barbados, to be supported, after 1958, by a cabinet. With Adams's strong leadership, Barbados was able to modernize its system of government in only two decades. The island was clearly heading towards independence. At the same time Barbados was also in the process of negotiating for similar changes within the West Indies and in the British Empire. Leaders of various West Indian islands began discussing – once again – the merits of federation.

With Adams representing Barbados, a federation was, in fact, inaugurated in 1958. Unfortunately, it never achieved the kind of momentum needed to grab international attention because each island seemed to have

Left, Prime Minister Grantley Adams, who put through revolutionary social reforms. **Right**, the Barbadian flag was first unfurled on Independence Day, 1966.

50

The Advocate

BARBADOS, WEST INDIES   WEDNESDAY, NOVEMBER 30, 1966   12 CENTS

Midnight: Darkness encompasses Savannah...then the Barbados flag emerges

© Duke photo P.M. Barrow constitutional Instruments

BARBADOS IS INDEPENDENT

By Tony Vanterpool

AT one minute after midnight today, Barbados threw off the shackles of colonialism, when during a tense and historic moment at the traditional Garrison Savannah the British Union Flag was lowered and the 166 square mile nation's ultra-marine blue and gold flag with broken trident was hoisted.

A deafening applause came from the thousands and thousands who came from every nook and cranny of the sugar coated territory, braving the threats of inclement weather, to witness the most significant achievement since the freedom of the island's slaves 132 years ago.

And so ended 339 years of association with Britain as a colonial territory and so began the membership of Barbados to the British Commonwealth of Nations as its 26th member.

After receiving the Constitutional Instruments from the Duke of Kent, who presided at the ceremony as the Queen's Special Representative, Barbados' Prime Minister, Mr. Errol Walton Barrow, 46, said: "This is a very crucial moment in the history of the people of Barbados.

In an address obviously packed with emotion, the Prime Minister added: "I am glad, and I am sure the members of my Government are equally glad, that we were born at a time when we would see this eventful day.

In his moments of glory the Prime Minister continued: "On behalf of the people of Barbados, on behalf of the Government, on behalf of the young people, I should like you to convey to Her Majesty the Queen, the heartfelt thanks of us all that she was on this eventful day the Head of the Commonwealth and that she elected to send you, her trusted cousin, to see us through the dawn of independence."

There was a road rush for the Garrison Savannah by Barbadians who wanted to get proper vantage points. And from as early as 7 p.m. traffic policemen were battling with numerous road blocks along the Street. At the Garrison some people gathered on roof tops and in trees. Virtually one half of the savannah was

filled and people even filled none of the grand stands which were not very close to the ceremonial apron.

Children and adults alike were crushed through pressure of numbers and first-aid had to be admitted at regular intervals.

Prime Minister Barrow and Mrs. Barrow arrived at 10.48 after attending to the state banquet at the Barbados Hilton Hotel, by the time they took their seats in the Royal Box, the stand for invited guests was practically filled.

But due to congestion, less than 10 minutes before the actual flag-raising, invited guests were still arriving.

The Royal party arrived at 10.55 which was already 15 minutes behind schedule and after a shortened version of the displays, which excluded the master-cycling Buckets due to the wet condition of the ground, four religious leaders recommended the Barbados Christian Social Council mounted the dias and read the prayers.

Then came the real prelude to the great moment as the Governor-general's designate, Sir John Stow, and the Prime Minister, left the Royal Box and took up positions facing the flagstaff.

At 11.55 the guards of honour saluted the Union Flag and the first verse of the British National Anthem was played.

Then at midnight the guards of honour saluted the Flag of Barbados and the first verse and chorus of the Barbados National Anthem were played.

Suddenly everywhere the Union Flag was lowered and the Barbados Flag hoisted. And when the lights went on again the ultra-marine blue and gold-coloured Barbados Flag with broken trident was fluttering in the wind.

● Barbados' Governor-General-designate, Sir John Stow, raises Prime Minister Errol Barrow's right hand as a sign of victory seconds after Barbados became independent today.

● Up goes the Barbados flag of ultra-marine blue and gold with broken trident (left), while down comes the British Union Flag. Within seconds of the completion of this operation, Barbados became an independent State within the British Commonwealth of Nations.

IMPROMPTU ROAD MARCH

A GROUP of Trinidadians who are in Barbados for the island's independence celebrations were the centre of attraction in Bridgetown yesterday when they staged an impromptu road march through Broad Street and Swan Street.

With their improvised steelband, the group notched up and down in true festive spirit and had soon attracted a large crowd of Barbadians to do likewise.

Meanwhile, the official road march in Barbados was staged early this morning when thousands of Barbadians and visitors marched and jumped to the rhythm of steelbands from the Garrison Savannah following the Flag-Raising Ceremony, down Bay Street to Pelican Village.

MISS BARBADOS ARRIVES

MISS JUDY ROSITA WALKER, 18, Miss Barbados (United Kingdom), arrived in Barbados last night from London to take part in Barbados' Independence celebrations.

Miss Walker, who was crowned at the Lyceum Ballroom, Strand, London, on Saturday night, beat five lovely Barbadian belles who were vying in the competition.

Second in the competition was Miss Marguerite Rocheford, Miss June Gill placed third.

Victor's hand is raised

Barbados' Governor-General-designate, Sir John Stow, typical of a referee in a boxing match, held Prime Minister Errol Barrow's right hand in the air in dramatic victory during the Flag-Raising Ceremony at the Garrison Savannah last night.

And, as if to be outdone by Sir John, Guyana's Prime Minister Forbes Burnham also raised the hand of his contemporary.

POPE'S CONGRATS

VATICAN CITY, Tuesday — Pope Paul today cabled his congratulations, best wishes and blessing to the island of Barbados, which becomes independent tomorrow.

He said he was confident that the Catholic members of the population would contribute generously to, and work effectively for, the good of their new country.

The Queen's thoughts are with us

QUEEN ELIZABETH II has assured Barbadians that her thoughts are with them as they step into independence.

The Queen's message on the occasion of the flag-raising ceremony, which was read at the Garrison Savannah last night by her cousin, the Duke of Kent, was as follows:

"I have asked my cousin, the Duke of Kent, to represent me at the independence celebrations of Barbados and it is with real pleasure that I send you this message at such an important and happy moment in your history.

"My husband and I are very glad to have been able to visit your beautiful island earlier this year and to meet its people. With that enjoyable memory still fresh in my mind, I join with you in celebrating your country's independence and in welcoming you as a member of the Commonwealth.

"My thoughts go with you as you step into independence. In sending you my good wishes, I pray that God may bless and guide you throughout the coming

MUD AND WATER ON THE GROUNDS

MUD and three inches of water in some parts failed to spoil an excellent show by the Royal Barbados Police Force, the Barbados Regiment and the Cadet Corps at the Garrison last night.

The display put on by these units drew applause from the Royal Box and from the thousands of spectators who had converged on the Garrison for this historic-making occasion.

The Regiment marched past and the display began. This was followed by the advance of the guards

SPECIAL ISSUE

The Advocate's special Independence supplement (96 pages) is being circulated today along with your regular copy of The Advocate.

This historic document carries stories of all aspects of Barbados life and Barbadian personalities.

Get your five in today's issue — a ten picture of the major contributors to this special publication.

Russia recognises Bimshire

THE Soviet Union has declared its recognition of Barbados as an independent and sovereign state. In a message yesterday to Prime Minister Errol Barrow, the Chairman of the Council of Ministers of the USSR, Mr. Alexi Kosygin, expressed the Soviet Union's readiness to establish diplomatic relations with Barbados.

Mr. Kosygin, in a congratulatory telegram, said: "On the occasion of the declaration of the independence of Barbados, please accept, Mr. Prime Minister, sincere felicitations and best wishes of well-being and progress for the people of Barbados on the road of independent development."

From Chou En-Lai, Premier of State Council of the People's Republic of China, came the telegram: "On occasion of proclamation of independence of Barbados, I extend sincere congratulations in Government and people of Barbados on behalf of Government and people of People's Republic of China. May people of Barbados achieve new successes in cause of consolidating imperialism, consolidation and non-colonialism, safeguarding national independence and building their own country."

West Germany also recognised Barbados as an independent State and declared its readiness to open diplomatic ties.

Traffic jams as thousands flock city

HUNDREDS of Barbadians, young and old, flocked the city last night to window shop and see the buildings and stores which were brilliantly illuminated and gaily bedecked with flags and bunting in Barbados' national colours of ultra-marine

Vice-president of Lions here

Mr. David Evans, vice-president of Lions International, arrived in Barbados last night to attend the island's Independence celebrations.

Mr. Evans, who lives in Texas, United States, leaves Barbados tomorrow for visits to Trinidad, Surinam, Curacao, Panama, Costa Rica, and Mexico City before returning home.

and gold.

The City Council's building cut a colourful show. City stores were also points of attractions and so, too, were the Public Buildings, and the Barbados Workers' Union building on Fairchild Street which has been illuminated since the start of the silver jubilee celebrations last week.

Other focal points were the Arch South of the Chamberlain Bridge.

Hours before the flag-raising ceremony, pedestrians, cyclists and motorists were seen wending their way to the Garrison to get early vantage points.

All roads leading to the Garrison from the East had traffic jams and many people who left home to get did not get to the Garrison for the ceremony.

One of the busiest places was Bay Street, the main road to the Garrison. Bay Street was seemingly never ending line of traffic, policemen at point duty were kept busy.

China rejected

UNITED NATIONS, New York, Tuesday — The General Assembly today administered a crushing defeat to advocates of Peking's admission to the United Nations rejecting their resolution to seat the Communists by 57 votes to 46 with 17 abstentions, one member (Laos) being absent.

748 die in U.S.

CHICAGO, Tuesday — More people died on America's roads during the long Thanksgiving week than in any previous accident period, it was announced today.

Pammastic: proof against any climate in the world.

Pammastic emulsion is based on a unique Acrylic Ter-polymer medium for longer-lasting protection, easier use and superior weathering. Its hardness and durability have been proved in sun, sea and storm the world over. Outside or inside, Pammastic dries in an hour to a perfect mat finish that can be washed or scrubbed, time and time again. Pammastic is available in a complete range of exciting contemporary colours. So look out for our sign. And choose Pammastic, every time.

MANUFACTURED LOCALLY

AGENTS:

JAMES A. LYNCH & CO., LTD.

McGregor Street, Bridgetown.

different goals for the union. Also, the Queen maintained legislative authority in matters of defense, external affairs and finance of the federation, and the governor had the power to veto any laws passed. These problems led to the dissolution of the federation on May 31, 1962, only four years after its inception.

When Adams returned from his dealings with the federation, much had changed in the political and social life of Barbados. And his nemesis, Errol Walton Barrow, had succeeded him. In 1961, Barrow, with his liberal Democratic Labour Party, held the reins of power in the government.

Barrow, the nephew of famous reformer Charles Duncan O'Neale, immediately in-

British West Indian islands. Yet, Barbados was ready for independence at a time when Britain was clearly liquidating her empire.

Although the decision to proceed to independence was one of the most significant in Barbados's history, it was accepted with little opposition or fanfare. After having fought so many battles for the cause of justice and equality, Barbados began a new life as a free nation on November 30, 1966.

The actual transition from colony to sovereign state in Barbados involved only a change of titles and functions. Errol Barrow and his Democratic Labour Party were reelected and, four weeks later, amid pomp and solemnity, the new flag was unfurled.

stituted reforms that were severely lacking during the years of constitutional rearrangement. He carried out a program of public works to provide relief for the unemployed.

Finishing touches: Although he, like all preceding reformers, had his share of problems and opposition, Barrow was able to put the finishing touches on an island prepared for imminent independence. After Adams' frustrated attempts to consolidate a Federation of the Caribbean from 1958 to 1962 and a subsequent attempt at a smaller Eastern Caribbean Federation from 1962 to 1965, it became clear that Barbados would not receive dominion status through any union of

As the nation's first leader, Barrow served for over 10 years. By 1976, Barbadians were ready for a change, and Barrow's DLP lost to the BLP. Five years later, the BLP led by Tom Michael Geoffrey Manningham Adams, won again. He took Barbados confidently into the 1980s. He entered 1985 without a political care, but on March 11, he died of a heart attack at the age of 53, leaving his party and the country bereft of his guidance.

Full circle: Adams's successor, the energetic Bernard St John, moved swiftly to allay fears of a disintegration of the ruling BLP, continuing the policies of his predecessor with the same dedication. Errol Barrow, then

65 and with 33 years experience in Parliament (a Caribbean record) seized the opportunity. His party hammered away incessantly at the St John administration as Barbados experienced an economic slowdown.

St John decided to hold the election in May – in order, some say, to avoid the harsh criticism in song that would come from the calypsonians during the Crop Over Festival. Despite a huge advertizing blitz by the BLP, the Barbadians went to the polls on May 28, 1985, and voted in the DLP, led by Barrow, by the largest landslide in Barbados history.

Tragically, Errol Walton Barrow died in 1986 while still in office, following a heart attack. The smooth transfer of leadership to

1966, it took years before its indigenous culture could flourish. Barbados was well-known for its Britishness and the conservative life-style of its people.

In the early 1970s, inspired by the Black Power movement in the US, Barbadian youths began forging a new identity. Many of them were also influenced by the Rastafarian movement from Jamaica. But the most powerful influence came from American television programs, trends, tastes and music.

Today, Barbadians are appreciative of things Bajan and more interested in preserving their *own* culture in the face of foreign influences. There is a movement to preserve aspects of the culture that are fast vanishing.

the Hon. Erskine Sandiford, of the DLP, testifies to the political stability of Barbados.

By 1994 the Sandiford government had become unpopular and, following elections, the BLP returned to power. Owen Arthur became the island's fifth Prime Minister, with Billie Miller as his deputy. She was the first woman to hold this office.

Coming into its own: Although Barbados was ready for independence way back in

Left, burning "Mr Harding," a symbol of hard times, at Crop Over Festival. **Right**, Kadooment Day Parade at Crop Over, a uniquely Bajan cultural tradition.

The enthusiasm the Crop Over Festival generates is a sign of cultural pride. Crop Over originated in the days of plantation society. Revived in the 1970s and managed by the National Cultural Foundation since 1982, it has played a major part in promoting cultural awareness, and is responsible for reviving the calypso tradition in Barbados. The wildly popular calypsonians are now a major force in every strata of Bajan society: they speak for the people, providing social commentary, gentle protest that grows out of concern for their nation, and a constant source of indigenous entertainment that delights Bajans and visitors alike.

ALL O'WE IS BAJAN

All o'we is Bajan!
Bajan to de back-bone...
Bajan black, Bajan white,
Bajan hair curly, Bajan hair straight,
Yo' brother red, yo sister brown,
Yo' mother light-skin, yo father cob skin...

This excerpt from local poet Bruce St John's *Bumbatuk I* reveals something of Barbadians that, given the island's many ethnic groups, may come as a bit of a surprise. That "something" is a sincere and deep-seated national pride, a sense of unity.

There are Afro-Bajans, Anglo-Bajans, Euro-Bajans, Bajan Jews and Bajan Hindus and Muslims. Smaller groups include an American community, a Canadian element, some South American expatriates and an influential group of Arab-Bajans from Syria and Lebanon.

Barbados is one of the most densely populated agricultural countries in the world, and the population is expected to increase from approximately 260,000 now to 300,000 by the year 2000. Given the propensity of Bajans to "get their quivers full," this substantial population growth is more than likely to occur, despite the efforts made by the local family planning association.

Over 70 percent of today's Barbadians are directly descended from Africans who were part of the greatest involuntary migration in world history – the slave trade. Another 20 percent of Bajans are of mixed black and white blood – described as "brown-skin," "light-skin," "fair-skin," "high brown," "red" and "mulatto." Another 7 percent of the population is white, either "overseas" white (of traditional Caucasian features and skin tone) or "Bajan" white (containing "a tip of the tarbrush," or a small amount of black ancestry). The remaining 3 percent is drawn from the immigrant groups mentioned earlier.

Still, despite this diversity, a national character, or sense of identity, has emerged. Bajans, on the whole, are pragmatic people with a native capacity for quick wit and irony.

Preceding pages: casting the net, the bay at Half Moon Fort; cocktails at the Colony Club Hotel. **Left,** before class at a private school. All schools, both private and public, require uniforms.

Quick sense of fun: Barbadians do not take offense easily, a trait which has led some visitors to believe they suffer abuses, particularly bigotry, without protest; actually, this trait has made smoother the social evolution from the modified feudal system prevailing before 1937.

There is a quick sense of fun among Barbadians, often quite subtle, and capable of being effectively directed, in true British fashion, against any form of pretentiousness. There is also a refreshing realism of outlook and a sturdy resistance to change for the sake of change – a characteristic which stands out in sharp relief against the apparent excitability and enthusiasm of some of the other Caribbean peoples.

Some have interpreted this Barbadian trait as smart-aleck cynicism, and it is not all that unusual to hear other Caribbean people use terms such as "smug," "smart Bajan," and "know-alls" to refer to Barbadians with whom they've had contact.

John Hearne, the Jamaican novelist, offered this analysis of the Barbadian character in the *New World Quarterly* (Barbados Independence issue, 1966): "The Barbadian is a problem... He is English in a way that the rest of us are not. History Englished him by giving him an exclusive association with the former Mother Country. This gave him some values, and a head-start in the development of education; Barbadians have been school teachers to the rest of the (British) Caribbean, at a time when education in Jamaica (a hundred times larger than your island) was at the level of reading, writing and arithmetic...

"In all this Englishness the Barbadian geography has played a significant role. It is the most un-West Indian of the islands in appearance, and in atmosphere... It is a sunburnt piece of England, modified by the Tropics, but still and stubbornly a corner of the English countryside, and Barbadians, black and white, have clung to that Englishness. But it has given the Barbadian a wholeness, a self confidence and self-discipline that is remarkable and enviable among West Indians..."

At least in one regard, however, Barbados and Bajans conform to the Caribbean norm: there is a slowness of tempo to which visitors must try to adjust to if the want to avoid frustration. This is balanced by a readiness to oblige, exhibited with such unforced courtesy that the recipient of favors feel no sense of obligation.

Earliest inhabitants: The story of the people of Barbados begins more than 30,000 years ago, when men of the Far East crossed the Bering Strait, which was then a land bridge, and made their way through the North American continent to the Southern landmass. Others came by way of the Pacific, their skill in navigation bringing them across the vast ocean until they reached present-day Brazil, Venezuela and the Guianas. Thus Barbados's Amerindian ancestors began to migrate from

South America to the West Indies. These hunter-gatherers eventually came to Barbados in search of new food sources: they settled in Barbados about 2,000 years ago. These earliest people, the Barrancoid, left relics at what are now Chancery Lane, Boscobelle and Golden Green. They left Barbados around the year AD 600.

Two hundred years later the Arawaks came to the island from South America, traveling to the island in long, narrow, flat-bottomed canoes. They inhabited Barbados for the next 400 years, settling around springs of freshwater in various parts of the island. They grew cassava, corn, peanuts, squash, guavas, paw-

<u>Left</u>, fruit-loving Belleplaine boy, St Andrew. <u>Right</u>, a woman from the parish of St George peeks out from the kitchen.

paws and pineapples for food; they also grew cotton and tobacco.

The Caribs were the last group of Amerindians to settle in Barbados. This warrior tribe arrived on the island sometime around AD 1200, and were gone by 1536. They either drove out or exterminated the Arawaks and established the island as headquarters for governing the nearby islands of St Vincent, St Lucia, Grenada and Tobago. In turn, the Caribs were captured by Spaniards some time early in the 16th century and shipped as slaves to Hispaniola. Thus, when the Portuguese, led by Pedro a Campos, first arrived on the island in 1536, the Caribs had vanished.

Off the beaten track: Present-day Bajans are

slightly miffed that early Iberian explorers by-passed Barbados and did not settle there. Apparently Barbados was off the beaten track – legend has it that Columbus never even saw it because it was so flat. And, after all, the Spaniards had their pick of large Cuba, enticing Hispaniola, mountainous Jamaica, exotic Puerto Rico and lush Trinidad. So this island was up for grabs until 1625 when some wandering Englishmen "discovered" it, and claimed it as their new colony in the name of King James I. The real settlement began about two years later when a group of 80 Englishmen came across in a ship called the *William and John*. They captured 10 Africans from a

Spanish galleon, and the group landed on the west coast of the island on February 17, 1627. Today, this landing is celebrated annually at the Holetown Festival.

The English who landed more than 350 years ago were men of substance who came to the West Indies out of a spirit of adventure. The first man to step ashore, William Arnold, was a businessman who had sold his shop in London to relocate in the sunny Caribbean.

Barbados quickly became the "Brightest Jewel in the English Crowne," despite the fact that St Kitts was the first Caribbean island settled by the English. To the British arrivals, Barbados was reminiscent of the rolling downs of Cornwall and Devon; after they became accustomed to the broiling sun, they soon reshaped Barbados into a "Little England," tropical style.

Henry Powell, the captain of the first ship of colonists, brought some Arawak Indians from Guiana to teach the new Barbadians how to grow tropical food. This was certainly a key to the successful start of the colony. The settlement thrived, and the English arrived in droves to join the original band of settlers.

Poor whites: Some of the English who made their way to Barbados were young men of solid families, anxious to make a quick fortune, but others were laborers, indentured to their masters for years.

Gradually, the conditions of work for the poor whites, and the quality of their lives, deteriorated to the level of the African slaves, and these resentful "Christian servants" joined the Africans to plan an uprising against the "higher-ups" and "better-offs," as the planter class was called behind its back. As it happened, the uprising failed and the indentured laborers found themselves worse off for their pains, still treated like slaves and now having to serve even longer terms of indenture. They became a sorry lot, herded into villages on the eastern sea coast and eking out a living by fishing, hunting turtles and land crabs.

The more adventuresome and intelligent of them escaped the island after their indentures were over and went to Jamaica after that island was conquered by England in 1655. A sizable group went on to North America, settling in the Carolinas, speaking their West

Left, taxi driver working in the heart of Bridgetown, city of entrepreneurs. **Right**, on the job in Speightstown, "metropolis" of the north.

Country brogue and bestowing a distinctly Barbadian flavor on those colonies. In fact, each year for the past 20 years, Carolinians have made an annual pilgrimage to Barbados, digging into the records of births and baptism lists, searching for evidence that will establish their Barbadian ancestry.

Meanwhile, the original English settlers were joined by some unwilling Scottish, Irish and Welsh men of various classes. They had been on the losing side in the English Civil War and were exiled, or "Barbadosed." They became bonded servants, and they stayed at the bottom of the social and economic pyramid until the 20th century. They married their brothers and sisters in defiance of the injunctions of the English *Book of Common Prayer*, thus keeping their bloodlines pure. The fact that they passed on debilitating diseases to their descendants was a price to be paid for their lily-whiteness.

"Red Legs": Over the centuries the Afro-Bajans have ribbed their fellow Bajans about these practices and lampooned them with such nicknames as "Red Shanks," "Red Legs," because the kilts their ancestors wore exposed their legs to the sun, "Ecky-bekky," "white niggas" and "Poor backra-johnnies." "Backra" comes from the West African word *bakara*, which means white man. These white Bajans were also called "Pawgees," a word from a plantation in St Joseph called the "Spa" or "Spaw" where many poor whites lived.

The sun-intolerance of Celtic skin aside, poor whites did benefit from the generosity of planters who were embarrassed to see their "kith and kin" in such a down-trodden state. Schools, jobs and even clubs were provided for them. The Haynes Memorial School in Bridgetown, Combermere School, the Alleyne School, Harrison's College and Boys' and Girls' Foundation Schools were all founded to help the poor whites pull themselves up by their bootstraps.

Likewise, the Young Men's Progressive Club was established in the 1920s to provide poor whites in the city with an alternative to delinquency. Here they could play cricket, soccer, and indoor games and attend lectures, debates and cultural programs. It is interesting to note that the earliest literary magazine in

Left, Gail Prescod, law student and runner-up in the controversial "Miss Barbados" beauty competition.

the Caribbean, *Bim*, was started by two early members of the YMPC, Frank Collymore and Therold Barnes, who were both descendants of poor whites.

From being scorned and pitied, the Bajan poor whites are now regarded as a remarkable people, "survivors of the crossing," and a group with a romantic heritage. Today they comprise a small minority existing in isolated poverty in the parishes of St Philip, St John, St Joseph and St Andrew. By the end of this century, these early settlers will probably not be recognizable as a unique ethnic group. For the most part, they will have assimilated into the middle class, a process which has been underway for the past 50 years.

The island's elite: And what became of Barbados's original English settlers? Approximately 20 families dominated the island's history and economic development during the early period of colonization. Even now many of these families still rank among the island's elite, known as "high whites." Sugar exporting was their vehicle to wealth, and many assumed the role of local lords, attempting to recreate patterns of English country life in the islands. An exclusive clique developed: they recommended one another for the Legislature, they bestowed knighthoods amongst themselves, they sat in the Anglican parish vestry councils and they served as Justices of the Peace. These privileges were passed on to succeeding generations.

But first and foremost, the planter class turned its energy to growing sugarcane and producing sugar on the 80,000 acres (32,400 hectares) of land available to them. They developed a deserved reputation as the most outstanding sugar planters in the region, coaxing high yields from the thin soil and driving their African slaves to extraordinary levels of human endurance.

To the planters, "Bimshire," as they fondly called their island, was their only home, and they gratefully spent their adult lives working to show the love they had for the island. Of all the West Indian planter classes, the Bajans were the most devoted to their island, never leaving it to live the life of luxury in England, as the Jamaican plantocracy did.

Today, the great wealth of Barbados's first planter families has been dispersed, but the descendants of these families still remain, along with some of their beautiful and well-preserved plantation houses. But gone is the era of exclusivity which saw the coining of the phrase, "The Sealys talk only to the Piles, and the Piles talk only to God."

The island's "high whites" still speak the purest Bajan dialect, with a rich West Country brogue. You can always tell a Bajan white by his expression "Gaw-blum-muh!" He is a cricket fanatic, a horse-racing addict, and a sturdy believer in the pursuits of polo, tennis, rugby and soccer, a love of which he has passed on to black Bajans. He named his houses and plantations after the Royal family

and British districts and towns, even though he might never have been to England. The white Bajan is a passionate supporter of the British monarchy, of the Anglican Church (termed "the planter class at prayer" by one West Indian cleric and wit) and British institutions. In fact, until independence in 1966, it was usual for white Bajans to openly support visiting English cricket teams over local host West Indian teams.

"High whites" continue to control much of the commercial and economic life of the island, just as they have since the 17th century. And many are actively involved in all the things that make Bajans a nation, from cricket

Left, Mr King of Martin's Bay farmed all his life. **Right**, a photograph for the family album, Martin's Bay, St John.

to calypso-singing, from loyally drinking Cockspur rum to unswervingly defending Barbados's institutions against reproach or criticism from outsiders.

"High Whites" heavily influence the island's cultural life as well. It was the privileged class which launched the tourism industry and founded a monthly magazine, called *The Bajan*. In the early 1960s, the revival of Bajan folk songs and early calypsoes was spurred by The Merrymen, a group of Bajan whites, which is still popular today. "Mighty Whitey" became, in 1984, the island's first white calypsonian.

Cheek by jowl: The coming together of blacks and whites in Barbados began during the slave clubs until as late as 1970 when St Winifred's became the last school to desegregate.

While today there is an easy tolerance between the black majority and whites on Barbados, there still remain areas of prejudice. The many interracial couples that are seen are almost all foreigners: the number of marriages between black and white Bajans can be counted on the fingers of two hands.

The best-known black politician of this century, the late Sir Grantley Adams, squeezed under the barrier by marrying into a white planter-class family in the late 1920s. Sir Grantley was, of course, a "man of the future" at the time: he was a Barbados Scholar, a lawyer, a better-than-average cricketer and an

period, when blacks and poor whites lived "cheek by jowl" on the plantation tenantries and in free villages. Afro-Bajan men had children with poor white women, and vice versa. Co-mingling was trickier with the "high whites," however. They didn't mind having a black "outside woman," because, as a rhyme says, "…de blacker de woman, de sweeter de tail…", but accepting blacks or mulattos socially was something else altogether. Open race discrimination was practiced in commerce, the civil service and, until the 1930s, within the Anglican Church, where whites sat at the front and blacks were relegated to the back. In sports, there were racially exclusive agitator for political reform. Today, Bajans of all groups will tell you that "it doesn't bother anybody." Others will reveal the not-very-secret secret that "black and white Bajans ent gwine marry one anodder, but nuff 'living-wid' does go on dat a lotta people don't know 'bout!" Attitudes are changing, if slowly.

"Bajanized" blacks: The Bajan black is a descendant of West Africans brought to the island between 1627 and 1807 as slaves. They probably came from the Gold Coast (modern-day Ghana) or the area that is now Nigeria. Unlike Jamaica, Guyana or Trinidad, Barbados was the destination of few African-born slaves after the year 1800. Thus African blacks became "Bajanized" relatively early on in the island's history. This tended to make them less resistant to local culture, with its Anglicized language, religion and customs.

On plantations such as Drax Hall (the largest on the island), Newton, St Nicholas Abbey, Kendal, Sunbury, Colleton, Bayley's Thicketts and Morgan Lewis, the African peoples and their children struggled to create a new way of life. Like those indentured everywhere, they resisted the slave system in whatever way they could. In Barbados, they had no mountains to run to, as in Jamaica or Dominica, St Vincent or Grenada. The only places they could escape to were the caves in the middle parishes of St Thomas and St

Experience and education eventually proved to be two great levelers, however. Hundreds of black Bajans served in the two World Wars and suddenly saw life in a radically different way. They saw whites doing menial jobs and even being ordered around by non-whites. Since then the agitation of Clement Payne and Marcus Garvey, the performances of Jack Johnson, Joe Lewis and Muhammed Ali in boxing, of Jesse Owens in athletics, Pele in soccer and Gary Sobers, Wes Hall and Charlie Griffith in cricket all prompted new pride.

Union organizers: When black Bajans went overseas, they often became militant and eager to defend the rights of the laboring classes of all races. In Panama, the United States,

George or the island of St Vincent, 95 miles (153 km) away.

The slaves attempted open revolts four times, in 1649, 1675, 1692 and in 1816, and after each showdown, the whites gained further ascendency. With their dreams of freedom thwarted, these oppressed people sometimes resorted to many forms of passive aggression and to indirect trickery, deceit and quiet defiance. Nevertheless, they had the reputation of being the most obedient slaves in the region.

Left, executives meet at international accounting firm in downtown Bridgetown. **Right**, the Forte family on Christmas Day in Queen's Park.

Canada and Trinidad, Bajan blacks helped organize workers and unions long before such action could be taken on "the Rock."

In the 1960s, many of the black politicians who worked towards independence had spent time abroad in their early childhood, and were proud to be black and Bajan. Among these men were former Prime Minister Errol Barrow, who had been a World War II airman and was trained in London as a lawyer and economist; Sir Grantley Adams, who was trained in London as a lawyer; and Sir Winston Scott, who was to become the first native Governor-General (1967–76) and had been trained as a doctor in the United States. By contrast, the leader of the island's blanket trade union, the Barbados Workers' Union, Frank Wolcott, came by his racial pride by remaining on the island and fighting discrimination. These men led Barbados into the 1970s and gave the next generation a new understanding of what it could mean to be a Barbadian.

During this period of ferment, two cultural foundations were formed which heralded the African heritage of black Bajans. Black Night, formed in 1969, and Yoruba Yard, created in 1972, were inspired by the philosophy of Elton "Elombe" Mottley, a confirmed Africanist. Blacks began to challenge the notion that to be a respectable citizen required rejecting African traditions. African folklore

Pakistanis, Lebanese and expatriates from America, Canada, England, Germany, China and South America. According to Eddie Brathwaite's poem *Negus* it is not enough for these "arrivants" to enjoy the "sweets" of Barbados without first becoming part of the culture and supporting the strides the country has made in race relations.

To be a Barbadian you have to respect the rights of the people, and this is non-negotiable. Modern Bajans, in other words, hope that outsiders won't jeopardize a hard-won culture, won't come "mashing our corns." A controversial decision in recent years, to elect a white Canadian as the representative to the International Beauty Queen pageant, inspired

and practices were resurrected; school children read the African-inspired poetry of Eddie Braithwaite and the writings of George Lamming, Bruce St John, Timothy Callender, Austin "Tom" Clarke and Jeanette Layne-Clarke – all literary explorations of what it means to be Bajan.

The "New" Bajans: Since the 1980s, a new national consciousness has emerged in Barbados. Ironically, the black Bajan is now more comfortable with whites and the other "original" settlers of the island. However, dealing with the "new" Bajans, recent arrivals of the 20th century, is a slightly different matter. These groups include Indians and

theses stinging lines from Mighty Gabby:
Miss Barbados – never hear 'bout ackee tree
Miss Barbados – never hear 'bout Sir Gary
   (Sobers) or even me,
Miss Barbados – never hear 'bout flying fish
Miss Barbados – never hear 'bout nutten so
When she get she Bajan citizenship leeme
   know!

Today, Barbadians "ent mekking no sport" about their national pride and can share in the refrain, "All o' we is Bajan."

Above, Mr Williams of Newcastle, St John, just awakened from an afternoon snooze, shares tales of life in the old days.

A SHIP ON LAND?

"What a strange idea, but then it is not so strange, considering that we are in Barbados!"
—a visitor's comment

A ship on land indeed. Founded in the 1860s by a retired black seaman, the Barbados "Landship" began as a collaboration of ex-sailors who sought to strengthen the camaraderie which developed among them on the perilous seas, and, at the same time, carry on the sights and sounds of

their former vocation. The founders, seeking to bring discipline and a sense of worth into their "evening years," styled a self-help organization using a naval theme and structure – a land-based "brotherhood of the sea."

Today the Landship has many facets: not only is it a group of talented performers, it is also a savings and loan society and a character-building "club" which has branches all over the island.

Local chapters are "ships," each with a complement of "officers," "mates," "engineers," "doctors" and so on. The "crew" dresses in white bell-bottoms and shirts, British Navy style, complete with epaulettes

and ratings. And – call it progressive or just a sailor's answered prayers – women were allowed to come aboard as "nurses" in the early 1920s.

From the start the most visible aspect of Landship has been its hilarious public performances. With all the starch and shoeshine afforded to a serious review of arms, the sailors, lively and straight-faced, demonstrate their formation marching discipline as only black Barbadians steeped in British pomp and circumstance can. The "wanglelow" is a semi-limbo, the "centermarch" is done in time to African rhythm and in a formation that would leave poor Lord Nelson spinning in his briny grave. In one of the dances, the sailors advance with the right hand swinging ahead together with the right foot – shamelessly contrary to tradition!

With titles such as "Rough Seas," "Sinking Ship," "Changing of the Guard", and "Admiral's Inspection," the Landship dances are spoofs of real life situations. They are performed to tuk band music – a sort of fife and drum corps with an African touch, a unique Barbadian accompaniment to the naval masquerade.

The burlesque public appearances of Landship has drawn attention away from its serious purpose. One of the most important features of Landship is the "Meetings Turn," whereby a community pool is funded through regular dues payments by members, to aid individuals in time of fire, flooding and unemployment. The Landship Movement is a credit to the ingenuity and resourcefulness of the Bajan people. ∎

A RELIGIOUS MOSAIC

Religion is not far from hand at any turn in Barbados. From the patchwork of staid Anglican churches (seemingly at least one to every village), to the ebullient "Tie-heads," to Rastafarians hawking coconuts on the street, the Barbadian people are, on the whole, believers and practitioners.

Almost all schools begin the day with prayer, and a substantial amount of radio time is devoted to religious programming.

"Gospel Bag," a weekly newspaper column, informs its readers of upcoming religious activities. It also serves as a local hit parade for new records released by gospel singing groups.

Each Sunday afternoon at three o'clock, CBC TV hosts a half-hour of religious choral singing. Island choirs join a year-long waiting list to appear on the popular "Time to Sing."

At last count, there were over 140 different religious denominations and sects practicing on the island: among these are Protestants, Catholics, Jews, Mormons, Bahais, Muslims and Hindus. Religious tolerance is almost as old as Barbados itself. The earliest settlers were British Royalists and Anglicans who, in 1627, claimed Barbados "at one and the same time for the king of England and the King of Kings." Later, at the time of England's Civil War, others fled to Barbados because of their conflict with Oliver Cromwell's Parliament. But when a Cromwellian invasion party gained a footing on the island in 1651, the two opposing factions quickly reached a compromise which proclaimed "liberty of conscience in matters of religion." Ironically, this pact was ratified by the English Parliament in 1652, at a time when religious freedom in England itself was denied.

The colonists' early religious tolerance was admirable, but it also served a practical end: to ensure the stability and profitability of the plantation system. Indeed, the sugar producers were so eager to avoid the disruptive forces of the English conflict that a local custom insisted "whosoever named the word Roundhead or Cavalier, should give to all that heard him a shoat and turkey to be eaten at his house.

Right, an intensely emotional Sunday service at one of the island's many "store-front" revivalist churches.

72

Yet "liberty of conscience" proved to stretch only so far. Irish Catholics exiled to Barbados as indentured servants were accompanied, at one landing, by 26 teachers and priests. Upon arrival, the teachers and priests were sold into seven years' labor, and many died as a result of the especially harsh treatment ordered for them by local authorities. A trickle of Catholic immigrants followed the first influx, but it was only after a military garrison requested a Catholic chaplain in 1839, and a mission was established, that this faith gained acceptance.

Expedience: By the mid-1600s, sugar was big business in Barbados. Realizing the advantage of a cheap, acclimatized and permanent black labor force over a motley crew of sick, white, indentured servants, landowners threw in their lot with the traders and began importing slaves by the thousands.

Unlike the Catholics, who considered it their duty to impart the civilizing force of Christianity to the "heathen" Africans, the British planters refused to let their slaves become Christians, often against the express wishes of the Anglican authorities in Britain. Their rationale, when offered, was primarily one of expedience. It was commonly believed that one Christian could not enslave another. By excluding them from the fold of Christianity, the British insured that the Africans remained fair game.

When the Church of England attacked this excuse in 1691, by declaring that conversion to Christianity did not make slaves free men, the Barbadian planters retorted, "What? Shall they be like us?"

Planters also developed rigid social divisions between Christians and the Africans to maintain order in circumstances in which they were dangerously outnumbered, sometimes by as much as 13 to 1. White indentured servants were given special privileges within the household. Christian ceremonies were always performed in secret in order to play on the African tradition of the secret society, which endows its members with special knowledge and power. This practice, coupled with the staggering control exercised by the planters over the lives of their slaves, created a belief that Europeans were witches and sorcerers, in the classic African sense of one who could cause harm or benefit by harnessing the powers of nature.

Right, the organist practices in solitude at St Patrick's Catholic Church in central Bridgetown.

Folk beliefs: While the massive disruption of enslavement and the intermingling of Africans from very different cultures prevented religious systems from remaining wholly intact, the absence of a Christian missionary effort undoubtedly encouraged the slaves to retain African folk beliefs and superstitions.

Some of these customs persist in diluted form in present-day Barbados. Until recently, the placenta and umbilical cord of newborn babies were buried in the ground near the place of birth in order to link the spirit with its homeland. Long and festive funerals were held to ensure that the deceased's spirit would rest in peace.

Some Bajans still speak of *duppies*, or wife – who shed her skin at night and traveled as a ball of fire in search of blood. If someone found the skin and rubbed it with pepper or salt, the hag could not re-enter, and so died. The last of the hags is supposed to have died in the 1920s.

By far the most notorious of these folk beliefs, however, is the system of *obeah*, a form of witchcraft. The practice is believed to have come from a West African religion called *Obi*. The presence of obeah in Barbados today is a matter of opinion. Many hotly claim that it no longer exists, while most will agree that its power is limited to that segment of the population that believes in it. As one Barbadian author writes, "What you believe in, you

spirits of the dead, who roam the earth at night, taking various forms and returning to their favorite "haunts."

Duppies are barred from entering a house by various herbs hung at the windows and doorways, by leaving one's shoes at the door, and scattering sand around the house. (This forces the spirit to stop and count each grain, a task that cannot be completed before daylight.) Gifts of liquor are particularly appreciated, and it's still a Barbadian tradition to sprinkle a few drops from a new rum bottle on the ground "for the spirits."

An especially hideous spirit of the night-stalker type was the hag – usually a planter's die in. If you believe that's a duppy 'pon the roof, then one is there."

Obeah "men" can be of either sex, and typically employ a bag of charms which may include rusty nails, feathers, broken glass and pieces of clay, to work their magic, which can be for good or evil purposes.

"Come-to-me sauce": Obeah potions are credited with the ability to make one succeed in one's endeavors and give one control over others. Not a few men are alleged to have been tricked into marriage after unwittingly consuming "come-to-me sauce," which makes its victim irresistibly attracted to the woman who slipped it into his food. Wives are also known to have given their husbands "stay-at-home sauce" to curtail extra-marital philandering.

These potent substances are administered in coco tea or in *cou-cou*, a traditional corn meal dish. Legend has it that one potential victim was saved from a tainted dish of cou-cou and flying fish when the cooked fish began to wink at him.

Control over others can also take more sinister, and even fatal, forms. "Duppy dust" – grave dirt or pulverized human bones – is a particularly dreaded poison, thrown directly on the victim or hidden in his food. Obeah practitioners can "read up the dead" and direct them to wreak the desired vengeance, sometimes by entering the bodies of their poor victims.

him. Eventually, the wretched woman was admitted to a psychiatric hospital.

This is no isolated incident, as indicated by a popular folk song:

De mother-in-law said to de son-in-law
What de hell it could be
Dat every fo-day morning
A man in Della belly.
O Conrad, O Conrad
Conrad come out de woman belly
and he gone to Trinidad
Tra-la-la-la, Tra, la, la, la
Conrad come out de woman belly
and he gone to Trinidad!

Though death is sometimes attributed to the force of obeah, induced insanity is the more

As recently as the early 1960s, one such demon reportedly entered the body of an unfortunate woman. Many people claim to have heard the little fellow, called Conrad, uttering the foulest curses in a high-pitched voice, and making all kinds of demands on his reluctant "hostess."

Nobody knows how or why he tormented this particular woman, but it is known that he defied all efforts of an obeah man to exorcise

Left, Spiritual Baptists, called "Tie-Heads" because of the colorful cloths they wear, in St Michael. **Right**, Sunday morning at St Thomas Church.

oft-mentioned result. Certain bush medicines are believed to act upon the nervous system to produce psychotic states, and just the fear of obeah is said to be enough to drive one mad. In the early 1960s, a young man charged with the murder of his wife's lover had his charge reduced to manslaughter on the grounds of temporary insanity due to obeah.

The British did their best to crush obeah from the start, forcing the practice underground. Today, obeah remains on the Statute Books of Barbados as a felony.

Conversion efforts: Prior to the emancipation of the slaves in 1838, several religious groups antagonized the planting community with their efforts to convert blacks. The Quakers were the earliest and most influential. They ignored a 1676 Act which prevented them from bringing Negroes to their meetings and riled the establishment with their controversial stands on such issues as war, and oathtaking in court.

Quaker's Road in St Michael is believed to be the former center of the Quaker community. A cemetery west of Government House, and a burial place just north of the St Philip Parish Church are the only other vestiges of the Quaker religion in Barbados today.

The Moravians, the oldest Protestant Episcopal Church in the world, became known for support of the slaves under its leader Benjamin Brookshaw. During the slave revolt of

the faith was posted on the town walls. This challenge to religious freedom was soon answered by Anne Gill, who defied the authorities and rallied her fellow Methodists into a united front. By 1826, the church had been rebuilt on James Street, St Michael. Over 20 Methodist churches stand on the island today.

Despite the presence of these denominational options, the majority of ex-slaves joined the Anglican Church following emancipation and the offer of salvation.

To many Barbadians, Anglicanism still represents respectability and an opportunity for social mobility. Yet its complete isolation from traditional African belief, and relative lack of "religious zeal," created a sort of

1816, members of this denomination were granted virtual immunity from the surrounding terror. Today, the majority of the 1,200 seats in the Moravian Church on Roebuck Street, once the site of a cockfighting pit, are filled with black Bajans.

The ranks of the Methodist Church were also swelled by the newly-freed slaves at whose side it had stood in the darker days before emancipation. Previously, the Methodist minister, William Shrewsbury, had so angered the landed gentry with his "forthright manner" that, in 1823, his church was systematically demolished, its furniture was destroyed, and a proclamation aiming to abolish

spiritual vacuum in the post-emancipation period, soon to be filled by the revivalist sects that were sweeping the American South.

"Store-front" churches: Barbados today hosts a staggering number of small sects, often similar in doctrine. As in some African societies, any man who could be a convincing intermediary between his fellows and his Maker was likely to establish a following. Many store-front churches took root in impoverished rural areas. The intensely emotional religious experience they encouraged and their joyous, hand-clapping gospel music was nearer to black African rhythms than the English hymns of the established churches.

Yet these religions still harked back to a white, Christian God who often did not seem to be listening to His black children. This was true throughout much of the Caribbean, where it seemed that God moved in mysterious, if selective, ways among the white people, but left the blacks to fend for themselves at the backs of the English-built churches or in makeshift churches of their own.

In Jamaica, social inequality and the search for an identity rooted in Africa fostered the Rastafarian movement. It has since had a profound impact throughout the Caribbean. The movement began, in spirit at least, in the teachings and beliefs of the Jamaican, Marcus Garvey, who founded the Universal Negro

When, in 1930, Ras Tafari was crowned in Ethiopia as Emperor Haile Selassie I, "King of Kings, Lord of Lords, and the Conquering Lion of the Tribe of Judah," many thought the prophecy was fulfilled, and a way of life was born.

Haile Selassie claimed to be a direct descendant of King David, and the 225th in an unbroken line of Ethiopian kings from the time of Solomon and Sheba. His followers stressed black pride, and the need to regain the heritage the black race temporarily lost by straying from holy ways. Thus, the true Rastafarian lives a peaceful and pious life, desiring nothing beyond material essentials, and engaging in contemplation of the scriptures.

A modern Babylon: At the same time, the

Improvement Association. In the 1920s, he called for self-reliance among Africans "at home and abroad." He advocated a "back to Africa" consciousness, and awakened black pride. He denounced the British colonial indoctrination that taught blacks to feel shame and contempt for their African heritage. He urged his followers to "look to Africa, when a black king shall be crowned, for the day of deliverance is at hand."

Left, members of an Anglican church choir. **Right**, the ebullient "Tie-Heads" singing at their annual candlelight procession, on "Old Year's Night" (New Year's Eve).

Rastafarian rejects the white man's world – the modern "Babylon" – and its greed, dishonesty, lasciviousness, meat-eating habits, "devil soup" (alcohol) and chemical-oriented technology. The two most obvious external marks of the Rasta – his "dreadlocks" and his proud, strutting walk – are inspired by the image of the lion in Selassie's title, Lion of Judah. Rastas are also known by outsiders for their use of *ganja* (marijuana) as a sacrament, a cause of frequent conflict with the police.

Rastafarianism was introduced to Barbados in 1975, and spread quickly. But in addition to faithful adherents, the movement soon began to attract various undesirables, including criminals. Local youths saw it as an extension of their rebellion against school and home, and welcomed the attention their dreadlocks, cocky strut and colorful garb attracted. Rastafarianism was an excuse, too, to smoke ganja.

Barbadians soon took up arms, sometimes literally, against this wave of "Rascals." Whenever a dreadlocked youth fell foul of the law, there was always a headline to trumpet the fact: "Rasta fined for possession of drugs"… "Rasta youth charged for larceny"… "Dreadlocked man arrested"…

In due course, however, the attention of renegade young people wandered back to the streets – to rollerskating, dancing and computer games. Criminals, too, realized that dread-

locks no longer afforded them anonymity, and the faddists got bored and cut their hair.

The remaining true brethren more or less accept and are accepted by the larger society. Many have made substantial contributions to the arts and to sports. Some better-known Rastafarians in Barbados are Winstone Farrell, an actor and rhythm poet; Adonijah, a university teacher, journalist and calypso musician; Ras Iley, another calypsonian; and Ashanti Trotman, a gifted wood craftsman.

Heard God's voice: The only truly indigenous Barbadian religion is the so-called "Tie-head" movement, founded by Bishop Granville Williams in 1957, after a 16-year self-imposed exile on the neighboring island of Trinidad, where he had been exposed to the Spiritual Baptists, a West Indian revivalist religion with its roots in Africa. Maintaining that he had heard God's voice and seen visions, Williams held his first open-air meeting in the fishing village of Oistins, within days of his return to Barbados. There was a terrific response, and soon after, he established the Jerusalem Apostolic Spiritual Baptist Church at Ealing Grove, followed by its Zion Sister at Richmond Gap.

Members wear colorful gowns, each color symbolic of a particular quality: white stands for purity, cream for spirituality, blue for holiness, gold for royalty, green for strength, brown for happiness, silver-gray for overcoming, and pink for success. Red stands for strength, as well as for the blood of Christ. Both men and women wrap their heads in cloth, hence the name "Tie-heads."

As a native faith of Barbados, the church is closely tied to African religious traditions. Its lively music is often accompanied by much hand-clapping, foot-stomping and dancing. "We can take 'Abide with Me' and make you dance to it," boasts Bishop Williams. No mean feat, as this Anglican hymn is traditionally sung at funerals and notorious for its dreariness.

The Tie-heads are also known for their mysterious "Mourning Ground" rituals. After accepting the faith, the members are baptized in "living water" and given instruction in the doctrine. The born-again then mourns "a godly sorrow which calls one away from the busy walks of life." The Mourning Ground is a sacred section of the church set aside for this purpose and tended by chosen members. Here, in isolation, the mind is cleansed by prayer and purification for a period of seven to 10 days.

The Spiritual Baptist Church now boasts a following of some 7,000 people, about 40 percent of whom are male. This is an achievement, as the seemingly innumerable rum shops tend to deprive the traditional churches of male membership. It is women who are the backbone of the family and the church, and the primary force behind religion's continuing importance on the island.

Left, Anglicans after a Sunday service. **Right**, the graveyard behind St John's Church, with sweeping views of the east coast and a tree that loses its leaves.

Eudora Brathwaite was in her fifties when she married Selwyn, the man she has lived with for over 26 years and for whom she bore six of her 11 children.

She looks back on her life: "In dem days girls didn't stay on at school like they do now. I left when I was 14 and had to stay home and help my mother do the housework. She work in the (cane) field. When I was making my first child she was so mad. She cuss and carry on and t'row me out de house. But she tek me back when the baby born 'cos she like how it look."

The relationship between Eudora and the father of her first child was short-lived and though he gave her money for the child during its first year, she stayed with her family.

At age 19, she became involved with Deighton. A child was born and she moved in with him. Only two of the four children born to the couple lived. Eudora explains in a matter-of-fact tone: "Women had lot of children in dem days – some had more than 20. But a lot died."

When Deighton migrated to England to work as a bus conductor, Eudora and her children moved back in with her mother. Deighton at first sent money to them, but later this and all other communication from him ceased, and Eudora was forced to earn money as a domestic servant. Her mother looked after the children. Life was hard, but they managed.

Major crisis: But then her mother died, and Eudora faced the major crisis of her life – the threat of destitution and the embarrassment of becoming a welfare case. She found a solution: "I had to find somebody to help me with the children. Selwyn was liking me at the time and he had a good job, so I decided to stick wid he."

Before her marriage, Eudora and Selwyn lived together for 26 years and produced six children. In the early years, Eudora continued to earn money to support her children from previous unions. Now these older children contribute financially to her maintenance. But Deighton recently wrote from London to ask that they join him there. Eudora is reluctant, for she feels she will lose their contributions if they go.

Left, champagne and a kiss for Mrs Scantelbury from her son Victor; on the table is "peas and rice." **Right**, "hanging out" in St Joseph.

Eudora's changing family pattern is typical of women of her generation and illustrates a number of characteristics of the families of poorer black Barbadians, who form the majority of the population.

A typical pattern for women is that of delaying marriage and entering into a number of different unions, serially and with different men. Often couples start out with a "visiting union," in which the man visits his girlfriend at her house. Children may be born, and the couple may either move in together and even-

tually marry, or they may remain casual for a while before ending the relationship. It is not uncommon for a woman to have given birth to children from more than one man. The distinction between legitimate and illegitimate children is of little importance and there is no stigma attached to being an illegitimate child.

While it is accepted that a woman will enter into unions with more than one man during her lifetime, to do so simultaneously and to "have children all about" (from a number of men) is cause for considerable scorn. There is a Bajan proverb that goes "When yuh pick corn 'pon more than one row, yuh don't know where you get yuh bag full up." It means that when a woman is involved with too many men, she will not be sure which one has made her pregnant. Most women are careful about this, and they are generally sure about who the father of their children are.

Fame and shame: For a man, however, the situation is different. It is often said in Barbados, "What is fame for the man is shame for the woman." Even when a man is married or involved with one woman, he often continues to maintain a relationship with another woman and produce "outside" children. This is often accepted by wives until money they feel is theirs goes to support the other household.

Though many women work, and have done so since the days of slavery, home and chil-

good live-with better dan a bad marriage," for most, to wear a ring and be addressed as "Mistress" signifies that they have really made it, even though they may have had to wait for years. Weddings are often put off until a couple is well into middle age and childbearing is complete, as in Eudora's case.

This ambiguity towards marriage is the result of expectations about what a husband should be. For a man, marriage means economic responsibilities – not the least of which is the cost of the wedding.

Foods for days: A Bajan wedding is a grand affair. No expense is spared. People nostalgically speak of the country weddings of years ago, especially the elaborate receptions with

dren are their main concerns. Children are so important to womanhood that it is a great insult to be called a "mule," or worse still, a "graveyard" (a term for a woman who has had an abortion). But while one or two children are proof of womanhood, males are esteemed for their success with a number of women and their fathering of many children.

Women are expected to be the carriers of respectability in the community. As one man joked, "Women in de church; men in de rum shop." Respectability for a woman has its roots in the family and the church and is symbolized primarily by marriage. Even though some women will tell you that "A

"food for days." These celebrations were often repeated the weekend after in what was known as a "second day" wedding. As Louis Lynch describes it in *The Barbados Book:* "For days friends had been bringing down trays of ground provisions, dozens of eggs, bananas, water coconuts and live cockerels… masses of corn pone, cassava pone, pudding, sponge, coconut bread, 'black cake', fricasseed chicken, baked ham, boiled salt beef, avocados, lashings of peas and rice and stew, baked pork and fried fish, and to wash it all down, coconut water for the children, cheap red wine or falernum for the ladies, and rum or gin for the lords of creation."

Some of this splendor has died out. Some say it is because people are "too cheap," others that it is difficult to keep up with the rising cost of living. Still, a wedding is an important celebration.

If the opportunity arises, a visitor should stop and take a peek inside the church at the beauty of a bride in white lace, satin or chiffon, the brillance of the bridesmaids, often six or eight in number, the bridegroom and best man in smart dark suits set off with orchid buttonholes. Nothing must be left out of a "proper wedding." Weddings may attract many bystanders to the church, and any perception of skimping, even by the use of a cheaper material for the bride's dress, is cause for "malicious" comment.

is recounted by Louis Lynch in *The Barbados Book* as he records a doctor's attempts to obtain information from a male patient:

DOCTOR: *What is your son's name?*
FATHER: *John.*
DOCTOR: *John what?*
FATHER: *I doan know. You see he can either go in my name or the mother name.*
DOCTOR: *What is the mother's name?*
FATHER: *Estelle.*
DOCTOR: *Her second name.*
FATHER: *I doan know.*
DOCTOR (becoming exasperated): *How many children do you have?*
FATHER: *Five, but I doan know she last name 'cos I doan tek so much notice o' she.*

Living separate lives: "Family is woman's business," and the mother-centered family is another feature of life in Barbados. Ties between the couple are weak and they generally lead fairly separate lives. They usually engage in different leisure activities. Money and property matters are rarely entered into jointly, and as we've seen in Eudora's case, separations are common.

The marginality of the father in family affairs

Something old, something new: marriage, Bajan style, circa 1900 (left) and modern-day (right). Weddings are often elaborate affairs where no expense is spared.

Paternal pride: A father often takes pride in his children, especially in their educational progress, but his responsibilities lie mainly with providing financial support. This means he wants to be sure the child is biologically his. Denials of paternity do occur, especially from men in casual, visiting relationships, but then, so do false paternity claims from women.

The financial obligations of fatherhood can be quite onerous for a poor man. A man is reluctant to support children that are not his own even if he is married to their mother and therefore legally bound to do so. Remember how Eudora continued to work to help support her older children from previous unions, even

after she and Selwyn were married? Fathers are expected to support their children even if they and the mother are not living together or when they are "outside" children, though as we saw in Eudora's case, such support may dwindle with time and then cease altogether.

Men are often accused of being "wut'less" (worthless) and "vagabonds" in evading their responsibilities to their children. Though these labels may well apply to some, it is not easy for men to keep up with the many claims to their often meager financial resources. As one man put it: "I got a lot of stretching to do with my money. Apart from the woman in the house, I got to give my mother something, plus I got to give some to the ones outside."

When the father's duty ends the mother's begins, for with the money he provides she performs all the other child-rearing tasks. As Eudora herself put it: "The mother is who raise the child. She does nurse it, feed it, dress it, send it to school and to church – mek sure she raise it the right way, decent-like, with good manners."

The relationship between a mother and her children is close and often lasts to the end of her days. Mothers assume responsibility for their children and take their duties very seriously, always making sure their children are well-groomed and neatly dressed. The sight of scrubbed young girls on their way to Sunday school, all dressed up in pink frills with matching bows in their tightly braided hair, is a delight to visitors and locals alike.

Discipline is strict with "plenty licks and lashes" (slaps) – licks for being late for school and for arriving home late, licks for forgetting to say "good morning" or "good evening" or "yes, please" to your elders. "To spare the rod is to spoil the child," yet as one mother says in George Lamming's classic novel of village life in Barbados, *In the Castle of My Skin*, "When all's said and done they is ours and we love them. Whatever we mothers say or do, nobody love them like we."

Eudora and many other women like her consider themselves mothers first and foremost; they devote nearly all their time and energy to mothering.

Help from granny: Yet there are times when such duties are by necessity exchanged or passed on to others. It is common for a mother

Left, homing it up and sporting their finest on a family outing to Queen's Park in Bridgetown.

to take a job to earn money and share the raising of her children with someone else.

When Deighton stopped sending money from England, Eudora took his place as breadwinner and her mother helped take care of the children. "Leaving de child at Granny – dat is my culture," sang the calypsonian Mighty Gabby in "Culture," his 1985 hit about life in Barbados.

The exchanges between female relatives go beyond that of occasional babysitting and borrowing of money, food and other goods. If a woman has a large number of children who prove to be a handful, one or even two may be "adopted" and go to live with an aunt, sister, sister-in-law, or even a neighbor or friend. This is not legal adoption, though the woman

assumes full maternal responsibility and may be addressed as "Ma" or "Mum." Children are shared rather than possessed in circumstances like Eudora's.

Tightly-knit villages and extended families make this kind of cooperation possible. In Barbados, a family can extend beyond the confines of mother, father and children. Supportive networks between female relatives – sisters, mothers and daughters – are especially strong, and sometimes include male relatives as well – uncles, brothers, cousins and grandfathers. These men can serve as father-substitutes when the biological father is not around.

Family relations, then, are flexible and open enough to extend into the wider community. Households may contain a mixture of relatives and friends, often on a permanent basis. Friends may call each other "Sis" or "Brother." A friend is often said to be "like family to me" or sometimes even "better than family to me." Indeed, it is difficult for a stranger to tell who is "family" and who is not.

No place like home: Three generation households are common, particularly those containing grandmother, mother and children. The question of "What to do with mother?" asked by many adults in Europe and America is less of a problem in Barbados, where grandmothers lead functional lives for much of their old age. The family home continues to play an important part in the lives of many Bajans; it is a haven to which they can return at any stage.

Family ties also stretch internationally, and although some links with migrants may weaken, they are likely to be reactivated in later years, as we saw in the case of Eudora and Deighton. Links with migrant family members are maintained by letters, remittances and visits, often for funerals and weddings. Starting in early December planeloads of Bajans laden with gifts arrive "home" for Christmas.

Changing patterns: But family patterns are changing in Barbados. For example, Eudora's first son Tony married when he was only 24 – 14 years before his mother. Both he and his wife, Michelle, completed secondary school; he is now a bank clerk and she is a secretary. She has one child, and continues to work. With the use of contraception, now generally accepted and widely available in Barbados, the couple intend to limit their children to two. Any more would be too expensive and a "keep-back" to their careers. They live in their own house in a new housing development and employ a half-day maid.

Some claim that as Third World countries industrialize and modernize, they will adopt the same cultural patterns as the developed world, with family life becoming centered on a nuclear family household. Maybe so, but tradition dies hard. While Tony and Michelle lead a very different life from Eudora, not everything has changed. Eudora looks after their child while they are at work. And when

Left, Christopher Phillips with icon appropriate to the season, in St Peter. Right, Rastafarian mother and son Heshimu in their hilltop chattel house.

Michelle suspected that Tony was involved with another woman, she went back to live with her mother.

Family flexibility: Traditional family life in Barbados is often described in derogatory terms as having "promiscuous" and "adulterous" sexual relations, "illegitimate" children, "unmarried" mothers and "absentee" fathers. But there is another side of the picture, one which stresses the flexible and adaptable nature of the family among the poor in Barbados.

Historically, these families have endured the transposition from Africa and the rigors of slavery, and now survive in conditions of unemployment and poverty. Migration also removes adult breadwinners from the family. In many societies, this might cause a crisis in family life. But the Barbadian family adapts relatively painlessly. The weakness of the bonds between couples cushion what seems to be almost inevitable separation.

We must look at these features within the economic and historical context of the society in which they exist. Only then can we come to a full understanding of what family life is like in Barbados. Where family duties are constantly being rearranged and reassigned to cope with life's contingencies.

FACTS ABOUT THE BAJAN HOUSEHOLD

- 60–70 percent of the houses are owner-occupied. (In contrast, around 62 percent of Americans and just over half of Britons live in houses either they or their families own.
- Per capita income: US$5,000.
- Adult literacy is 98 percent.
- Over 74 percent of Bajans aged between 15 and 44 have never been married.
- More than 38 percent of households are headed by women.
- Almost 100 percent of households have running water.
- 80 percent of Bajans households have a TV and refrigerator.
- 24 percent of the people have cars.
- Over 55 percent of households have a telephone.

Right, The Yearwoods outside their chattel house in the parish of St Lucy. "Chattel" means "movable property."

A LETTER FROM "THE ROCK"

Almost every family has relatives living abroad. Yet even emigrants think of Barbados, affectionately called "The Rock," as home, and try to keep in touch. This letter from a mother in Barbados to her daughter in England provides some insight into the everyday life of a Bajan village:

Dear Grace,

I got yuh last letter and I glad to hear yuh keepin' well – yuh old mother her alright too.

white people nose 'cause dey keep slippin' down on my wun. Dese pas' months de pressure 'ent botherin' me so much – de doctor call it hypertension or some such fancy name. I tryin' to keep down de weight like yuh tell muh. I cut down 'pon de starches and trying' to eat de greens – but dey so expensive doh!

Yuh father still here de same way. Yuh would tink now he gettin' old – he did 65 las'

I hope yuh tekin' care o'yuhself and de cold weather in England 'ent killin' yuh. Yuh mus' remember to use de mixture – dat candle grease and coconut oil and camphor – which I send up for yuh to rub yuh feet 'gainst de cold. Doan' mind de smell – it good.

Yuh ask muh so many questions 'bout so many people here in Maynard's village in yuh las' letter dat it goin' tek a long time fuh muh to write 'bout all o' dem. And muh eyes 'ent so good now. Las' time I went to de doctor he tell muh to wear de glasses all de time but yuh know how it is – Mum 'ent get 'custom to dem yet. Dis old grey head o' mine can't deal with dis new-fangle ting. And besides de glasses mussee mek for

birthday – yuh would tink dat he would change. He still chasin' de women – dey goin' kill he! But I lef' he to de Lord. I know yuh doan like muh to bad talk yuh father and he 'ent all bad – I should know after 50 years!

He still usin' de money dat yuh send good – fixing up de place. We change de winders in de front from de old-time jalousies to glass ones. Dat wasn't so much problem. But dis changin' from de wood to de wall is a real headache. De dust from de cement and de cleanin' up every day after de workmen gone. So far de back part finish – paint up and everyt'ing. It 'ent so much to be done now – Praise de Lord! And I hope he goin' let muh live to see it done.

Yuh know dat yuh sister Shirley daughter staying wid me now. We does call she "Tammy" for short. But she's a sweet girl doh! And helpful too – washin' wares and tidyin' de house and so every mornin'. I gotta admire she 'cause she doan get on like dese young vagabonds o' today. Yuh can't speak to non o' dem 'cause dey 'ent got no respect and no shame neidder. When you did commin' up any big person could correc' yuh and yuh would have

Well, nobody 'ent see she for a few months very well. And yuh know what – jus' yesterday I did commin' from in town and I butt up 'pon lickmout' Doreen. She tell muh dat Mavis got a baby boy – 6 weeks now. And nobody 'ent see it yet. To tink dat Bertha is muh friend and she 'ent tell muh – not a word! But Doreen now – she does know everyt'ing 'bout everybody – she say dat de child ugly, ugly like de Pastor. De Lord sure

to hear. But today yuh know dem too hard ears.

But I was tellin' yuh 'bout Tammy. She bright too yuh know. She jus' pass de exam and she reach der de top. And its does mek muh old heart feel so good to see she steppin' out 'pon a mornin' in she school uniform.

But child I gotta tell yuh dis – yuh remember Bertha daughter dat name Mavis – de foolishy, foolishy one – dat used to play dat she more Christian dan anybody else? And de only place dat she used to go to is church.

Left, outdoor haircuts, such as this one in St John, are a Bajan tradition. **Right**, the girls of St George shake and jam to the beat of calypso and the American Top 40.

does move in mysterious ways nowadays!

I going stop writin' for now I goin' to look for something to put in de pot. I still can't do like de young people and cook Sunday for Monday. I goin' cook some stewfood wid sweet potato, a piece o' pumpkin, some breadfruit and a piece o' pigtail and some light dumplin's – 'cause yuh known yuh father like dat. Doan' mind de women – he still doan' eat out. He mussee frighten for what dey might put in the food to mek he bewitch. Doan' mind me – I know he does like muh cookin'.

I doan' know ef I remember to tell yuh but I did get a invitation to Tiny weddin'. At de St Michael Cathedral – ef yuh please! So yuh know me – I did had to go.

And de talk, girl – everybody wonderin' who de groom is. He name write 'pon de invitation – Sylvester MacDonald Dacosta Broome! Some say dat he livin' in America, some say England. One body say he white, but yuh Aunt Cintie say doan' mind de name – is de skinny little boy dey used to call "Bones" – dat used to run 'bout here barefoot. But she vex 'cause she didn't get no invitation.

For an occasion like dat dis old girl had to look real smart – everyt'ing new from head to toe – hat, dress, shoes, bag and gloves 'cause gloves in fashion now. I didn't bother you 'bout sending de outfit 'cause my meeting turn was commin' up and dat money was sufficient.

De big day come. Riding in de taxi wid yuh father mek muh remember de day we get married. And yuh father lookin' something like he did den – t'ree piece suit and all. I did feel too sweet.

Tiny did look real good but she mother – I'ent know what it is dat she had on! De hat did like a upsided-down lampshade. She face didn't make-up bad but de eye shadder did too blue and too tick and when she start to cry all o' it run down she face. Lord what a mess!

De bridgegroom look dapper. He is a Bajan – but he been 'way for donkey years. She mussee find he when she went to England – only 17 days and she come back talking like she swallow a dictionary.

Anyway everybody enjoy duh self. It didn't really nothin' to find fault 'bout – but yuh know de village people. It did a nine-day-talk 'bout here.

But I did tellin' yuh 'bout de changes in de village. Mos' people try to improve de house. Everybody got in electric now. No more oil lamps – doh I still keep mine – one in each room jus' in case – 'cause yuh doan 'get no warnin' when de light goin' off. Nowadays everybody got dey little fridge and TV – some even got videos.

Mos' people got in runnin' water now but de standpipe still dere. Sometimes we old folk still find weself by de standpipe talkin' like de old days. Look how t'ings change nuh! Yuh remember how you and Shirley get dere 'bout five o'clock 'pon a mornin' to avoid de cussin' and quarrellin' and pushin' in de line?

Mr Pilgrim rum shop still dere and yuh father still teking one dere in between. But dat is one place I would like to see move from 'bout here. De young boys tek over from where de old men lef' off. Yuh see dem 'pon a Friday or Saturday – as dey get pay. De money dat shoulda gone to feed dem family gone in Pilgrim pocket. Dis is de second house he buildin' now.

Edna doing well too. She 'ent got no more shop – is a Mini Mart now – ef yuh plese! And move out to de front road – sellin' all kind o' fancy t'ings. And she doan' trust no more – no credit for we poor people again. One or two girls in de village get work in de Mini Mart doh – so she didn't forget she roots altogether.

But de big news now – Praise de Lord – we get de roads fix. Dat been a eyesore for years 'specially when de rain fall. And if yuh did by a pot-hole when a car passin' yuh would had to gone back home and change yuh clothes 'cause dem did get wet up and dirty. But now de road get pave. No more carryin' de extra pair o' shoes.

Dis mussee de longest letter I ever write in muh life but I goin' stop now. Give muh love to muh grands – How dey doin' nuh? I hope dey behavin' duhself. And muh best to yuh husband.

May de Lord bless yuh, real good.

Your lovin' Mum.

Left, watching the world go by in St Philip. **Right**, young "Philipians" never trouble trouble until trouble troubles them.

A DAY IN THE LIFE OF A FISHERMAN

Above, the clouds whisk by at a steady clip, their shapes altering every minute. The mind's imagination conjures heads of lions, shapely mermaids and gliding flying fish. Below, the white-cap sea pulsates with the forces of wind and gravity. Between these two natural elements is the fisherman.

In Barbados, a fisherman's day begins before dawn. At 4 am Speightstown residents Philip and David are pushing their small rowboat down to the water's edge. Sensing a lull in the sets of rolling breakers,

wind is strong, bucking the swells and current, creating a frothy, turbulent sea.

By the time these two brave fishermen reach their destination, shut off the diesel engine and set adrift, light is just beginning to break over the distant silhouette of Barbados's west coast. David begins his chores: inspecting the engines, sharpening hooks, preparing the nets and palm fronds. Philip turns on the radio to channel 16 and gives fellow fishermen their location and a weather report. He then washes some pots and cups

they quickly hop aboard the dinghy and row under the stars to their fishing vessel, some two hundred yards offshore. This pre-dawn ritual is a daily one during the fall and winter months. They start early so they can bring in a big catch of flying fish – one of the island's staple foods and the visitor's favorite treats.

Loading their supplies onto the single engine fishing boat and untying the anchor line, Philip and David get ready to set out on a course 12 miles (19 km) due west. It's a long, slow, bouncy journey. Near the coast, the island's land mass blocks the strong southeast trade winds, keeping the water smooth as glass. But a mile or so offshore the

and prepares the day's meal: a stew of macaroni, pork and fish and a batch of hot tea. The two men have some tea, along with cold fried fish and home baked bread, for breakfast.

Now there's light to work by: they carefully dip one net about 60 yards (55 meters) long with palm fronds attached to each end, in the water. The palm fronds create a shadow: flying fish gather under it to hide from the sun, and become trapped. This net will stay out until the end of the day, when Philip, a strong husky man, will haul it in.

The men drop a shorter net about 30 yards (27 meters) long right next to the boat. A chum bucket filled with cut fish and oil dangles from the side of the boat and attracts the fish to the net. David and Philip works this net every hour or so; pulling it in, cleaning it of its catch – usually about 500 fish – and setting it back out again.

In between the hauling and dropping of the net, they spend the time fishing with handlines. One, a thick monofilament with a large hook and live flying fish for bait, is set a fair distance behind the boat in hope of hooking a blue marlin or any of the other large fish that feed on flying fish. They also use smaller handlines, with tiny hooks and

and on news of the last crew to be lost at sea.

In the back of each fisherman's mind is the thought that one day his engine may fail to start after a day of drifting. If that happens, he must simply roll with the tides and waves and hope that eventually he will be found by a passing freighter or run aground on the island of St Vincent or St Lucia. That's why fishing boats are painted such bright colors: they're easier to spot if lost at sea. This fateful uncertainty has led to the daily sermon and prayer that comes over the boat

cut bait, to catch the fish that are swarming around the chum.

All the while the seas ceaselessly roll and tumble the boat in every direction. After years of such an environment, though, the two are oblivious to the 7-foot (2-meter) swells. David stares out at the horizon as if in a trance and Philip loudly sings his favorite calypso song. In the background, the non-stop chattering of other fishermen comes over the radio – seamen trading all kinds of information on their fishing luck

Left, and **right**, flying fish (*Hirundictys affins*) is a national dish. It accounts for 60 percent of the weight of all fish landed on the island.

radio at 9.30 every morning, given at sea by one of the fishermen who is also a minister.

The work is hard, the hours long, the danger imminent and the rewards fair but not great. It is a life that calls to hardy and adventurous souls. Philip and David are two such characters.

At the end of the day they have netted three or four thousand flying fish. On their way back to Speightstown they bag their catch, wash the boat and themselves down, and change into dry, clean clothes. All that is left to do is to hand over the fish to the market vendors. The fishermen then head home for a meal and hot shower, hoping tomorrow will bring the same results.

AFRICA
UNITE.
JAHLOVE
SEEN.

A LIVING ART

Recognizable African influences still lurk in the works of many Barbadian artists and craftsmen. Walk through the Temple Yard district, at the westerly end of Bridgetown, and watch the Rastafarian craftsmen bend their dreadlocked heads over leather and straw, clay and wood. Listen to their joyous humming, the sounds of their mallets and chisels. Before long you are transported to that faraway continent.

The African cultural memory springs forth in the colors, themes and styles of many of the island's most creative citizens. It expresses itself in the unique blend of art and craft that so dominates Barbadian art.

The Barbadian artist will boggle the minds of those who try to distinguish between art and craft. Throughout the centuries, the Barbadian artist-craftsman has ornamented, embossed and embellished the functional, making it a work of art. He has taken simple, everyday items and made them into expressions of his personal and cultural self.

Community of craftsmen: At Temple Yard, you'll find artists who have been able to combine old and new, East and West. There is Ibo, an artisan, who designed a building made entirely of bamboo: doors, windows, roof – all skilfully plaited, rainproofed and heatproofed, too. There is also Akyem, who studied at the Jamaica School of Art. A master of clay, Akyem produces plaques, sculptures in the round, low-relief scenes, and some unusual paintings which explore and reject Western concepts of art.

At **Temple Yard**, the creations of a whole community of craftsmen are laid out, leather bags, shoes, purses – there are countless items created from wire, bamboo, coconut husks, shells and fronds; images of local fish, birds, fruit, animals, seashells clustered into fans and jeweled vases. Many of these are functional, yes, but they are still created with the art-spirit of Africa.

To many of the brethren in Temple Yard, "making with the hands" is part of the Rasta-

Preceding pages: rocky reverie on south coast; young Rasta by mural; whirling dancers at the show *1627 and All That**. **Left,** Bajan art often incorporates themes from everyday life.

farian creed. You will find painted images of Marcus Garvey, the Jamaican leader of the Back-to-Africa movement, reggae musician Bob Marley, former Ethiopian Emperor Haile Selassie, lions – the Rastafarian symbol – and maps of Africa resplendent in red, green and gold.

Exquisite boutiques: The Rastafarians are only one group of craftsmen on the island. Nearby, in **Pelican Village**, you'll find small, exquisite boutiques, galleries, craftsmen in their workshops and their goods on display.

The Barbados Arts Council, an old and respected institution, has its Art Gallery here. And there is Karl Broodhagen's painting and sculpture gallery, where the island's art con-

Broodhagen has also made exquisite portrait heads of many famous Barbadians, including the famed Sir Grantley Adams, whose bronzed features are forever immortalized on a pedestal at the Government Headquarters on Bay Street. Perhaps the most impressive of Broodhagen's works, some dating to the 1930s, are those he keeps at his house in Strathclyde, St Michael.

Avant-garde sculpture: Pelican Village is where the fashionable and the knowledgeable gather after sightseeing and shopping. Nearby, there is the Barbados Investment and Development Corporation (BIDC), a statutory body which oversees handicrafts on the island. On its grounds is a massive piece of

noisseurs gather. Broodhagen is a living legend in Barbados and a master craftsman, painter, thinker and researcher. He began his career as a tailor and grew to become a virtuoso artist.

If you have the opportunity, take a look at his statue, "The Freed Slave," commemorating the 150th anniversary of emancipation. It stands in the center of a traffic circle in St Barnabas, where the parishes of St Michael and St George meet (*see page 195*). A larger-than-life figure of a man with his arms upraised, head thrown back, broken chains dangling from his wrists, the statue speaks eloquently of pride and freedom.

sculpture called "Pelican in Flight" consisting of three pylons welded together and rusting under the sea-breeze. Some consider this piece an insult, foisted on the Barbadian public at exorbitant cost, by an avant-garde architect.

The BIDC looks after local craftspeople. It has Handicraft Sales Shops at Pelican Village, Grantley Adams International Airport, Sam Lord's Castle is in St Philip and Almond Beach Village is in St Peter, and at Harrison's Cave in St Thomas. The BIDC also has workshops, where beginners and veterans alike can practice their crafts. Products from these workshops include dress accessories: hats, shoes, handbags; table accessories: place mats, coasters, utensils of coconut and clay, straw and bamboo grass; handy items: baskets, lampshades, beautyboxes and rugs.

Hill of clay: If you are interested in pottery, you will find Barbados filled with collectable treasures. The tradition of making household vessels from clay started long ago in the parish of St Andrew, at Chalky Mount, a hill of stratified clays sandwiched between thin strata of shale (*see page 274*). Here, the sedimentary core of Barbados is laid bare; red, yellow, brown and white clays can be seen in the massive cross-section of Chalky Mount visible from the East Coast road.

are operating on Chalky Mount, many of the older, traditional hand- or foot-operated wheels are still in use here.

Often the master potter has a boy to turn the flywheel. In these workshops (often just sheds tacked onto the side of the houses where the potters live) you'll find shelves displaying the finished work and the traditional ovens nearby in the yard; strong structures made of thick brown fire-bricks, encasing hundreds of degrees of heat when running full blast.

Creative spirit: The potter's craft is handed down in the family from one generation to the next. Courtney Devonish is a son of Chalky Mount, a purveyor of a long tradi-

Throughout the centuries, the ground of Chalky Mount supplied the material for numerous household items: the clay pot served as the stove for many homes; clay lamps and candlesticks were a necessity; cups, plates, bowls and that strangely beautiful utensil called a "monkey"(designed for cooling and dispensing drinks) were very much part of everyday life.

Although modern, electric potter's wheels

Left, a Bajan artist paints a village scene in vibrant colors with a palette knife. **Right**, Ras Akyem Ramsey with his prize-winning "House of King David."

tion, though he operates from a modern workshop at Pelican Village. Some of the best examples of traditional pottery can be found at his place. He has been trained formally in Italy, and you will also find pieces crafted in classic European styles in his gallery.

The creative spirit is restless in Barbados. People turn from one art form to another. Goldie Spieler is like that. She's a marvelous manipulator of material. She has some first-class ink and watercolor studies of local plants, with authentic landscapes in the background. She also paints in oil and acrylic. And her earhworks at the Potters House in St Thomas is worthy of a visit.

Open-air markets: For a small island, Barbados boasts a surprisingly large number of artists. You'll find them coming out in droves at the festival markets. There is Bridgetown Market, in early August, at the end of the annual Crop Over Festival, a very old and recently revived activity.

Crop Over is a real explosion of calypso, costumed bands, street fairs and dancing. At its culmination, special stalls are set up to show off the wide range of Barbadian arts and crafts.

The costumes of the revelers who participate in the Crop Over Festival are a delight in themselves, and are evidence of the great creative talents of the islanders. It's a pity that the art of the carnival costume is so ephemeral; beautiful creations are left abandoned in backyards a day or two after having dazzled spectators on the roads.

The Oistins Fish Festival, another island favorite, is growing yearly. It concentrates on things of the sea; and here, on Easter weekend, the fishermen have their day. For the little town of Oistins in Christ Church, fishing has always been a major occupation. The fishing boats can be seen lining the beach like washed-up shells, equally colorful and sparkling.

Boatbuilding is one of the oldest activities of the islanders, and the painting of these boats is an art in itself. But the craft of the fisherfolk doesn't stop here; they also make fishing nets and fish-pots. These pots are clever, box-like structures with a tunneled, twisted entrance through which fish can swim, but once inside, they are trapped. The traps are made of wire and bamboo, plaited and tied. They are among the best examples of Barbadian craft.

The **Holetown Festival**, in mid-February, focuses on the historic traditions of Barbados. It was at Holetown that the first English settlers landed and set up their little wooden pioneer huts in 1627. The festival that takes place here is filled with costumes and pageantry, and art and craft displays abound.

Batik and silk-screen: You'll also find plenty of art and handicraft pieces in the little shops attached to the hotels on the St James coast

and along the Christ Church roads. They have a wide range of printed fabrics: batik and silk-screen dresses, wall-hangings and scarves. At Best of Barbados, a shop with many branches, there are the famous Jill Walker prints. Her scenes and landscapes of Barbados adorn the walls of Bridgetown offices, hotels, guesthouses and public places. Her representations of island life are delightfully ironic, and Jill is one of the most hardworking and popular artists around.

The **Barbados Museum**, at the Garrison, houses some extremely interesting items of old Barbados, and has a fine art gallery. There are some interesting old prints, maps, landscapes and colorful portrayals of the activities of an earlier era. The most famous old painting in Barbados is that of *Christ* by Benjamin West which hangs in the St George Parish Church. It was once placed in a storehouse on one of the plantations, and neglected for a long time. A thief, entering the storehouse, was frightened by the piercing eyes of the portrait, and began to dig them out. Though the portrait was later sent to Britain for repairs, one eye remains missing.

The National Cultural Foundation organizes regular art exhibits at the Queens Park Gallery, and around Independence Day (November 30) there is the National Independence Festival of Creative Arts (NIFCA), which

Left, traditional crafts like blacksmithing are alive and well in Barbados. **Right,** Henry Harding, an old-school potter, holding one of his "monkey jugs."

features shows and presentations of many local art forms. The NIFCA visual arts and crafts exhibition usually presents the creative work of schoolchildren.

Ornate murals: The Cultural Foundation also helps local communities and schoolchildren to create murals in community centers and schools. These depict the cultural, historical and social aspects of their neighborhoods, as well as popular local personalities. There is a large and complex mural at Eagle Hall, St Michael, on the wall of the Post Office; others are at Springer Memorial School in Government Hill; at Ellerton Primary School, St George; at the Bathsheba Community Center, on the East

Coast in St Joseph; and one at Boscobelle.

The first murals in Barbados were simple paintings done on the outside walls of shops and nightclubs on Baxter's Road and Nelson Street in Bridgetown. They advertised the activities to be found inside. The carts and stalls of vendors carry smaller versions of this kind of art. The modern-day spate of mural-painting began with the staging of the Caribbean Festival of Creative Arts in Barbados in 1981. CARIFESTA is the biggest arts festival of the region, hosted in turn by the various islands. At the St James Secondary School and the Barbados Community College, there are several murals created during the last CARIFESTA. Several artists worked on each, so that in one mural you will find a variety of styles and techniques.

Preserving culture: Many of the artists are driven by the urge to portray aspects of their culture which are fast vanishing. They make the effort to record the ways of life of the farm worker, the fisherfolk, the peasants; the places where such people lived and the materials they used. A striking painting of plantation life by one of Barbados's most prolific artists, Alison Chapman Greaves, is displayed in the Barbados Museum.

The little chattel houses of the villages are a favorite subject for these culture-preservers. Fielding Babb has painted hundreds of them, mainly in oils. You'll also find paintings of chattel houses by Adrian Compton, Omowale and Sundiata Stewart (twin brothers), Winifred and Harriet Cumberbatch (twin sisters), Oscar Walkes (a self-taught painter with a sharp, bright, detailed style), Briggs Clarke and Kathleen Hawkins. Their scenes of plantation life in old Barbados are collected by many art connoisseurs.

Artists also seek out old buildings about to be demolished and capture their image before they are pulled down. Others have painted historical events and eras: of slavery, of struggle, of sailing ships; of insurrection and rebellion; of hurricanes, rain and flood.

Startling hues: Art in Barbados runs the whole gamut of themes. Some artists, like Ena Power, specialize in flower-painting. Others, like David and Indra Gall, have moved into the realm of the symbolic, using local images to project their message. Coral Bernadine, blends the themes of African heritage and Catholicism, and also paints more intimate studies of local subjects.

You may notice that the color of the older, oil-based, European-style paintings is subdued, even dull. By contrast, the color in Caribbean paintings is sometimes startling. But no more startling than the colors of the landscape. There are seas so turquoise, skies so ultramarine, flowers and foliage so crimson and yellow, butterflies so multicolored, that often a stranger from the North, seeing West Indian paintings and not knowing the islands, thinks that the artist is exaggerating.

Left, sculptor Karl Broodhagen at work in his studio. **Right**, every summer brings an explosion of creativity for the annual Crop Over celebration.

"Bajans, Come Back to Calypso!"

Box-cart and stick for wicket
Dat is my culture
Mauby and marble cricket
Dat is my culture
Slamming domino in competition
With the calypso and sweet steel band
So now you see what I really mean
Dis is my true culture in the Caribbean...
— "Culture," Mighty Gabby (1985)

No doubt about it: calypso in Barbados is here to stay. For centuries, church and state tried to banish this African-derived music. But the musical culture of Afro-Barbadians survived – and indeed thrived – underground. Today this tuneful, topical music is, as Mighty Gabby, the island's foremost calypsonian, proclaims, an integral part of Barbados's "true culture."

On one level, the lively calypsoes are pure entertainment – the ultimate party music. But they also function as a kind of auditory news-paper, spreading information about current issues. No topic is too trivial or too touchy to be the subject of a calypso song – themes range from corrupt politicians to potholes in the road, a controversial beauty contest to a nosy neighbor. A visitor who wants to learn about the true social and political situation in Barbados need only listen to the current crop of calypso tunes. And today's visitor will be spared a subterranean search, because you can hear the music everywhere: on the radio, at nighclubs, in the hotels.

Social commentary: Calypso's ancestors were the slave songs brought by Africans to the West Indies in the early 1600s. Historians suggest that the slaves brought two distinct types of music: work songs and ribald songs of commentary. The work songs, sung by laboring slaves to lift their spirits and pass the time, were usually laments on the hardships they suffered. The lighter, satirical songs are more like the social commentaries of con-temporary calypso. Surprisingly, the slaves rarely attacked their masters in tunes. The songs were basically channels for the spread of local gossip about plantation people.

Left, the Sunshine Orchestra Band at a south coast hotel. **Right**, emotion-filled music at Mount Hillaby Pentacostal Church in St Thomas.

"Forever England": By the 1640s there were 20,000 Africans and 23,000 British colonists in Barbados; social and cultural life was patterned on that of England in their quest to create "some corner that is forever England." The cultural heritage of African slaves was not welcome in such a society. The British viewed the Afri-cans' music, dance, dress, food, languages and religious rituals as pagan and barbarous.

In 1649, the indentured servants and Afri-cans rebelled against the white landowners. Legend has it the bondservants roused each

other to battle by lively music on horns, drums and conch shells. Another uprising in 1675 led to the enforcement of a slave code that banned the beating of drums. The law provided that due care was to be taken "to restrain the wanderings and meetings of Negroes and other slaves at all times."

In 1688, the plantation society passed an-other law stipulating that any drums or loud instruments had to be burned if discovered. But the planters could not wipe out the musi-cal heritage of the slaves; music was a vital part of the Africans' daily life. They sang while they worked. They celebrated with songs on holidays and at funerals (they believed the dead would be transported back to Africa, away from the brutal slave society).

In response to the masters' strict policies, the slaves hid away their African customs. And these were carefully preserved and handed down to younger generations through secret ceremonies and rituals. Slave music had much in common with present-day calypsoes. The melodies included spontaneous vocal effects such as cries and yells, verses alternated with choruses, and the songs were based on clearly discernible short phrases.

Even after the slaves were freed in 1838, the planter class deemed any vibrant expression of African cultural heritage dangerous and a "relapse into barbarism." Indigenous music ish military bands. The regimental rhythms are superimposed on a persistent and recognizable African base. What results is a seductive, semi-martial rhythm that excites even the most staid villagers to dance or "work up," as Bajans would say.

Tuk bands travel from village to village playing popular tunes and inviting villagers to contribute their own compositions – as long as they fit with the lively tempo. People dress up as donkeys or bears and dance suggestively. Men put on dresses and stuff them with rags to suggest pregnancy. The melodies of tuk songs are simple and the subjects are trivial. But these tunes have kept the laboring classes in high spirits on many a Sunday afternoon and

therefore stayed underground and survived as folk music. This "little tradition" of communal singing, religion, dance and customs became embedded in the life-style of little villages and tenantries away from unfriendly eyes and ears of the leaders.

Seductive beat: At the time, the primary form of resistance to cultural pressures was the music of the tuk band. The name comes from the onomatopoeic sound "Boom-a-tuk, boom-a-tuk" that the big log drum gives out. For the last 120 years, tuk music has been played at picnics and excursions and on public holidays.

The music is lively, with an intricate, pulsating, quick beat strongly suggestive of Brit- have become synonymous with holiday revelry in Barbados today.

Calypso country: In the early 20th century, the calypso that had developed in Trinidad began to influence Barbadian folk music and helped revive the calypso tradition. The songs from Trinidad influenced not only the melodies of the Barbadian songs but, more importantly, the lyrics. Themes widened beyond gossip and scandal to include satire and social commentary, but it took many years for calypso to become an influential medium of satire and a legitimate vehicle of musical expression in Barbados.

Although a few performers like Da Costa Allamby, Frank Taylor and Mighty Charmer were hard-working calypsonians in the late 1930s, not many Barbadians were drawn into the music. Most citizens were preoccupied with British standards of respectability. People were concerned with getting ahead, which to them implied losing touch with all vestiges of plantation life. The more closely an individual approached the British in his manner and speech, the more cultured he was considered. Ironically, the phrase "he ain' got no culture" referred to those whose behavior revealed the vitality of their African ancestry.

Up to no good: Singing calypsoes was certainly not a way of achieving positive social status and prestige in Bajan society. Early calypsonians were seen more as jokers and

(By this time, the art form in Trinidad had acquired a measure of commercial value.) The only performer to make much of an impact was Mighty Charmer, the first recognized Barbadian calypsonian, who went professional in 1947 with "My Dear Mammy." Even then, Barbadian calypso was held to be far inferior to the "real thing" from Trinidad. This lack of acceptance of indigenous calypsonians was a serious obstacle and those who could afford it – like the Mighty Charmer and the Mighty Sugar – went to Trinidad. Charmer left Barbados in 1950 and stormed Trinidad with his composition "Flying Saucer." The exposure he gained there was important for the development of calypso in Barbados. He arrived in

comics than as serious singers. They functioned like the strolling minstrels of earlier decades, wandering from rum shop to rum shop and from street corner to street corner. Mothers would pull their children inside and shut the door when they saw these minstrels. They forbade their daughters to talk to the singers. In the mothers' eyes, the calypsonians were up to no good.

Yet calypso pioneers persisted, lured perhaps by the chance of making some money.

Left, a band parades through the street at a "village meet" in Market Hill, St George. **Right**, celebrations in Bridgetown on Independence Day.

Trinidad when calypso was functioning as a powerful political weapon. He was also there at the time of the rise of the Mighty Sparrow, the master of satirical calypso.

For this reason, when Charmer first recorded in Port of Spain 1961, his lyrics had become more critical, though he retained his sense of humor. His hit, "The Laughing Stock," satirizes the clearly divided social classes in the West Indies:

You could tell some people's class
By de way dat dem does laugh
Every time you go to a social or party
De Big Shots laugh – Ho! Ho! Ho!
De middle class laugh – He! He! He!

But when de woman began to laugh
You could tell she was from de ordinary class
She bawl out, Wullos! muh belly! Oh lawd
Ah going dead! Wuhlaw!

Charmer was an exception. Popularity – not to mention stardom – was elusive for most Barbadian calypsonians for almost two decades more. Ironically, it was a group of white, middle-class men called The Merrymen who kept the Barbadian calypso tradition alive in the 1960s and early 1970s.

Hit after hit: Led by Emile Straker, The Merrymen's repertoire consisted of old calypsoes played in a sing-along style that crossed the boundaries of folk, country and western, pop and calypso. They perfected a

when Barbados experimented with a Trinidad-style Carnival, a bacchanalian festival occurring immediately before Lent. At first, this Carnival contained none of the island's enduring folk forms such as tuk music, folk singing, calypsoes or folk dances. In the third year, when black calypsonians finally played a role in the festival, they were treated as comics and burlesque performers.

By 1963, however, the government-owned station Radio Barbados came on the air, and together with Rediffusion (the former Radio Distribution) provided a channel for budding calypsonians. More calypso shows were being organized at theaters and community centers on the island, and visits from estab-

beat called the Caribbean. This has and remained their signature for more than 30 years, during which they produced hit after hit.

The group's first big Caribbean hit was "Archie Brek Dem Up," a catchy song about carnival revelry. Before this they had a string of hits with old calypsoes like "Brudda Neddy," "Millie Gone to Brazil" and "Sly Mongoose." By the late 1960s they were the only Barbadian group with a Caribbean-wide reputation.

Meanwhile, black calypsonians in Barbados found the going rough and either stopped singing altogether or switched to ballads and American pop. Perhaps they were frustrated by the treatment they received from 1958– 64

lished Trinidadian singers got the public more interested in stage-presented calypso.

By independence in 1966 a new crop of performers had entered the Barbadian calypso scene, including Mighty Gabby – who became the high priest of calypso in the 1980s – Mighty Dragon, Lord Deighton, Lord Summers and Mighty Viper.

These men helped calypso reclaim its rightful position as the real music of the people. And in 1968 and 1969 there were major calypso competitions that attracted wide public attention. But then a new sound came on the scene and drove calypso underground once again.

Sound called spouge: The new sound was spouge. It was originated by Jackie Opel who had started out in the early 1960s as a calypso singer. He migrated to Jamaica, where he was successful as a ska and rock-steady singer, but when Jamaica started turning to the reggae sound in 1968, Opel returned home to introduce his calypso-reggae hybrid.

Opel and spouge dominated the Barbados music scene from 1969–73, although Opel himself died in a car crash in late 1970. The Draytons Two and Sandpebbles, Troubadours, Blue Rhythms Combo and the Outfit all cut original spouge records, which filled the airwaves until 1974.

However, Barbadian calypso came to life

Calypso in Barbados has become the voice of the people. A current saying holds that no matter what political party holds power, the calypsonian is always a member of the opposition, always keeping politicians on their toes, reminding them that they hold a sacred trust from the people and that it is their duty to be sensitive to their needs.

Satirical assaults: In recent times more than 50 percent of Barbadian calypsoes have dealt with politics. Gabby is the foremost exponent of this type of satirical assault on politicians.

Grynner, Gabby's colleague, often takes the same tack, as in his vicious "Mister T," in which he describes the way he'd like to punish a deceptive politician:

again when the Crop Over Festival was revived in 1974. At first the response from calypsonians was slow, but within a decade the calypso contest had become the single most important event of Crop Over. And the artists have responded by presenting thought-provoking and rib-tickling songs about politics, politicians, youth, education, tourism, public transport, crime, religion, social prejudice, apartheid and male–female relationships.

Left, The Merrymen combined folk and country music with Bajan calypso. Right, the Barbados Police Band plays in Queen's Park for special occasions.

Your tricks and lies and pleasant smiles
Can't win my "X" again
You come with big tricks, corned beef and
biscuits to instill hurt and pain...
I gine rip yuh pants. I gine mek yuh dance
You gine feel dat I is a nest of ants
I gine milk yuh goat, I gine sink yuh boat
And next I gine beat yuh wid my "X".

Other calypsonians are more subtle in their attacks, though no less serious or critical. Sir Don's "Tom Say," Romeo's "De Microphone Hey," Black Pawn's "Sucking the Country Dry," Stranger's "De Government Loco," and Viper's "Message to the Prime Minister" all criticized government's policies and defended the poor. But all managed to couch their satire in more or less tolerable lyrics although Romeo and Viper's tunes were banned from the airwaves.

The best exponent of this type of subtle satire is probably Gabby's arch rival, Red Plastic Bag, who rocketed to fame in 1982 with "Mr Harding Can't Burn," a tune which won him the first of his two titles of calypso monarch. In 1997 he won the crown again with his song "Massa Day Done."

The Bag, as he is known, uses all the possibilities of language: irony, pun, sarcasm, allusion and double entendre. In the hilarious but biting "Holes," he complains about the wretched condition of the island's roadways:

Neighbor, neighbor, neighbor, neighbor
Leh me 'lone!
Leh me 'lone!
Neighbor, neighbor, neighbor, neighbor
Mind yuh business, not me own.

Creative vision: Each of the performers plays different roles and has distinct specialities. Grynner, for example, is the "King of the Road," and a comedic entertainer without peer. Viper and Romeo are both young men who have emerged on the scene since independence. Viper is good with songs of revelry. And Romeo, the "Love Man of Calypso," is a charming and polished performer.

Barbadian calypso is alive and well and in the capable hands of many talented performers.

A friend of mine from the USA
Here on a holiday
Wanted me to show him around
I took him all over the town
But goin through the countryside
My face I wanted to hide
The condition of the roads was a sight to see
So many times he had to say to me
Look a hole! A big big hole!
Watch that hole! Shun that hole!

There are plenty of other calypsonians who use the music more as social commentary or just plain entertainment. One of the best examples of this is "Sousie" by Director, in which nosy neighbors are criticized:

Gone are the days when a calypso singer was ostracized for his lack of respectability, or when less indigenous music kept the development of calypso underground. Today's calypsonians offer a wide range of perspectives on social issues, and this is what keeps the public interested and entertained. Calypso is an indispensable component of contemporary society, providing the people with a clear mirror image of the land they live in.

Left, calypsonian Red Plastic Bag sings on "Old Year's Night" at the Crane Beach Hotel. **Right**, Rasta calypso singer Adonijah, also a scholar and journalist.

THE MIGHTY GABBY: KING OF CALYPSO

Listening to the island's calypsonians is a good way to understand the issues that concern Barbadians today. The Mighty Gabby's award-winning music typifies Bajan calypso: his lively songs are more than entertainment – they are a form of protest and a means for seeking positive change within the culture.

The Mighty Gabby's 30-year influence has steadily grown within the world of calypso – he first won the Crop Over Festival competition in 1968 and then again in 1976, 1977, 1985 and 1997. His songs often speak of the challenges Barbadians encounter in their daily lives. A 1976 tune that hit close to home was "Needles and Pins," a comment on a common feature of working-class life:

Johnny got two women
he wife and he girl frien'
Johnny got two women
You know dat is problem
But what really, really cause de strife
He love de girl friend' better dan de wife
An every time de two o' dem meet
It is bacchanal in de street!

The more political song "Jack," named for a bureaucrat who tried to limit the use of beaches by vendors and beachcombers, asserts the joint ownership of landscape:

Jack doan want me to bade on my beach
Jack tell dem to kick me outa reach
Jack tell dem I will never make de grade
Strengthen security, build barricade
Dah can't happen here in this country
I want Jack to know
Dat de beach belong to me.

His criticism of those who minimize Barbadian culture is evident in the song "Miss Barbados," written in response to a Canadian woman being chosen to represent Barbados in an international beauty contest:

Miss Barbados never hear 'bout flying-fish
Miss Barbados never hear 'bout cou cou dish
Miss Barbados 'ent know 'bout bread-fruit and that's no lie
Miss Barbados is as Bajan as apple pie!

Gabby's songs can also be saucy and spicy, as in the delightfully tongue-in-cheek "Hit It" (1983), in which he relates the events of a cricket game between himself and a young woman. On the surface, the song is about cricket – but it is filled with sexual innuendos:

Hit it-why yuh missing so?
Hit it-you used to brag before
Hit it-if you could handle me
Hit it and let me see
Hit it, Hit it, Hit it!

Gabby, whose real name is Tony Carter, began singing at the age of six. As a teenager he competed in his first calypso contest, placing third behind Sir Don (Marshall) and The Mighty Romeo. In 1971 he moved to New York, where he worked to refine his writing and performing skills, returning to the island in 1975. Gabby has become to Barbadian calypso what Bob Marley was to Jamaican reggae and what Sparrow means to Trinidad's calypso. He is the spokesman of a musical form as well as of a culture. His recognition as Folksinger of the Year in 1977, 1978 and 1979 further illustrates the place Gabby has carved out for himself as a Bajan musician.

His music speaks for the thousands of Barbadians who see their culture awash in foreign influences. In "Culture", he sings:

All o'dem shows pon TV you must agree
    are not for we
Show me some Castle in My Skin by
    George Lamming
Instead of that trash like Sanford and
    M.A.S.H.
Then we could stare in the face
And show dem we cultural base.

This is music that provides the visitor with a glimpse of a world often known only to Bajans. Gabby's songs, however critical, are infused with a love for his homeland, and hearing them will inspire a true appreciation of Bajan culture. ∎

If all the world's a stage, everyday life in Barbados is high theater, from the musical pulses and pitches of community gossip to the rhythmic swaying of hips as the beat of calypso fills the street.

There is much more to the performing arts of Barbados than flaming limbo and a poolside calypso band playing "Yellow Bird." Although the many local dance performances, plays, concerts and annual festivals are not always marked as stops for visitors, the adventurous traveler who seeks out these delightful extravaganzas will be treated to an inside look at real Bajan culture.

A walk down a busy street is a drama in itself. Listen to the rhythm and use of the language. The sounds of words, it becomes apparent, are as important as the words themselves; double meanings; expressive folk sayings, stories told with much gesturing and emotion are entertainments without an admission charge. The repartee and haggling at an open-air market easily makes co-stars of vendor and customer.

Dancing? Music is everywhere: at parties, at church, on the mini-buses, at home. Portable radios take music to the streets and to work. It is said that Bajans dance before they can walk: watch any toddler, barely able to walk, hoist himself up, grasp his mother's knee, and stand and sway to calypso.

Out of this verve comes performing arts infused with spontaneity and energy. Little wonder that a strong ballet tradition doesn't exist on Barbados, and that most island dance companies are interpretive, modern, ethnic.

Love of dance: From earliest times, there were two dance traditions on Barbados: the more formalized, European dances of the planters, and the energetic, spontaneous dances of the slaves, rooted in West African tradition. Both groups loved to dance, and though the plantation owners originally tried to prohibit slaves from gathering to play music and dance out of fear that they would

organize rebellion, they quickly came to realize that the slaves worked more productively if they were allowed to enjoy their own form of dance and music one or two nights a week.

The dancers "hollered and bellowed in an Antique manner, as if they were all madd," wrote an early observer. Some dancers would tie rattles to their legs and wrists; others looked on, clapping their hands and chanting "Alla, Alla!" A description from 1750 com-

mented on the use of the entire body, which is typical of West African dance, observing that "their bodies are strongly agitated by skipping, leaping and turning around."

Many of these early reports by white witnesses of the African-inspired dances and rituals revealed both fascination and astonishment: after all, white visitors and plantation owners had never seen anything quite like this. They were ballroom dancers, at best.

"Supreme excellence": An account from 1880 said that "the twistings of the body seem to constitute the supreme excellence of the dance," and went on to describe the

Left, drummers provide African rhythms for performance given by children's dance group (**right**), headed by dancer-actor Robert Ifill (smiling drummer).

dancers' "indecent, wanton, and lascivious" movements in great detail. Today, the West African tradition of pelvic gyrations is still seen in West Indian dance – Bajans call it "wukkin," and you're most likely to see it on holidays as tuk bands joyously parade through the streets.

Today, the rift between "formal" dancing and folk dancing is still evident in Barbados. Ballet, for example, for many years suffered under negative connotations and a class bias. It had been taught exclusively to wealthy white children, and became a symbol of class separation. However, over the years, aspiring jazz and modern dancers have studied classical ballet technique weekly at the Penny Ramsey or Sheila Hatch Schools of Ballet, with such names as Louise Woodvine.

Modern dance on Barbados – abstract and expressionistic – began as a rejection of formalism and sterility. It was introduced to the island in 1968 by Mary Stevens, founder of the Barbados Dance Theatre Company. One of the island's leading dance groups, the company conducts training classes, promotes community spirit through dance, and develops greater interest among young people in cultural affairs – a worthy mandate.

Some of BDTC's performances remain indelibly etched in the memories of its audiences. "How Greed Traps Anansi on an Island" tells the story of Anansi (also known as "Anancy"), a clever and daring spider-hero of many popular West Indies folktales.

Another Bajan folk "celebrity" is the Hag, an old woman who turns into a vampire. Choreographer Rosemary Wilkinson used the story to symbolize, "the schizophrenic complexities of women." Combining native folktales and modern dance technique in this manner makes the dance especially West Indian.

Current issues: Some performing artists feel that the themes of island dance are too diffused. Says Anthony Payne, one of the directors of the Rontana Dance Movement, a company formed when the Rontana Dance Company merged with the Awade Drummers in 1975, "Dance is a communicative art, and it ought to mirror its community. There must be current issues worth dancing about, but dance in Barbados has no focus."

One of Rontana Dance Movement's most exciting pieces is entitled "Follow the Drum." Choreographed by Beverley Griffith, its danc-

ers interpret the sound of four sets of percussion instruments: the continuous flow of tambourines, the more guttural bass drums, the faster, lighter bongos, and the loud, staccato timbales. The piece is gloriously African-inspired.

One of the pioneers in interpretive dance was Yoruba Yard, a small theater in the Bridgetown suburbs that, during the late 1960s, housed a broadly based cultural organization founded by Elton "Elombe" Mottley, who later became director of The National Cultural Foundation. Yoruba Yard explored Barbadian folk material and researched the island's Caribbean and African past. It contracted Shola Olaoye from Ni-

geria to provide technical assistance in dance, and staged the still memorable "Landship" dance, which translated the movements of sailors on a ship into dance steps that seem to float to tuk band rhythms. Though financial problems forced their theater to close, the Yoruba Dancers flourished as a semi-professional group. Dance Experience, a young group of talented dancers, was formed in 1981 by internationally acclaimed Barbadian dancer Richild Springer, a professional dancer in Europe. Despite its youth and many obstacles, the company grew from strength to strength, entertaining Barbadians and conducting workshops in folk, modern and jazz technique. Many of their folk performances are accompanies by the Wesahh Singers. The dance "Croptime," which portrays the last days of the sugar crop season and the rejoicing of its workers, is accompanied by the refrain:

To we economy it's essential
We all know as every Bajan should...

Grassroots effort: Country Theatre Workshop, founded by Patrick Cobham, was introduced to promote and develop the performing arts in the rural parishes where "the audience prefers folk dances." They have also performed at a weekly dinner show at the Plantation Garden restaurant as well.

Both Cobham and Tyrone Trotman, the the Yoruba Dance Company, also believes in this approach to dance and drama. As president of the company called Youth Creative Expressions, he staged in 1982 a multimedia production entitled *Black Heritage*, a portrayal of the West Indian black man through the generations. The music was drawn from the haunting melodies and rhythms of Jamaican reggae superstar Bob Marley, from the lively beat of calypso, and from the emotive soundtrack of the movie *Roots*.

Devoted to the development of Afro-Caribbean dance, two groups emerged from Youth Creative Expressions: New Generation and Seitu (the Nigerian word for "art-

director of Tyrona Contemporary Theatre (a group of dancers and musicians who perform on the hotel circuit), believe the performing arts should reflect an awareness of society and be the artist's inspiration. "Study your people – the way they walk, act, gesticulate – see people the way they are, go into villages, talk to the old folk," Trotman tells his dancers.

Danny Hinds, a young dancer trained in

Left, a song from the musical "Barbados, Barbados" at Balls Plantation. It is the story of the infamous Rachel Pringle. **Right**, "Laff It Off" at Queen's Park.

ist"). In 1981, Robert Ifill, the former president of New Generation, began to bring African and jazz dance to 50 energetic children in an afterschool workshop called Creative Arts for Youth, which staged occasional public performances. The same year Danny Hinds also formed a new group – Bim International – which entertained visitors with polished folk dance performances at a west coast hotel.

The first plays: Theater in Barbados began in the late 1600s, with plantation improvisations called "tea meetings" in which individuals recited passages, presented slapstick skits and gave spontaneous speeches. Just as spontaneous were the alfresco performances given by troupes of actors who pulled into port and presented plays in the shadow of their ships.

The first mention of theater in Barbados occurred in, of all things, the diary of former US president George Washington. He noted that, on December 15, 1751, on a trip to the island, he attended a presentation of *The Tragedy of George Barnwell*.

By 1783, a theater called the Patagonian, complete with boxes, was presenting English plays, including performances of Shakespeare. An advertised billing of a performance of *Richard III* notes that the Duchess of York was played by "Miss McIntosh (being

gan to stage productions of local and international plays. From light farce to serious drama, the Green Room Players' extensive and efficiently produced offerings have pleased several generations of Barbadians and visitors. Among their popular comedies, playing to packed audiences, are *Let's Go Bajan*, *Move Over Mrs Markham*, *Absurd Person Singular*, and *See How They Run*. Their 1978 production of *Colly!* was a celebration of the work of the late Frank Collymore, a distinguished Barbadian writer of mime, dance, song and poetry.

In the 1960s, the now-defunct Barbados Writers' Workshop produced several West Indian plays under the directorship of Earl

her first appearance)" and also included "on the programme, Lady Pentwenzle from Blow-Bladder-Street." The Patagonian Theatre soon received swift competition from another theater, referred to in newspaper accounts as the "New Theatre." Comedies and pantomimes drew crowds, exclusively from the plantation-class whites. A newspaper review of one performance noted that no "profligate or abandoned women were admitted."

Until the early 20th century, in fact, the small theater groups in Barbados were exclusively white. Then, after World War II, the Green Room Players emerged, and be-

Warner. The non-profit Stage One Theatre Productions, established in 1979, carried on the tradition of producing works relevant to the Caribbean experience. The company's goal: to encourage greater interest and participation in the theater.

Raw energy: One of Stage One's most successful productions was Errol John's *Moon on a Rainbow Shawl*, set in a Caribbean backyard in the late 1940s and suffused with raw energy. The play, winner in a 1957 competition sponsored by a London newspaper, is both warm and powerful. Its lingering question: how far have the Caribbean territories evolved from colonialism towards an independent future? The beginnings of an answer to the questions lie with Esther, a child gifted at needlework and embroidery. The patterns she creates, however, are not those that her society encourages. Still, she finds her own patterns "prettier, though much harder to do." The embroidered shawl created by Esther becomes a symbol of the diversity and identity of the Caribbean territories. As the stage lights dim and then extinguish, the vision of this multicolored shawl of hope remains in the minds of the audience.

Folk and popular theater are the winning efforts of a newer island group. Community Theatre Productions, which grew out of a demand for entertaining theater that makes

use of Barbadian material. The company's first event, an improvised folk comedy called *Laff it Off*, played to packed audiences at the Queen's Park Theatre. *Laff it Off* delighted Bajans and visitors alike with its amusing exploration of the wit and talent found within the everyday goings-on at a village rum shop. The rum shop, called "Nook and Cranny Bar," is transformed from bar to court to church to parliament to cultural center.

Left, the dance company BIM International, headed by Danny Hinds (in front), performs at the Divi St James on the west coast. **Right**, *1627 and All That*.

Productions such as *Pampalam*, social and political comment in witty sketches and songs, popular with locals, have also found audiences in Britain, Canada and the US.

Weekend entertainment abounds in Barbados. In the villages, you'll find Friday and Saturday are often filled with the sounds of music and laughter as residents are entertained by a "village meet," a beauty contest, a "dub" contest, a tuk band, or a local dance, called a "fete," "bram" or "jump-up."

Dinner extravaganzas: Most likely to snare the visitor, however, are the many dinner shows, entertaining demonstrations of Bajan history and mores. Originally produced by entrepreneur Andrew Nehaul, the show *1627 And All That*, for instance, portrays the folk culture of Barbados in music and dance in the spacious Sherbourne Conference Centre.

Living theater: Festivals are living theater, and Barbados offers many special celebrations and events. The Oistins and Holetown festivals are annual affairs which showcase the island's talented performing, visual and culinary artists.

The National Independence Festival of the Creative Arts, in late November, is a forum for professional and amateur performing artists. The Crop Over Festival in July/August is the island's largest fête, a month-long celebration inspired by what was once the island's main economic event, the harvesting of the sugarcane crop. Crop Over opens with the ceremonial delivery of the Last Canes, during which the Champion Cutter and the Piler of the last crop are named and honored. This is followed by a decorated cart parade.

Bridgetown Market, also part of Crop Over, is an open-air emporium of hundreds of decorated crafts and food stalls on the Princess Alice Highway in Bridgetown. Local tuk bands, steel bands, hot Jamaican reggae, the latest calypso hits and American disco rhythms compete for attention.

The Cohobblopot, held at the National Stadium, is another potpourri of drama, music and dance, although more formal and organized than the Bridgetown Market.

Kadooment Day climaxes and closes the Crop Over Festival. Costumed bands portray themes of Bajan life, uninhibited revelers dance in the streets, fireworks explode in the sky – and the month's festivities end in a dazzling display of color and light.

BAJAN DIALECT: A GOOD COOK-UP

"When yuh poor, yuh very speech poor." So say the Bajans about the pervasive effects of poverty. But they speak an untruth about their unique language, for Bajan, rising out of the clash between African and European speech, has crystallized into a rich form of expression.

Bajan was born about two centuries ago, the child of a mixed marriage. The mating began on the west coast of Africa, continued on the Atlantic crossing, and was finally consumated in the West Indies, which gave birth to a "hybrid" language.

In its infancy, Bajan combined features from both languages: English words were pronounced with African intonations; African expressions were translated literally into English. But the African elements of Bajan's formative years have slowly eroded; now the English influence is much stronger.

It is said that when a hybrid language remains exposed to the influences of one parent, it grows more like that parent and less like the other. When a hybrid and parent language exist side by side, the hybrid is often seen as inferior, the tongue of the illiterate, a medium for jokes and light matter. The parent is considered the language of the church, the school and the judiciary – the language of the learned, the one more suitable for any and all serious subject matter.

Cinderella language: Bajan, like other dialects in the Caribbean, is known as a "Cinderella language." For a long time, most Bajans accepted this judgment, and thought that their language, like Cinderella, should be restricted to the kitchen and the backyard. But as in the Cinderella story, fairy helpers appeared – this time as writers, poets and linguists. They began to wipe out the image of Bajan as a "broken" version of English. They showed that, like Cinderella, Bajan had its own beauty, seen in the variations of its stress patterns and pitch levels, which combine to shape a language that is neither English nor African, and yet is both.

Local poet Bruce St John defends the language against those who say that it is limited:

We' language limit?
Who language en limit?
Evah language
Like a big pot o' Bajan soup:
Piece o' yam, piece o' potato,
T'ree dumplin', two eddoe,
One beet, two carrot,
Piece o' pig-tail, piece o' beef
Pinch o' salt, dus' o' pepper,
An' don' fuget okra
To add to de flavour.
Boil up, cook up, eat up
An' yuh still wan' rice...

Crash course: Let's use this poem as crash course in Bajan. Line 1 translated is, "Is our language limited?" In Bajan, unlike in English, one form of a pronoun may be used as subject, object and possessive: "we know"; "tell we"; "it is we book."

Bajan does not invert the subject and verb when forming this type of question; the sentence looks like a statement, but by raising your voice at the end, a listener will know that you have asked a question.

Verbs, even if used as adjectives, have no participle endings such as -ed, so you hear: "it finish," "it cook."

In line 2, "en" means "is not," and "who" is used instead of "whose."

The numbers "two" and "t'ree" make plurality obvious in lines 6 and 7, so no final "s" is needed. This feature is not as widespread in Barbados as it is in the other islands, so you will still hear "four steps" as well as "four step."

Note that from any powdered substance, you can get "a dust" (line 9), which means a small portion.

Line 12 gives a brief insight into the subtle differences between Bajan and English: "boil up" means "bring to the boil," but you can also hear "boil down" used when referring to the practice of allowing most of the liquid to boil out of your sauces or sous, giving them a thick consistency. "Cook up" means "cook all of the items together."

The Bajan speaker does not pronounce the ending of most words which end in two consonants. This is shown in line 6 – "dumplin'," line 10 – "an'" and line 13 – "wan'."

There is no "th" sound in Bajan so wherever an English word has this sound, the Bajan speaker has either "f," "v," "t," "d," "z" or "k":

English	Bajan
breathe	breav
with	wit/wid/wif
clothe	cloze/clove
think	t'ink
the	de
strengthen	strengken/strengfen

The verb system of Bajan is somewhat different from that of English. For instance, Bajans use the present tense of a verb even when speaking about past action – "he run home last night," instead of "he ran home…"

Expression of present time also differs in both languages. Whereas speakers of English would say: "the dancer casts strange shadows

as he moves to the pulse of the drum," the Bajan speaker would say: "De dancer t'rowing strange shadows all de time he moving to de pulse o' de drum." This is because the Bajan speaker usually speaks of present action as ongoing activity, while the English use what is called the "simple present tense."

"I does sing": To express habitual action, the English speaker would say: "I sing on Tuesdays, he dances on weekends and we relax when we get the chance." A Bajan speaker says: "I does sing 'pon Tuesday, he does dance 'pon a weekend and we does relax when we get de chance." Bajans don't worry about subject and verb agreement in sentences like this.

Bajans seldom use the word "very." Instead of saying, "It's a very pretty morning," a Bajan would say, "De mornin' pretty, pretty, pretty!" A speeding car might inspire a description such as "de car went 'long fast, fast, fast," or "de car went long real f-a-s-t," spoken with great emphasis on the word "fast."

Even though most Bajan words are English words, sometimes their meanings are quite different from what we might expect. For instance, in Bajan, to be "ignorant," is to be mean or very aggressive, not stupid. A woman has "gone cross," or is "pushing bread cart," when she is pregnant. If a Bajan promises to "pass by" your place, he would not be intending to go past, but would be planning to visit.

Outside of the law courts, being "malicious" does not mean that one is harboring malice, it simply means that one is inquisitive or nosy. It is therefore possible to hear a mother telling her two-year old infant: "Come out of my bag, you too malicious." In this context, "come out of" means "do not look into" or "take your hand out of."

During your stay, you may be asked whether you've had a "sea-bath" (swim) yet. If you're both going into town, "all two" are going. When you need a pencil, ask for a "black lead." And if you've gained weight since your last trip, your Bajan friends won't hesitate to tell you that you've "put on some size."

Note the Bajan use of the word "mind": it means "move" in the statement "mind you' foot out o' my way"; it means "take care" in the request "mind this child 'till I come back"; it means "ignore" in the expression "don' mind she" and "mind you' mout," means "be careful about what you say."

All visitors should therefore be advised to "mind" how they interpret words they seem to share with Bajan speakers. But do take the opportunity to savor the symmetry of the Bajan language, its various contours of thought and its unique turns of phrase. As language is the fabric of thought, be sure to take time to listen and to enjoy the lively patterns, to see the cloth this hybrid language has fashioned. You may come to see how well Bajan suits the life of the island. With an open mind and an attentive ear, any stranger to these shores can leave quoting the final line of Bruce St John's poem: "de cook-up is a beautiful soun'."

Left, "News don' lack a carrier." **Right,** it's time to eat a "home-cook" meal at the Swizzle Inn.

In Bajan homes, words of wisdom flow freely. Proverbs embodying folk values are uttered in almost every conversation, especially in the countryside. The proverbs listed below give one a palpable sense of the rhythms of rural Barbadian life.

Expressed with a sing-song jingle, proverbs capture the cadence and melody of Bajan speech. They provide information about the world view and morals of the Bajan. Yet their common-sense wisdom applies to people everywhere. Shrewd, biting and witty, their purpose is to instruct, admonish and judge people in the matters of everyday life.

● "One bellyful don' fattan a hog."
It requires sustained effort to achieve anything worthwhile.

● "Hansome don' put in pot."
Having physical beauty does not offer any practical benefits.

● "De sea en' got no back door."
The sea is not a safe place. ("en" = ain't)

● "Yuh can' want it in de glass and de bottle too."
You can't have it both ways.

● "Goat head every day better dan cow head every Sunday."
It is better to be given reasonably good treatment all the time than first class treatment occasionally.

● "If greedy wait, hot will cool."
Wait patiently, you will get what you want.

● "Every bush is a man."
Be careful how you talk; someone may well be listening.

● "A eyeful en' a bellyful."
Just because you can see it doesn't mean you can have it. (Said by women to men.)

● "Ole stick o' fire don' tek long to ketch back up."
Old love affairs can hot up again.

● "Dirty water does cool hot iron."
Once a man is aroused, practically any woman, good or bad, can satisfy his lust.

● "Cut pumpkin can' keep."
Once virginity has been lost, it is almost impossible to abstain thereafter.

● "Egg have no right at rockstone dance."
People should not get into situations with which they cannot cope.

● "One-smart dead at two-smart door."
No matter how smart you think you are, there is someone who can outsmart you.

● "De more yuh peep, de less yuh sih."
People will devise ways to fool those who try to spy on them.

● "Every skin teet' en' a laugh."
Outward signs of friendliness aren't always genuine.

● "Head en' mek fuh hat alone."
One should always use common sense.

● "Good name fuh blasted fool."
It is foolish to make big sacrifices when there

is nothing to be gained but the reputation of being a good Samaritan.

● "Mek-sure better than cock-sure."
It is better to make absolutely sure rather than assuming all is well.

● "News don' lack a carrier."
There is always someone to pass on a gossip.

● "Pretty-pretty things does fool li'l children."
Superficial things impress superficial and naive people.

● "Tek time en' laziness."
Much can be achieved by taking one's time.

● "Talk does mek talk."
Stay silent if someone tries to pick a quarrel.

- "Yuh does rust out before yuh wuk out."
Laziness harms the body more than work.
- "Coconut don't grow 'pon pumpkin vine."
Children inherit the traits of their parents.
- "Fisherman never say dat 'e fish stink."
People never give bad reports about themselves.
- "Duppy know who to frighten."
People will take advantage of those known to be weak. (Duppies are spirits of the dead.)
- "Manure can' mek ole plant grow."
You can't improve a hopeless situation.

- "De higher de monkey climb, de more 'e show 'e tail."
The more one shows off, the more one's faults are brought into the open.
- "De las' calf kill de cow."
Taking the same risk too often can have disastrous consequences.
- "Evah (every) pig got a Saturday."
Animals are slaughtered on Saturdays: everyone has his day of retribution.
- "Gold teet' don't suit hog mou'."
Elegant trappings look out of place on those

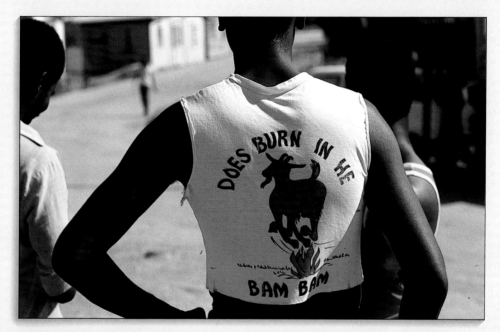

- "Trouble don't set up like rain."
Misfortune can arrive unexpectedly.
- "Yuh can hide and buy ground but yuh can' hide and wuk [work] it."
It's impossible to hide all of one's actions.
- "Better fish in de sea dan wha ketch."
There is always someone who will make a better lover than the present one.
- "Cat luck en' dog luck."
What one man can get away with might cause a problem for another.

Preceding pages: "Go so, up de hill, an' swing so," Bajan directions. <u>Left</u> and <u>above</u>, words of wisdom.

who aren't used to them.
- "Hungry mek cat eat salt."
Necessity causes people to do things they wouldn't normally do.
- "Two smart rat can' live in de same hole."
Two tricksters can't get along.
- "When hog dance, look fuh rain."
Unusual signs are omens of unusual events.
- "De new broom sweep cleaner, but de ole broom know de corners."
Both the new and the familiar have their advantages. (Used in a sexual context.)
- "Coo-coo never done til de pot turn down."
An issue is never settled until there is a definite sign of finality.

George Lamming

IN THE CASTLE OF MY SKIN

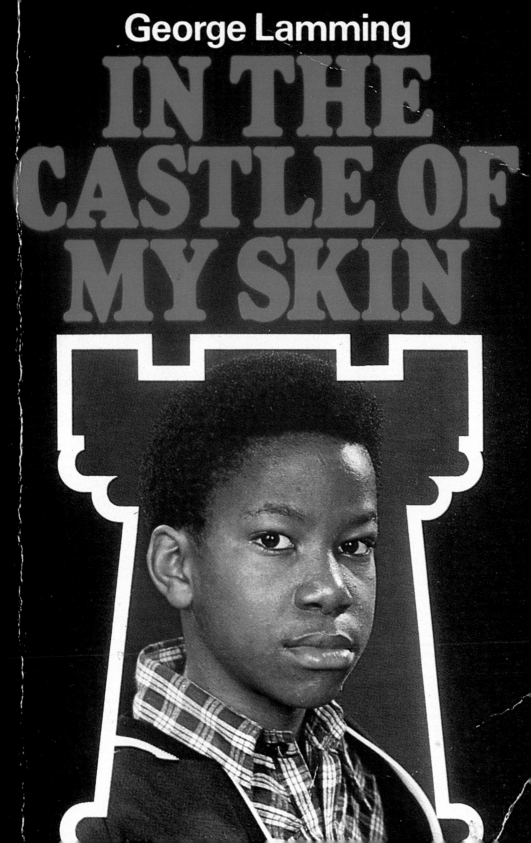

A STORYTELLING TRADITION

On a moon-swept night in Pie Corner, St Lucy, two men entertain one another with stories of ghosts and spirits. And over a family supper in Bridgetown, a grandmother admonishes children not to "throw stones at a dog or cat when yuh meet them at night – it might not be a cat or dog at all." Shared myths, legends and musings like these are part of Barbados's social currency, as traditional a part of life as flying fish and *cou-cou*.

Barbados also has a rich literary tradition, a number of respected novelists and one of the world's highest literacy rates: over 95 percent of the people can read and write. Here, folk beliefs and literature exist side by side, each preserving the culture and expressing its hopes and fears. Both sensibilities are an integral part of the many-sided Barbadian character.

As for the folklore side, it's replete with looming imaginings and supernatural beliefs. The *duppy* of Bajan folklore is a spirit, a "shade" of a departed person. The *Conrad* is an avenging ghost that possesses the body, racks it, and shouts nasty things at people. Many are the tales of a Conrad in someone's belly, talking in strange voices, and interrupting its host when he tries to speak.

There are also many accounts of *heartmen* who seem to appear and vanish with the sugarcane crop season. Heartmen supposedly kill children, offering their hearts to the devil for sacrifice, or using them to make concoctions of magical power.

No less puzzling is the *baccoo* of Barbados, a small man who reportedly often lives in bottles. In the baccoo one finds good or evil, prosperity or failure, heroism or villainy, depending on the amount of attention showered on him by his human owner. Local legends also feature entities that throw stones on the houses of the obsessed, and slap the victims of magic with invisible hands. Stories of witchcraft, spells and miracles abound.

African heritage: The many Bajan tales and folk beliefs are survivors of an oral tradition that harks back to the African heritage of the

majority of the Barbados population. From the villages of West Africa to the village communities of the Caribbean, from Blue Fields of Nicaragua and Limón of Costa Rica, to Afro-Brazilians and South American bush people, the oral tradition is used to transmit cultural mores and values.

In Barbados, these folk tales and songs describe legends, fragments of history and social events. Many contain a moral or a lesson: they are teaching tools. Others are

sheer entertainment, vehicles for grassroots creativity. Of all popular Bajan folk tales and practices, however, those that have the most powerful hold are religious. These are the stories and beliefs directly descended from old-time African lore.

The African deity Shango, once enjoyed a cult following in Barbados. Several other African gods are heroes of ancient, and now obscure, Barbadian tales. The West African "Anancy" folk tales, for example, inspired the phrase "nancy story," meaning a tall tale or a fib. "Don't give me no 'nancy story!'" a mother might scold her child.

The demons of West Africa's folklore have

Left, the young George Lamming on the cover of his novel about growing up in Barbados. **Right**, the author, near the Alantis Hotel in Bathsheba.

had an equally strong hold on the Barbadian imagination. Myriad are the tales of voodoo and *obeah* (witchcraft), of magicians that transform themselves into balls of fire and animals, of duppies and spirits of the dead.

Many Barbadians, for example, will tell you that a dead person will "dream" you a few nights after he dies, and that an important message will be conveyed to you in this way. They will hold vigils or wakes, called "nine-nights," to ensure the soul's safe passage to the other world. As in Haiti, there are ceremonies in which the living talk to the dead, inviting the dead to rectify unhappy situations they might have caused while still alive.

Local lore: Legends that originated locally cles. The tale *The Metaphysical Prank* is a case in point.

Stories describing local mysteries circulate freely as well. The Merrymen, a popular singing group, tell of a now-famous steel donkey who would appear at night and wreak havoc:

The steel donkey coming down...
An' he jumping and prancing 'bout
A long thing like a muffler sticking out behind him
And 'e tongue sticking out he mout'

In the 1960s and 1970s, there were people who swore they saw this steel donkey, surrounded with blue light, bawling and galloping along the country roads of Barbados. One woman said: "I believe it. I *see* it. We was

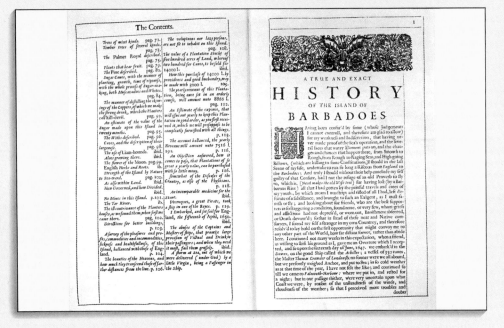

are vivid and entertaining. Even today there is a persistent folk rumor that certain people can transform themselves into animals and move about inconspicuously. There is currently a Bajan who, his neighbors insist, has been seen in his backyard changing into a duck.

Folk tales about theft and cunning abound and are especially evident because of popular stereotypes concerning the character of the Barbadian male. He has acquired a reputation for craftiness not unlike that of the heroes of the African Anancy tales. Though this behavior has more to do with thriftiness than stealth, this identification of the male as a "smart man" of cunning is widely accepted in Caribbean cir- living in Orange Hill, St James, that time. One night late I hear a strange noise. I peep out through the flaps o' my jalousies. If I lie I die: I see this light, blue, and inside it, a thing like a donkey, hollering, kicking up, galloping. It stop outside a shop. Days after, noises was coming from out that shop. I was in there one evening. All of a sudden, I see things falling off the shelves o' the shop. Not all together, one by one, like something picking them up and dropping them. Tins o' sardin, tins o' milk. I get out o' there fast. Few weeks later, the shop close down. Ask anyone in Orange Hill, then, if you doubt me."

History and social events are preserved in

folk songs as well. One Bajan folk song documents the activity of a petty thief:

Sly Mongoose, the dog know yuh name.
Sly Mongoose, you ain't got no shame.
You go straight in the lady kitchen
Take up half of she big fat chicken
Hide it down in yuh we'estcoat pocket
Sly Mongoose.

And then there is a song about a West African king, captured by the British, and brought to Barbados under a kind of house arrest in the late 1800s. There he became something of a folk hero; crowds thronged around him everywhere he went. He fell in love with a local woman, Rebecca:

King Ja-Ja won't leave Becka 'lone

to help in the construction of the Panama Canal, and whose riches, on their returning to Barbados, were legendary: they tossed coins in the street. "Da Cocoa Tea" reveals the power of obeah: with one drink, a man is overwhelmed by a powerful desire to marry the woman who gave him the drink. These and other folk songs can be found in the fascinating and readable *Folk Songs of Barbados*, a collection edited by Trevor Marshall, Peggy McGeary and Grace Thompson.

True and exact history: For generations, Barbados's folk traditions have been passed on orally, but rarely written or recorded. The earliest writings were not by Barbadians, but by visitors who reported the island's history

King Ja-Ja won't leave Becka 'lone
King Ja-Ja won't leave Becka 'lone
Wha' Becka got is all she own...

The song "Lick and Lock-up done wid" commemorates the ending of slavery on the island. "Murder in the Market" is about a woman who killed her common law mate in the 1870s. "Ah ain't kill nobody but muh husband," the song goes. "Panama Man" reminds us of the hundreds of Bajans who went

and conditions. The first study of the island is Englishman Richard Ligon's *A True and Exact History of the Island of Barbados*, published in 1673. A more definitive work is Robert H. Schomburgk's *The History of Barbados*, published in 1848. Past editions of two island newspapers, the *Barbados Mercury* and the *Bridgetown Gazette*, also contain a wealth of historic information and insights. The Barbados Public Library, with its headquarters on Coleridge Street, just outside the main bustle of Bridgetown, preserves copies of these books and newspapers, and is well worth a visit.

Indigenous literature, meanwhile, first came to public notice in the 1940s and 1950s through the efforts of a BBC program called *Caribbean Voices*, and through a Barbadian magazine called *Bim*. First published in 1942, *Bim* encouraged local creative writing. Highly acclaimed novels were to flow from the pens of *Bim* contributors – novels which may not have been written without such a forum or the encouragement of its editor, the late Frank Collymore. Back volumes of *Bim* are a Who's Who of Caribbean writers, including George Lamming, Oliver Jackman, Geoffrey Drayton, Derek Walcott, John Wickham, Monica Skeete, Austin Clarke, Andrew Salkey, Edward Braithwaite, Bruce St John and the late Timothy Callender.

It was to *Bim* that many foreign publishers of Caribbean prose turned in their search for authors. The English were becoming increasingly interested in West Indian culture, as immigrants poured into the country. Many books about West India, by West Indians, appeared in England. Back home, meanwhile, the spirit of independence was rising among now-educated, upwardly mobile blacks. Trade unions, political parties and calls for self-government were the order of the day.

Coming of age: Much of Barbados's best writing grew up in this ferment. Many early indigenous novels deal with childhood, with coming of age, with the search for self, with questions about color and race, bondage and freedom. George Lamming's *In the Castle of My Skin, The Emigrants* and *Season of Adventure* are classic cases. In *Season of Adventure*, the beat of drums in a voodoo ceremony sends a mulatto woman into a frenzied search for meaning and value in her life. Geoffrey Drayton's *Christopher* is about a white Bajan growing up and coming to terms with black society. Austin Clarke's *Amongst Thistle and Thorns* tells of a black boy doing the same with white society. John Wickham's autobiographical stories touch on this theme too.

The search for self also pervades Oliver Jackman's *Saw the House in Half*. Its title comes from an old Bajan folk rhyme:

Saw the house in half
An' gimme the bedroom part.
I ain't want no mash' up potato
Gimme me dumpling whole...

Although born of some domestic quarrel, the image of the divided house was, for Jackman, an image of Barbados itself; that is, a clash of British and African cultures.

Today the island's writers do not treat the themes of independence and identity with such urgency, an interesting comment on the ongoing and successful synthesis of these two Bajan ways of life. Contemporary novels and writings often bubble with humor, and capture the lives of ordinary people, in a positive way. Many Barbadians take special delight in local radio broadcasts of West Indian stories which often focus on popular culture and village life. Such readings brought to life the stories of Jeanette Layne-Clarke, Monica Skeete and Timothy Callender. Barbadians love these broadcast stories. They take pride in hearing about themselves, and the dialect of Barbados lends itself to public readings.

Today, there is a vigorous, vibrant springing up of writing in Barbados. There is a movement to record the oral tradition of the island, and capture its dialect in writing. And Bajan authors are writing more honestly and confidently, describing fuller, rounder characters than ever before; writing less for the overseas reader and more for their own people. It's a spirit kindled in the following poem by H. A. Vaughn, called *Revelation*, written about 40 years ago and certainly ahead of its time. The most quoted and anthologized poem to come out of Barbados, it is the first Barbadian poem dedicated to the black woman:

Turn sideways now and let them see
What loveliness escapes the schools,
Then turn again, and smile, and be
The perfect answer to those fools
Who always prate of Greece and Rome
'The face that launched a thousand ships'
And such like things, but keep tight lips
For burnished beauty nearer home.
Turn in the sun, my love, my love!
What palm-like grace! What poise! I swear
I prize these dusky limbs above
My life. What laughing eyes! What
*   gleaming hair!*

The literary magazine *Bim* published *Sandy Lane and other Poems*, H. A. Vaughn's collection. Another essential for the enthusiast of Barbadian verse is Frank Collymore's *Collected Poems*. And anyone wishing an overview of the spirit of Bajan folk culture, and its influence on Barbadian literature, will want to read *The Barbados Book* by Louis Lynch.

Two Bajan Folktales

The Metaphysical Prank

A very sick man went to a practicing metaphysician who worked in Bridgetown. The practitioner explained to the man what "pain" was all about. He told him that pain really only existed in the mind. He claimed that all the man had to do was to affirm and believe that the pain was gone and gradually it would be relieved. With neophyte's zeal, the man successfully made the affirmations.

However, when the practitioner asked for the fees for his service, the man, who by now was fully recovered, said: "Wha' fees? All you have to do is affirm and believe dat you have receive de fees and you have dem."

The Baccoo from St. Peter

Mrs. Barbara lived in Speightstown, St. Peter. Her daughter was cleaning the house after her death. In the bedroom of the deceased, she saw a blanket under the bed and attempted to remove it. To her surprise, the blanket showed resistance and seemed to pull itself back under the bed. When Mrs. Barbara's daughter examined the blanket, she discovered that it contained a baccoo. The tiny man defied all her attempts to root him out. Finally a Roman Catholic priest was called to rid the house of this demon.

The priest bagged the baccoo and paid a fisherman $50 to carry it out to sea.

The mysterious small man in the bag proved too much for the curious fisherman. He opened the bag and peeked, and the baccoo escaped.

According to legend, soon afterwards, the fisherman's house was destroyed by a fire. ∎

THE BOYFRIENDS: A SHORT STORY

Elmina Griffith had two boyfriends. One was short and one was tall. One was ugly and the other was good-looking. One had a lot of' money and the other didn't have none. And Elmina did like all two of them.

But from the start she grandmother was giving trouble when it comes to this boy-talk. She start from the time she first see Elmina with James. James was the short one, the one who was ugly and didn't have no money either. One night he come home there and sit down and talk to the grand-

got them coming in the house sitting down in all o' we morris chairs like if they own the place. What you want with boyfriend already, Elmina? And he ain't even nice-looking. I wonder where he come from? I aint know he nor none of he family, though he say he born up in St Peter where I used to live meself. And I know everybody that is anybody in them parts. But I ain't know *he*. And you hear what sorta job he doing?" she say, turning to Grandpa. "Says he does work with Patterson's Garage. What he

mother and grandfather good good, and they were all talking to he nice too, trying to find out things 'bout he and where he come from and who he family is, and when James get up and went 'long, seeing that he ain't going get no chance to talk lovey-dovey with Elmina that night, the grandmother ups and says:

"But Elmina, what you getting on with though? This is what I bring you up to do? You mother gone and dead and lef' me with you, and looka how you wanta mek she memory shame after I try so hard with you. What a young little girl like you want with boyfriend already? When I was your age I couldn't even *look* at a man, and now you

does do? Motor-mechanic or does drive taxi?"

"Grandma, nothing ain't wrong with them jobs! You got a lot o' old-fashion ideas that collar and tie work is the only work decent men could do. What wrong with honest work? The man only trying to make a living. He got to mek money and he doing the job that he like doing best too. He tell me that."

"What you talking 'bout? You wanta tell me you really like he? Why you tekking up for he so strong? You think he like you? How you know he don't go 'round the place chatting down every girl he come across? You know how these men does behave when they reach a certain age. Listen, I want you to get married and thing, but what is you hurry? You still too young to tek on the responsibilities of a wife. You is only twenty-six."

"But grandma, that is old enough."

"Old enough? Girl, when I was *thirty* my mother beat me because I was walking the road and I speak back to a man that speak to me."

But Elmina only chupse and say, "But Grandma, I *like* James, though. I can't help it. I like he bad, and he say he like me too."

see Elmina, the grandfather comes out and sits down in the rocking chair, all dress up in coat and collar and tie like if he feel that this give the atmosphere the sort of seriousness that it demand; like if it is a business conference or something. And he looks at James and say;

"Ahem. Young man, this is the second time I see you and I would like to find out some things 'bout you. You have a family?"

"Well, my father dead, but my mother still living. And I got two sisters that went to

"Hey, but you ain't got no respect for me and you grandfather? How you can talk that sorta thing in front of we? Look, Zedekiah, you better watch that girl, hear! She feel that she too old to get lashes. You better watch that girl, Zedekiah."

"Listen, however, she mek up she bed she got to lie down 'pon it, yuh know," the grandfather say. "But if I see the young man again, I going ask he a few questions."

So when James pass by another time to

"Elmina would sneak outa the house and go and meet he, and they use to walk to the beach and hold one another hand and mek plans 'bout getting married and thing..."

school at St Leonard's and St Michael's."

"Them is good schools to go to," the old man say. "So what you sisters doing now?"

"Well I ain't know. They wasn't home when I left."

He had the old man there. He like he is a fool, yuh, Zedekiah start to think. What sorta idiot this girl encouraging in my house though? Listen, I talking too decent to this idiot. I better talk in language he understand.

"Ahem. Listen, you man, you have money?"

The young man put he hand in he pocket and scratch 'bout.

"Lemme see... 'bout three dollars. How much yuh want?"

The grandfather bend down and hold he head in he hands.

And Elmina, sitting down 'pon the couch beside James, was very embarrass because she did know what the grandfather was getting at; in fact, she did want to find out sheself. So she turn to James and she says:

"All grandfather want to know is what your intentions is."

"Well, right now I intends to ketch the ten o'clock bus," the young man say.

"Listen young man. I ain't want you to ever come back inside this house o' mine!" Zedekiah shout out. "Don't ever come here again or I will do as I say as sure as my name is Amos Zedekiah Joshua Zechariah Hedoniah Griffith."

"I believe you, man. You ain't got to tell me you name too," the young man say. "And Elmina, I want you to know that whatever happen I still love you with a eternal love, and I building a house and anytime you ain't feel like standing here no longer, you know what you kin do. I gone for now."

And James went 'long.

"You hear what he say?" says the grandmother, coming out from the bedroom where she was listening behind the partition. "But looka this wussless nigger-man though nuh, trying to encourage a nice decent young girl like you to come and live with he. You see what he been intending for you all the time now? You see that we did right?"

So James never went back inside Zedekiah's house again, but every now and then when Elmina coulda think up a excuse she would sneak outa the house and go and meet he, and if it was night, they use to walk to the beach and sit down 'pon the sand and hold one another hand and look out to sea and look at the lights and tell one another how much they like one another and mek

plans 'bout getting married and thing, and so on.

Then one day Elmina get a job in a store in town and that is where she meet Bannister. Bannister was the Assistant to the Assistant Manager, so that mean that he had to do all the work. But he still had time to come and chat down Elmina though. And while Elmina ain't like he as much as she like James, she did still like he enough to take on, and she realize too the old people woulda like he better too.

And man, you should see the first evening when Elmina drive up in the car with this good looking young man at the wheel all dress to death in white – white suit, white shirt and collar and tie; and all the neighbors come pepping out through the jalousies and admiring the way he look and the other girls in the village jealous and saying that this time she must be work something 'pon he to get he to like she so. And Bannister gets outa the car and slam the door hard and gone 'round to the other side and open the door for Elmina and Elmina gets out with she head straight in the air and goes inside the house with Bannister. And Zedekiah comes out and starts shaking hands and laughing and talking good good good.

Then out runs the grandmother talking with the best words she could find and says to Bannister that he must excuse the condition that the house in.

So they sit down and talk a lot of small talk and then Bannister ask the grandparents if he could take out Elmina from time to time, and the grandfather say yes, of course, sure, that he know a decent man when he sees one, and that he certainly does admire the way Elmina does pick her friends.

After that Bannister make a date to go to the drive-in theater with Elmina, and then he left. So that is how the two of them start going 'round together. Elmina living it up now, every Saturday night she feting and coming home early in the morning, and she always going this place and that place with this Bannister fellow. And the grandparents watching with interest, wondering when the time going come that Bannister going mek the move to get married to Elmina.

Now Elmina was getting through all right: she dressing up in a lot of nice clothes and looking real sweet, and though she ain't got time to see James as often as she use to do in the past, sometimes 'pon a night when the old people think that she out with Bannister, she really gone off somewhere to meet James. And is true that she like James more, but she like Bannister too, and it looking like if Bannister is the man most likely to succeed in the long run. James feeling bad 'bout it, and asking she why she don't just stick to he and wait till he get enough money to married she, but she was so excited with the new life she living for the first time that she can't stick to James alone and leave out all o' that fun.

But some trouble start up that make a big scandal in the village, and all the people say, I tell yuh so, I know it would happen. And the grand parents feeling shame and crying and thing. "Where that man Bannister? What he doing 'bout it?" Zedekiah ups and asks. "Elmina, you know where he live? Looka, come lewwe go up there right now."

So the two of them ketch the bus and gone up by where Bannister live and knock 'pon the door and wait. And then a woman open the door and says she is Mrs Bannister, and

that Mr Bannister ain't home. And the old man ask, "Well, when he coming back? I got something important to tell him."

"I ain't certain," the woman say.

"Where he gone?"

"Well, this morning he ketch the plane for South America, where he gone to see after opening a business, and after that he got to go up to Canada to see he uncle, and after that he got to go to Norway and Czechoslovakia and I think he might got to pass through Jerusalem too. So I really can't say when he coming back."

"Well when you see him again, tell him I want to see him," the old man say. That was all he coulda say, too.

So then they gone back home and the old people quarreling and saying that they did know all the time that Bannister wasn't so good but that they was hoping that he woulda behave heself like a gentleman.

And they turning on 'pon Elmina and asking she why she couldn't keep sheself to sheself and things like that, and saying that they got five minds to put she outa the house.

So one morning Elmina get up and went straight to where James living and say that she staying there, that she ain't going back home, that she fed up with everything there. And James straightway gone and start taking out marriage license and thing and next thing you know they married and living in the house that James build.

And a lot of people was saying that James is a idiot to act that way after she stop seeing him for such a long time, but they didn't know what was going on for after the baby born and they look at it, it did so ugly, that everybody realize that Elmina had marry the right boyfriend after all.

—from *Bim* Magazine 52 (1971)

"You should see the first evening when Elmina drive up in the car with this good looking young man at the wheel all dress to death in white…"

THE LAND OF FLYING FISH AND COU-COU

Barbadians contend that the way to a man's heart is through his stomach. The Bajan woman's ability to cook is therefore highly praised, and a woman who cannot cook is hesitant to admit it. In fact, not long ago, this was reason enough for a man to "leave out" a prospective girl friend, or to eat at his mother's, to the girl friend's embarrassment. A popular folk song recounts just such a pickle:

Such a pretty little girl
Like Jessie Mahon,
She lazy since she born,
De girl can' cook,
She won' read a book
So pack she back to she ma. . .
Pack she back to she ma ma. . .

Bajan cooking is especially creative, and hence praiseworthy, for two reasons. One is that there are limited native foods available. The main protein sources for Barbadians have traditionally been milk, cheese, fish, imported salt beef and pork, corned pork, local fresh mutton and pork, and some imported frozen beef. In recent years, fast-food chicken and chips, hamburgers and hot dogs have become staples, too, although a Bajan cook would never consider these quick meals competition for "a sweet Bajan stew" or "cou-cou and salt fish."

Another reason a good Barbadian cook has a talent to treasure: for most islanders, the food budget doesn't stretch that far. Many households raise and slaughter their own chickens and pigs, for example, as an economy measure.

Culinary hybrid: The many influences which have shaped Barbadian life are perhaps nowhere as apparent as on the dinner table. Bajan cooking is a culinary hybrid, drawn from African and English traditions, as well as Amerindian, Spanish, French, Chinese, Indian, American and Caribbean cooking techniques.

The Bajan national dish, *cou-cou* and salt fish, is African-inspired. *Cou-cou* is a cornmeal and okra pudding, a relative of a basic food-

stuff of Africa called "foo-foo." It is ladled with gravy and served with salt fish.

Cou-cou in the making is a wonderful sight, and a challenge: much energy is put into the stirring, for if any lumps are allowed to form, it is considered a failure. The finished mixture is packed into a bowl and then turned out onto a plate. The center of the mound is sunk with a spoon and a light gravy ladled into the center and around the golden mound.

The love of this dish inspired the following poetic flight of fancy:

Salt fish like slabs of wood,
Onions like bangles and
Tomatoes like cartwheels
Cover the cou-cou, which floats
like an island in a sea of sauce.

Salt fish – much tastier than "slabs of wood" – is a food originally imported to feed slaves; it was an inexpensive source of protein. Today, salted cod is as expensive as some meat and poultry. Cod fish balls and cod cakes are now considered a delicacy, and served at cocktail parties and other festive occasions.

Tasty fish dish: Another Bajan specialty is flying fish. These silvery blue specimens, 7–9 inches (17–23 cm) long, abound in clear warm waters in many parts of the world. Yachtsmen and those traveling by ship have often reported seeing schools of fifty to a thousand flying fish suddenly leap from the water, and glide through the air for up to 75 feet (23 meters). In Barbados, these fish are most plentiful, and cheap, from December through June. They are bought in large quantities during these months and stored in freezers or dried.

A spicy Barbadian seasoning makes flying fish an especially tasty national dish. The seasoning is made of finely chopped onion, parsley, thyme, black pepper, paprika, garlic, finely chopped red pepper and any other herbs or spices available plus a little salt and a few drops of lime juice. This is all mixed together to allow the flavors to blend and then packed into the seams of the fish and left a while to penetrate before the fish is fried or steamed.

Other fish on Bajan menus include king fish, dolphin, red snapper, chub and bonito. Small fish such as sprats, jacks and fray are also skillfully transformed into tasty favorites.

Barbadians are pork lovers, too. It is often said that the only part of the pig which the Bajan cannot convert into a tantalizing dish is the hair. One traditional pork dish starts with several pounds of pork, which is "corned" or pickled in a stone jar with coarse sea salt, saltpeter, spices and water. After two weeks in the jar, the pork is removed and desalted by soaking several times in cold water. It is then boiled with white beans, onions, tomatoes, parsley, thyme, pepper, butter and gravy.

Even finely chopped pig's tails, snouts, heads and feet are served in a dish known as "stew food," with what are called "ground provisions" – that is, root vegetables, such as yams, sweet potatoes, white eddos, cassava (a

by a British sea captain. Breadfruit can be cooked in stews, fried, boiled, or pickled.

Sunday buffets: If late-week meals are inexpensive and imaginative, weekends in Barbados bring their own customs. Pudding and souse is a pork dish that is a traditional Saturday night meal. Leftovers are usually fried and served for breakfast on Sunday. And the custom of entertaining friends on Sundays is still popular; these occasions often assume a festive atmosphere, complete with popular music and buffets of local dishes.

To encourage Bajans to appreciate and cultivate more home-grown foods, the island's Hotels' Association organizises a culinary competition called "Taste of the Caribbean".

native root vegetable) and breadfruit. This particular dish is often cooked with green vegetables, such as okra, cristophenes (a green pear-shaped squash), cabbage and spinach. "Stew food" was traditionally cooked in the middle of the week, on the days furthest away from payday, when fresh or expensive food supplies could be counted on to be somewhat depleted for the average household.

For nearly two centuries, breadfruit has been a staple in the Bajan diet. It is a starchy fruit, white in the middle with a bright green skin, that grows on trees throughout the island. The breadfruit tree originally came from Tahiti, and was brought to Barbados in 1793

Local chefs have a "cook off" to determine who represents Barbados, with the Barbados team usually performing very well.

The National Independence Festival of Creative Arts (NIFCA) also celebrates Bajan culinary arts. This festival culminates on Barbados' Independence Day, November 30. Gold, silver and bronze medals are awarded for preparation and presentation of popular native dishes.

Left, roadside fruit stands abound in Barbados, especially in urban areaas. **Right**, Bridgetown's Cheapside Market is especially busy on Saturday mornings.

"Whole peas 'an rice is very nice upon a rainy day..." —Bajan folk song

Caribbean cuisine is a tasty medley created by combining the dishes and flavors of the peoples who settled the island. African, Arawak, European and Asian cooking influences are evident in Barbadian specialties.

Peas and rice: A popular main dish. Rice is cooked with one or several kinds of peas, including green or dried pigeon (gunga) peas, blackeye and split peas, cow peas, or

is 'turned' by adding cold water and mixing to a paste, which is added to okras. The dish remains on the heat and is turned until the mixture is quite stiff and ready to eat.

Sea egg: This is the roe of a white sea urchin caught on reefs around the island. The yellow roe is picked from the shells and piled into other cleaned shells. Each shell is topped with a sea grape leaf, steamed and sold. Unfortunately, sea eggs have been over fished. The government has declared limited seasons in which roe may be taken.

lentils. Salted pig tails or other salted meats are cooked in the rice to season it.

Pudding and souse: This is an old island dish available everywhere. The pudding is made from grated and well-seasoned sweet potato which is stuffed into the cleaned pig's intestines. This is steamed and the finished product looks like a long dark sausage. This is cut into slices and served with the "souse," which is pig's head, feet and flesh cooked until tender, cut into slices and "soused" or pickled with lime juice, onion, hot pepper, salt, chopped cucumber and parsley.

Cou-Cou: This is a corn meal dish commonly served with flying fish. The corn meal

Roti: Although this food is of Indian origin, it is so popular that it at least seems Bajan. It is a version of the dish well-known in Trinidad and consists of a flat, unleavened bread with a spicy meat and curry mixture inside. Vegetable roti is also growing in popularity. It is often made at home but is also available at many food shops.

Conkies: The name of this Bajan dish comes from "Kenke," a similar African dish. Conkies are made of cornmeal, coconut, pumpkin and spices, mixed to a thick consistency, placed on steamed young banana leaf squares, then folded like a parcel and steamed over water in a deep pot.

Fruit drinks: Popular drinks are coconut water, lemonade made from fresh lemons, and punches made from fruits like mangoes, guavas, soursop, golden apples, gooseberries, pawpaws, passion fruit or tamarinds.

Mauby: A drink made from boiling pieces of a bitter bark with spices. It is then strained and sweetened, and can be brewed to make it frothy like beer. It is a very refreshing drink, that is also said to have medicinal properties.

Sorrel: Prepared from the fresh or dried red sepals of the plant and boiled or infused in

Corn and oil: A drink consisting of equal parts of refreshing rum and falernum.

Coconut bread: A delicious Bajan favorite that can be served plain or lightly buttered:

1¼ lb flour
3 teaspoons baking powder
3 cups grated sugar
6 oz brown sugar
6 oz shortening
½ teaspoon salt
1 teaspoon powdered cinnamon
1 teaspoon powdered nutmeg

hot water with spices and rum added. This is the local Christmas drink.

Ginger beer: Caribbean ginger beer is usually still, strong and served chilled. Made from green or dried root ginger, the drink is made in a similar way to sorrel.

Falernum: A local liqueur made with lime juice, granulated sugar, rum and water, flavored with almond essence.

Left, Rastaman serves up some *itals*, an all-natural vegetarian stew. Right, bike loaded with sorrel, for making a traditional Christmas drink. Below, old-time mauby seller; grated coconut or coconut milk is used in many Bajan dishes.

2 teaspoons almond essence
1¼ lb raisins or mixed fruit
1 cup milk
1 large egg

Cream together the sugar and shortening. Beat the egg well, then mix it in. Add the grated coconut, spices, almond essence, raisins or fruit, and milk. Sift the flour with the salt and baking powder, and mix it in. Put the mixture into one greased 2lb loaf pan and one 1lb pan. Bake in a moderate oven, at 375°F (140°C) for about one hour, or until it is golden brown. Take the sweet-smelling loaves out of the pans and cool them on a rack before serving.

Nature was Barbados' first pharmacy, or "doctor stop." While "modern" medicine has superseded traditional folk cures throughout most of the island, ancient medical remedies are once again attracting a following among Bajans.

Folk cures seem to have sprung from three diverse sources on the island. The original Arawak inhabitants probably used indigenous plants and herbs in teas and "cures." It is also likely that African folk cures and bush medicines made their way to Barbados with the island's African inhabitants. More recently, the development and growth of the Rastafarian movement has spurred a resurgence of interest in nature cures: Rastafarians look mainly to nature for their needs; they have initiated research and experimentation with nontraditional teas and cures, and in doing so have extended that range of Barbadian folk medicines.

Unfortunately, much of the open pasture where many wild plants and herbs once thrived has been cleared for housing or cultivation. Some bushes have been overused and are very difficult to find. A good example is a bush called finger grow; it has very sharp thorns and reportedly is an aphrodisiac for men. (You may therefore guess which "finger" it helps to "grow.") Of course, some bushes still thrive all over the island, such as Christmas bush, cure-for-all and circee.

Groundnuts and Coconuts: The Rastafarians have revived the use of groundnuts (primarily peanuts) and coconuts. They call these foodstuffs "itals," a derivation, in their dialect, of "victuals." On almost every street corner, Rastafari brethren trade in coconuts.

Coconut water is praised by most Bajans

as a preventive and cure for illnesses of the bladder and kidneys. Coconut oil is also a long-standing cold remedy: it may be rubbed into the head to break up a cold. It is also used on the scalp a day or two before washing the hair to help loosen dandruff flakes. And of course coconut water is lauded as a refreshing beverage. The everuseful coconut inspired this ditty:

Coconut woman is called out
An' everywhere you can hear her shout
'Get your coconut water
Man it good for yuh daughter
Coco got a lot of iron
Make you strong like a lion...

The song goes on to advocate "if you tired and feeling down/Get coconut water an' little rum."

Peanuts are another Bajan "health" food. Barbadians have always eaten them raw for general health; and in large quantities peanuts are supposed to stimulate sexual desire or increase sexual prowess. For this purpose, the nuts are soaked in milk, gin or beer for one night or one week, depending upon the potency desired.

"Brings the Blood Down": A melon-like fruit

called pawpaw is put to many uses in a Bajan home. The fruit itself is delicious and it is often pureed into a beverage as well. Either way, it prevents constipation or, as the Bajans say, it helps to "keep the bowels moving."

Green pawpaw is reportedly useful for reducing the effects of hypertension, or high blood pressure; it "brings the blood down," goes a local expression. The pawpaw for this purpose is taken one or two ways, either as two small cooked slices of green pawpaw, or

Left, Rasta preparing coconuts that can make you "strong like a lion." **Right**, versatile Bajan health food.

in an elaborate concoction that involves grated nutmeg, candle grease and an optional few drops of coconut oil.

This versatile fruit is also used to prevent infection from cuts and bruises. Two or three thin slices are placed over a cut and bandaged for two or three days to promote rapid healing without infection. Pawpaw is used in this same way in parts of Africa, with excellent results.

The cactus-like aloe plant is another Bajan all-rounder. For colds, itching throats and constipation, the outer skin is removed and a small piece of the inner pith is swallowed with a pinch of salt to reduce the bitterness. A thin "inside" slice of aloe can also be bandaged on cuts to aid the healing process. For mild over exposure to the sun, rub the cool, soothing aloe over the affected area.

The green brew made from yet another native plant, the circee bush, is also a bitter medicine; it is used to help reduce fever and relieve the symptoms of influenza. Some people refer to the circee bush as "miraculous bush," a tribute to its healing powers. A cousin, in name at least, to the miraculous bush is the "wonder-of-the-world" plant (pronounced wonda-worl') which, when chewed with a pinch of salt, is supposed to bring relief from mild asthmatic attacks. Others believe firmly in a bowl of green-lizard soup to get rid of asthma.

Creative cures: Some Bajan herbal teas and home cures have merit, while others are definitely doubtful to the modern mind. For example, a child with asthma would be taken to a young pawpaw tree and made to stand upright against the tree. A nail would be driven into the tree just above the child's head. People believed that as the tree grew, the illness would gradually disappear.

For a child afflicted with worms, a piece of bitter worm-wood would be steeped in rum and the liquid fed to the child for nine consecutive mornings. If that failed to work, raw aloe in milk was administered instead. Hiccups mandated a different "cure": a match stick was pushed into the child's hair, or a small piece of brown paper was moistened with saliva and then placed on the child's forehead.

Ring-a-ding-ding, Ring-a-ding-ding,
Rum from Barbados is very sweet thing.
–Bajan toast

On this tiny island of just 166 square miles (432 sq. km), there are estimated to be nearly 1000 "rum shops." Barbados is the country in which the name "rum" was coined, and the first to export the golden liquor. It is the home of some of the best rums in the Western hemisphere.

Rum is made by distilling the juice extracted from molasses, the thick liquid residue left after most of the sugar has been taken out of the sugarcane juice.

Most of Barbados's dark rums are made in the traditional pot stills. The longer they are aged, the better: a five-year-old rum is good, but a rum aged for 10 years in barrels made of American white oak is even smoother and mellower. The rum acquires its dark color from the wood and from a small amount of caramel added later. Lighter rums are made in modern stills and aged for less time.

Kill-devil: Delicious and sweet today, Barbadian rum wasn't always carefully refined. In the 1640s, the first batches of native distilled spirits were referred to as "kill-devil" by Englishman Richard Ligon, a Royalist refugee who wrote the first book about Barbados. The rum in those days was not very tasty, but it was very strong. Those who imbibed it quickly felt its effects; as Ligon put it, "It lays them to sleep on the ground."

It is likely that the name "rum" itself was first coined in Bridgetown's taverns or on its waterfront, where it was loaded onto foreign ships for export. Around 1650, an anonymous island visitor left behind a description that "the chiefe fudling they make on the Island is Rumbullion, alias Kill Divill, and this is made of sugarcanes distilled, a hot, hellish and terrible liquor." Rumbullion may simply have been a descriptive word, or an English version of the Dutch and German *roemer*, meaning a large drinking glass.

Rum helped to make Barbadian planters prosperous. It was bought by planters who did not have their own sugar works, and sold to the taverns and to ships both for consumption by the crew, and for resale overseas. The

taverns sprang up all over the island following in the tradition of the British ale house and later made the transition to rum shops. With all this indulgence, consumption on the island reached 70,000 gallons (265,000 liters) a year by the late 1700s.

"Leh we fire one": Rum is unquestionably still the social drink of Barbados today. It is drunk at births, Christenings, weddings, wakes, funerals and at all other rites of passage. The invitation "Man, leh we fire one on dat!" could be prompted by a promotion, a lucky bet on the horses or on the pools, or

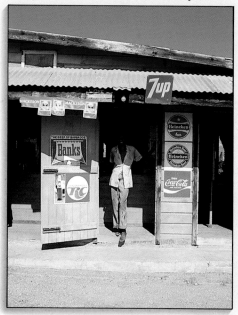

anything which causes happiness, and the "one" to be "fired" (that is, drunk) is usually rum. Rum is drunk straight from the bottle; with each person taking turns in a spirit of community, or from small "snap" glasses on the rocks, or with a chaser to dilute its strength and taste.

Rum is even used as a political instrument in Barbados. Politicians regularly provide rum and corned beef before and after elections, and woe be to the greenhorn political aspirant who doesn't fulfill this tradition. Voters have been known to "eat out, drink out, and vote out" many a candidate who was miserly with the supplies of rum.

It is considered bad manners and maybe a little foolhardy to drink a politician's rum and then not vote for him. A folk song made popular in the 1940s tells of one such candidate's revenge:

Speightstown people drink Marshall rum
And then vote fuh "Labour"
Speightstown people drink Marshall rum
And then vote fuh "Labour"
Doan pass here, doan pass here
For de dog will bite yuh ...

Apparently "Marshall" unleashed his dog on all those people who had unashamedly but it's a point hardly worth considering when instead you could be tipping a glass to:

Rum is sweet, rum is sweet
Doan let this drink
Sweep you off your feet

Some of the best rum-drinking rhymes come from the Christmas season and the best known is:

Hark the Herald Angels sing
A gallon o' rum is just de t'ing
Peace on earth and mercy mild
A pint for a man and a gill for a child.

Sociologists tell, in stark statistics, the

"drunk him out and then voted him out."

Where tongues are loosened: The "rum shop" is the place where liquors are dispersed. It is more than a store selling liquor, however. It is also a village store, often selling groceries and fuel, and an informal community center, where tongues are loosened, politics discussed and rumours spread. It is not a bar, a café, or a restaurant, though it may be all of these at one time or another.

There are fewer rum toasts than rum shops, story of rum consumption in Barbados. It is true that the typical rum shop patron is male, middle-aged, and sometimes too likely to spend at the rum shop what he could be putting towards child support or other obligations. Women rarely frequent rum shops, generally attending only occasionally, and with a male escort. The rum shop, in other words, is primarily a male bastion, and its liquid pleasures – like most pleasures are sometimes abused.

Still, it seems impossible to separate "Barbados" and "rum". In the words of one devotee, "No matter how long the world lasts, rum shops will go on."

Left, passing the time at a rum shop in St Philip. **Right,** oak barrels for aging rum at the West Indian Rum Refinery in St Michael.

BARBADOS TEAM v. REST OF WORLD — March 8th — 13th, 1967

Cortez   D.   P.   R.   A.   A.   G.   A.   R.
Jordan : Holford : Lashley : Brancker : Taylor : Howard : Greenidge : Bethel : Bynoe : S. Buller
(Umpire)   (Emergency Fieldsmen)   (Umpire)

S.   C.   E.   G.   W.   C.
Nurse   Hunte   Weekes   Sobers   Hall   Griffith
                    (Manager) (Captain)

When Barbados became independent in 1966 after more than 300 years of British colonialism, it chose to proclaim its political coming of age by challenging the rest of the world to a cricket match.

Barbados lost – an appropriate reward, perhaps, for such arrogance. Yet no one doubted the ability of this country to hold its own against the might of an international all-star team. Barbados may be no more than a pinprick on the -world map, but the game of cricket brought it instant and universal recognition. Often called its "national religion," cricket in Barbados is nearly a way of life.

Most of Barbados's national heroes are cricket heroes. The pages of *Wisden Cricketers' Almanac*, the Bible-size tome that has chronicled the game for well over a century, are filled with the records of brilliant Barbadians who have fashioned this most intricate sport into an institution.

Exuberant pride: In Barbados today, cricket is a source of exuberant pride. After all, even if Barbados did lose that 1966 match against a world team, it has trounced several international touring teams. It has taken the Shell Shield, the annual regional tournament, more times than not.

The game of cricket was introduced almost two centuries ago by the British military. The local white planter and merchant classes soon set up their own clubs, and organized regular competitions. It seems there would be other pastimes more suited to the tropical heat, yet cricket flourished in the Caribbean. Cricket, more than any other sport exported throughout the empire, was seen as a character-builder, a reflection of the noble values of British culture.

In the early years, cricket clubs mirrored the clear class and racial structures of Barbadian society. The Wanderers, formed in 1877, drew membership mainly from the white mercantile community. The Pickwick was the club of the plantocracy, and like The Wanderers, strictly white. Spartan's members mainly came from the growing group of

black and mixed-race professionals. When Spartan members blackballed Herman Griffith, a public health inspector, because they felt he was socially beneath them, objectors broke away and formed the Empire Club. Griffith became one of the great players of the game, a fast bowler (pitcher) who could sprint 20 powerful strides before hurling the 5½-ounce (160-gm) leather ball at over 90 miles an hour (145 kph). He was the first black captain of a Barbados team. These four clubs are still active, although the class

---

WHAT IS CRICKET, ANYWAY?

The best way to understand cricket is to experience a match firsthand. It is an intricate game with idiosyncratic rules and traditions. Matches run long hours, and can span five days, at the end of which no clear winner is guaranteed. Perhaps the enigma that is cricket is best summed up in this description, attributed to an English cricket club:

You have two sides, one out in the field and one in. Each man that's in the side that's in, goes out and when he's out he comes in and the next man goes in until he's out. Then the next man goes in until he's out. When they are all out the side that's out comes in and the side that's been in goes out and tries to get those coming in out. Sometimes you get men still in and not out. When both sides have been in and out including the not outs, that's the end of the game. Howzat!

---

and racial structure of their membership has subsequently changed.

All of this early activity was once centered around Bridgetown and confined to a small segment of the population. Yet, artisans, laborers and other workers would not be excluded, and soon formed their own clubs. Plantation bosses recognized the game's potential for fostering community spirit. They encouraged workers to play, providing them with land for a pitch, and passing on second-hand kit and equipment from their own clubs. Largely ignored by the official Barbados Cricket Association, these lesser teams arranged their own competitions. The rivalry

---

Left, the national cricket team at the time of independence included some of the world's best cricket players. Gary Sobers was captain.

was usually intense, particularly on the sugar plantations where outsiders could qualify for membership only by living on or near the plantation or by marrying or courting a girl from the village.

This spirit gave momemtum to the formation of the Barbados Cricket League at a time of significant social and political upheaval; the League is now recognized as a step towards Independence. Ironically, this game that once segregated the classes and colors so neatly, eventually brought disparate groups together in a way not otherwise possible. White plantation managers and business executives found themselves playing against black lawyers and civil servants: camarade-

time. In 1958, at the age of 21, he recorded the highest individual score ever made. In an international Test Match for the West Indies against Pakistan at Kingston's Sabina Park in Jamaica, the lithe left-hander scored an incredible 365 runs. He was stopped only when the jubilant crowd invaded the pitch to hoist him shoulder-high in triumph.

He was an explosive batsman, a bowler of three distinctive styles, and an incomparable fielder. He played 93 international matches, from 1954 until 1974, when the cartilage in his knees finally gave out. Trinidadian calypso king the Mighty Sparrow described him as "the cricketer on Earth or on Mars" in a 1965 song. And in 1975, Queen Elizabeth

rie and respect emerged. It would be some time, however, before the stevedore of the cane-cutter found a place "at the stump."

The new heroes: Today's best-known players are black, many from humble backgrounds. In the 1950s, the West Indies scorelines were dominated by three batsmen of grace, style and endurance known as the Terrible Three Ws: Frank Worrell, Clyde Walcott and Everton Weekes. Worrell was knighted by Queen Elizabeth in 1964; his image even graced the five-dollar bill.

Garfield Sobers, born into a family of six in the Bridgetown suburb of Bayland, grew up to be the undisputed finest player of all

overturned a tradition and knighted Sobers, not at Buckingham Palace, but in an open-air ceremony on the Garrison Savannah, the site of the earliest recorded matches on the island. The versatile Sobers has captained the Barbados golf team.

Making it big: Barbadian cricket has inspired many personal hopes and dreams as well as national pride. It is a vehicle for young boys who want to escape from poverty and "make it big." They know that mastering cricket may mean more to their future than any other skill. So they play cricket everywhere, year-round.

They sharpen their reflexes and techniques

playing in the street and on the beaches, using anything that approximates a real ball and a real bat. Top players earn at least US$50,000, a very good living in Barbados. The West Indies team has been by far the strongest on the limited international circuit for at least a decade. This means that its star players are in demand as well: Malcolm Marshall and Joel "Big Bird" Garner, for example, have had contracts with English county teams and wealthy clubs in Australia.

Even those not quite on their level can find jobs coaching and playing abroad. Barbadian cricketers head overseas every year to make the kind of money they could never earn from cricket at home.

Sunday morning is when more than 100 softball league teams compete with one another for places on the Barbados teams that regularly tour the United States and Canada.

Teas and trees: One of the peculiarities of cricket is that there is no legal definition of the playing area. A batsman on some pitches may need to hit the ball 70 yards (64 meters) over the boundary, while other pitches are smaller, requiring hits as short as 50 yards (46 meters). Some clubs are equipped with dressing rooms and showers and serve elaborate teas. In country areas, things are a bit rougher: the shadiest tree serves as a pavilion, the grass on the pitch is kept trim by a flock of sheep, and the "tea" is more potent.

The two controlling organizations of cricket in Barbados, the Association and the League, cram 100 matches into the limited space at their disposal every Saturday afternoon throughout the season, from early June until mid-September. A "softball" association controls a modified form of the game which uses tennis rather than leather balls, and slim bats of local mahogany in place of the regulation willow bats imported from England.

Left, a print by local artist K. Hawkins depicts the first intercontinental cricket match in the Caribbean, at the garrison. *Right*, beach cricket at Bathsheba.

The fans come no matter what the conditions of the pitch or its surroundings. A day of cricket is a social ritual. An international match runs from 10.30am to 5.30pm each day for up to five straight days, with breaks for lunch and tea. When the action on the field is sluggish, and the sun is hot, diversions become mandatory. So fans make a picnic of it, toting their baskets of peas and rice, salted pig-trotters, pickled breadfruit and other delights, as well as the island's famous rum.

Kensington Oval is always crammed to its 15,000 capacity on days of a Test Match against England or Australia, and the atmosphere is electric. It can seem even more crowded at key club matches where as many as 4,000 enthusiastic fans encircle much smaller grounds.

Until the 1960s, businesses closed and Parliament was adjourned when international teams came to town. Productivity drops when the West Indies are on tour in England, as the ball-by-ball commentary is heard on thousands of radios concealed in desk drawers and behind service counters.

All the activity surrounding the game has produced some characters who like nothing better than to entertain the fans when the players are failing to do so. The late "Flannagan" (no one seemed to know or really care

match was recorded in Barbados, cricket has remained much more than a game. The island has changed enormously in that time, and cricket has both reflected those changes and helped bring them about.

When Barbados finished fifth out of six in the regional senior and junior championships in 1985, everyone threw their hands up in horror, predicting the end. Yet, Barbados had won the senior pennant five times in the previous eight seasons, and the junior title for two consecutive years before that.

Social statement: In an editorial *The Nation* newspaper pointed out that the cricket club of 50 or 60 years ago was "first and foremost a social statement." It stated: "When cricket

much about his real name) traveled with Barbados teams throughout the 1930s and 40s, serving as a sort of mascot, heckling and teasing opponents on and off the field with his loud, sharp-witted comments.

The late "King Dyal", Redvers Dundonald Dyal, was a regular for more than a quarter-century, unfailingly supporting the other team, particularly if it is the English. He always makes a grand entrance to the most conspicuous seat in the most conspicuous stand – and each interval reappears in a different, resplendent, three-piece suit: flamboyant scarlet, canary yellow, emerald green.

In the nearly 200 years since the first

became a mere game, then an occupation, it was the beginning of the end of what it once was. It may have become better organized, the players more technically competent, but they have become less committed to club, country, and ideals."

Perhaps, but then, Barbados has changed as well, and through most of the changes something has been gained, not lost. Always a barometer, cricket and its social climate will continue to evolve along with Barbados.

Left, the Barbados team today. **Right**, Sir Gary Sobers, a Bajan cricket hero who was knighted by the Queen.

PLACES

No matter how addicted you are to sea and sand – and it does have a special allure in Barbados – it's worth tearing yourself away to experience the "other" Barbados, the one many visitors don't see. Though you can learn quite a bit about the island by chatting with the locals you'll meet on the beach and in the hotels, it's well worth renting a car or mini-moke to see for yourself.

Of course you'll get lost – that's part of the fun. Road maps are a good guide to the island's seven main highways, but with 800 miles (1,300 km) of paved roads in a country 14 miles (23 km) wide and 21 miles (34 km) long, it's best to relax and enjoy the adventure. You'll never be more than a 20-minute drive from one coast or the other – and don't hesitate to ask for directions. Barbadians speak English and react enthusiastically to any visitor's interest in their country.

For ideas about some offbeat things to do and see, tune into the "Voice of Barbados" radio station. You'll hear ads in Bajan dialect, short stories, the latest calypso hits and announcements of upcoming events – festivals, concerts, picnics, dances – all of which welcome visitors. To help you find your way around and discover more of its hidden delights, we've grouped the 11 parishes of Barbados into four categories – Bridgetown, The West, The South, The North and East – and mapped out a tour of each section.

So four times you can "go an' come back," taking a separate tour of each section. Or you can see a fair portion of the island in a single excursion – "one time," as the Barbadians would put it.

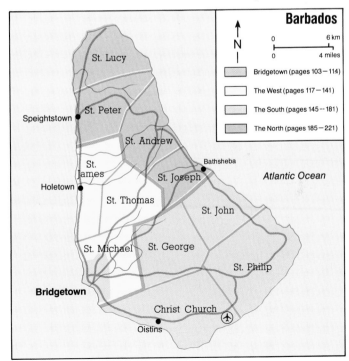

173

BUSTLING BRIDGETOWN

Though small in size, Bridgetown pulses with all the energy of a major Caribbean capital – and with something that is uniquely Barbadian. In brilliant sunlight, and in the shade of colonial buildings and modern offices, the city hustles and bustles to an ageless quick tempo; women bearing baskets hurry to be the first to market: curbside vendors hawk their wares; well-dressed business people hurry towards their office buildings. You will not find a busier, more industrious population anywhere else in the Caribbean.

Overseeing it all, at the head of Bridgetown's main thoroughfare, is the statue of **Horatio, Lord Nelson** probably the city's most popular backdrop for photographs, taking precedence even over the picturesque wharf and the bridges from which the city takes its name. Yet the gallant bronze monument, erected in 1813 (preceding Nelson's Column in Trafalgar Square, London, by 17 years), has long been a figure of great controversy. From as early as 1833, people have petitioned to have it removed from its commanding position. It has been an object of ridicule, a dumping ground for garbage and a platform for protesters. But Lord Nelson, sculpted by Sir Richard Westmacott, stands firm, despite the cries of "Take down Nelson and put up a Bajan Man," as sung by calypsonian, the Mighty Gabby.

As in London, the area around Nelson's statue is called **Trafalgar Square**. Lord Nelson, and the flagship *Victory*, accompanied by other ships of his fleet, arrived at Barbados on June 4, 1805. When news of his death in the Battle of Trafalgar later that year reached Barbados, patriotic citizens dedicated the square to his memory.

The square is also home to the **Dolphin Fountain**, installed to commemorate the introduction of piped running water to Bridgetown in March 1861. You will also find here the **War Memorial**, unveiled on May 10, 1925. Many Barbadians fought bravely in World War

I (1914–18), and the decision was made to erect the monument just six months after the Armistice. The names of those who died in that war are listed on three bronze panels. A fourth panel, bearing the names of those who died in World War II (1939–45), was added in 1953.

Nelson's statue faces east, away from **Broad Street**, Bridgetown's busiest shopping street and thoroughfare. It is as if the old war hero is trying to show his contempt for the worldly materialism in the department stores and Duty Free shops. On Broad Street, the old colonial buildings struggle to retain their old-world charm amidst the steady proliferation of more modern neighbors. Some buildings, like those of Dacosta and Co., C.F. Harrison's and the Barbados Mutual Life Assurance Co., still retain the proud grandeur and architectural flourishes of the turn of the century. All along this street you will find a wide and varied selection of attractive goods, services and banking facilities, rivaling in quantity and style many of the world's larger duty-free ports.

Trading on Broad Street goes back to the mid-17th century. In a statute of 1657, the street was declared reserved "for a market-place and other publique uses of this island." It was then called Cheapside, but today only its western end – where you'll find a modern post office and an old-fashioned farmer's market – still bears that name. During the latter half of the 17th century, Broad Street was also called The Exchange or Exchange Street because the Merchants' Exchange was situated there.

Settlers and swamp: Bridgetown was never planned; like many towns, it just grew. It was founded on July 5, 1628, when 64 settlers, led by Charles Wolverstone, arrived on the spot. The proximity to a swamp, together with the town's haphazard development, provoked criticism from early visitors, including one Richard Ligon who came in 1647. He wrote: "A town ill situate, for if they had considered health, as they did convenience, they would never had set it there, or if they had any intention at first to have built a town there, they could not have been so improvident as not to force the inconveniences that must ensue by making choice of so unhealthy a place to live in…"

One of Governor Wolverstone's captains, John Swan, who was a surveyor, reputedly laid out the principal streets of the early town. According to tradition, the secondary business street was named after him.

Bridgetown derives its name from a primitive bridge built by the Indians to span the waterway. In the early years, names such as Indian Bridge, Indian Bridgetown or just simply The Bridge were given to the town. Bridgetown now has two bridges, situated to the east of the city. They span the **Constitution River**, which is actually not a river but an arm of the sea which once ran some distance inland. The lower reaches of the river form the **Careenage**, a basin so called because it provided facilities where schooners could be careened and their bottoms cleaned and painted. It was the presence of this arm of the sea which, undoubtedly, inspired the first

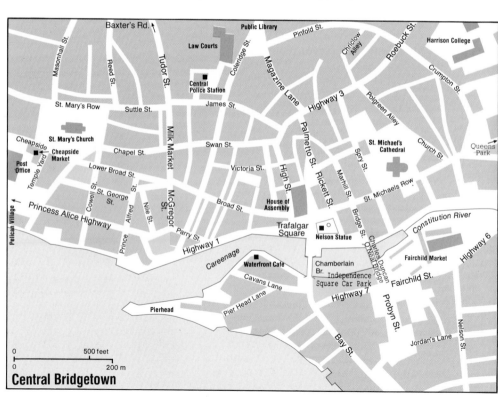

Central Bridgetown

settlers to choose this site for a town.

For hundreds of years, the Careenage was the berthing place of many small ships from all over the Caribbean. The sea, of course, was the only means of communication with the world. The busy area around Careenage thus became the center of trading and news for the island. This prominence slowly became a thing of the past as aircraft travel became more popular and facilities for handling cargo at the ports were modernized. Now, instead of seeing bananas, mangoes, plantains and other fruits loaded from the old wooden schooners and other vessels, one will see sleek, slender-masted yachts berthed in the basin and their passengers sunbathing on the decks. A number of boats which offer sightseeing excursions and deep sea fishing trips dock here*.

The bridge which separates the inner basin from the outer is called the **Chamberlain Bridge**, named after Joseph Chamberlain, the great Colonial Secretary who, during the late 1890s, was instrumental in saving the West Indies from European competition in the vital sugar trade. This bridge was once a fascination to visitors and locals alike, who used to stop to watch it swing back to allow boats to pass into the inner basin. But the Chamberlain Bridge swings no more; mechanical problems several years ago forced the government to make it into a stationary structure.

The eastern bridge is named the **Charles Duncan O'Neale**, after the founding father of the city's Democratic League and the Workingmen's Association, the forerunners of democracy and trade unionism on the island.

On the banks of the Constitution River, next to the Charles Duncan O'Neale Bridge, is the city's main bus concourse. This multimillion-dollar terminal on **Fairchild Street** is indeed an improvement over the old terminal, where harried commuters had to fight their way to the buses during rush hours, with very little shelter from the weather.

On the waterfront: Across the Careenage at the western end is the **Pierhead** and **Willoughby's Fort**. It is not gener-

Shoppers in turn-of-the-century Bridgetown.

ally known that the fort once occupied a small island. In 1656, Willoughby's Fort was constructed on Little Island by William Withington, who was paid some 80,000 lbs (36,300 kg) of sugar for the job. Today the Barbados Coast Guard uses it as its headquarters.

The Pierhead, once across from the island and now connected to it, originally consisted mainly of pasture, marshland and ponds. Over the years, warehouses were constructed there and on the island, and today some of these are of enough historic and architectural interest to be preserved by the Barbados National Trust.

One of these former warehouses is now the **Waterfront Café**, which as its name suggests, is perched on the waterfront, offering a most spectacular view of Trafalgar Square, the Public Buildings and the upper end of Broad Street. Diners have the option of sitting in the cool indoors or on the sidewalk – European style – to watch the world go by as they savor a flying fish sandwich and a Banks beer.

Heading east from the Pierhead, you will find **Independence Square**, a car park by day and a meeting place by night. Because of its proximity to the main bus terminal on Fairchild Street, it is very popular with politicians who stage many of their public rallies there.

Until early in this century, Fairchild Street was a residential area, though today it's the busy provenance of commercial tenants. Colonel John Fairchild, from whom the street get its name, was a prominent citizen who lived there in the mid-18th century. He served as a vestryman of the Parish of St Michael, was a member of the Assembly, and was appointed Chief Justice in 1752.

The area between Fairchild Street and Nelson Street was once a disreputable residential neighborhood called **Racoon Quarters**. The origin of the name remains unclear, but racoons were once considered to be vermin in Barbados, and this neighborhood was probably a haven for these creatures at some time.

In the 19th century, a devastating cholera epidemic swept this area at as-

Central Bridgetown, with Careenage. St Elizabeth's hospital is in background, to the right.

178

tonishing speed. On May 14, 1854, a resident of Fairchild Street died under suspicious circumstances. Within three days, similar deaths occurred in Nelson Street and its vicinity. By mid-June the epidemic had spread throughout the island, and by August 6, the known death-toll was 15,243. When the pestilence finally ended, between 18,000 and 20,000 people had died.

A Moravian minister who lived through the epidemic said the disease "increased in town steadily... until it reached 340 per diem... In the most erratic manner it went from street to street, omitting one or two in its course and returning to them when the residents thought they had escaped, and taking off more in such cases than in the street first visited."

Another bit of history from this area is that the site of the **Harbour Police Station**, in **Bay Street**, was once the Hospital for Contagious Diseases, better known as the Lock Hospital. This building was constructed in 1869 after the British government passed an act in 1826 for the better prevention of contagious diseases at certain naval and military stations. The objective was to safeguard members of the armed forces from venereal infection. But the hospital was closed in 1887 when the act and its supplements were repealed; it was then used to house the Constabulary, the Harbour Police and the Fire Brigade.

Off to market: Next door to the bus concourse you will find **Fairchild Market**, one of the two big public markets in this city. Though it sometimes seems that every street-corner in Bridgetown is a mini-market selling everything from baskets and sunglasses to a refreshing drink of coconut water, the public markets are something special.

In bygone days, the public markets were a riot of color and full of gaiety, especially on Saturdays when housewives from all over the island came to shop for the week's supply of food. Yams, potatoes, breadfruit, lettuce, cucumbers and tomatoes still fill the stalls.

Amidst the development of supermarkets and mini-marts, both of Bridge-

The
Barclays
Bank
building.

town's public markets are slowly losing their appeal. But tradition dies hard in Barbados and every Saturday both Fairchild and Cheapside public markets are lively places – and definitely worth a visit. The Mighty Gabby captured the spirit of the market in his song "Bridgetown Early Saturday Morning":

See de women
How dey calling, singing:
Come for your breadfruit,
Come for your corn,
Come for de apples –
fresh as de morn.
Come for your guava.
Your guava, your guava

Across from the public market the city's red-light district starts in **Nelson Street** and extends south into Bay Street. A residential estate back in the 18th century, it was part of Racoon Quarters. The modern development of the city has passed this area by, but the government has, in the past, designated this area for development which would bring new housing along the lines of the others around the island. It is interesting to note that in the heart of this district is a church, the St Ambrose Church, which was consecrated on January 1, 1858.

An extract from *The Barbadian* newspaper of March 14, 1857 stated: "The Rev. Joseph S. Meyers, on his arrival from America, having been placed for a brief period in charge of St. Paul's District, saw at once that there was want of a church–the adjoining Church of St. Paul's accommodating 1,200 in the population of 13,000. The place known as Rebitt's Ground had in it an amount of spiritual destitution startling in the extreme, and was covered with a pall of darkness too deep to be fancied, and only realized by those who have explored the district.

The place, once the abode of filth, misery and vice; the scene of cockfights, indignities and other degrading dances; whose very atmosphere was polluted with the dreadful imprecations of the blasphemous, became an object of extreme solicitude to his mind. His appeal was not in vain…"

Parliamentary pomp: Back at Nelson's

Bay Street by day; red-light district by night.

statue, look northward and you will see the neo-Gothic facades of the **Public Buildings**. Erected in the 19th century, they house many of the island's public records and accommodate the Houses of Parliament.

The earliest parliamentary building, called the State House, was built around 1640, somewhere in the vicinity of Upper Broad Street. It was burnt down in 1668, and for the next 30 years the House of Legislature met in people's homes and public places, often taverns, a situation frowned upon by many. In 1695 Governor Francis Russell proposed allocating funds for a new State House. But it took six years before a building was finally erected in the vicinity of James Fort. Three years later, this building was assigned for use as the jail, forcing the politicians back into the taverns. They only got their building back when a new jail was built in 1730.

The present Public Buildings became a dream of John Glasgow Grant, member for St Michael in the Assembly, in 1856. A bill was introduced to the As-sembly, a committee set up and adver-tisements published inviting plans and estimates. The west wing of the present building was finished in 1871, and the east wing was ready for occupation in 1874. It is ironic that it took so long for the physical structure of the **House of Assembly** to be erected when Barbados boasts the third oldest parliamentary body in the Commonwealth, founded in 1639, after Bermuda and Britain.

But the House of Assembly was elabo-rately done up, with a Speaker's chair and mace, Government and Opposition benches, and a stained-glass window representing the English monarchs from James I to Victoria. Interestingly, the stained-glass window carries the image of Oliver Cromwell, the Great Protec-tor, despite the staunch Royalist sympa-thies of Barbadians during the English Civil War.

Heading east after the Public Build-ings, you will soon see **St Michael's Cathedral**. This edifice was first built in 1665 to replace the old wooden struc-ture which was located where St Mary's

Marathon with House of Assembly in the background.

Church now stands. It was destroyed by the hurricane of 1780, and the present cathedral was built in 1789.

Northwest of the cathedral was the site of the old Harrison's Free School, founded by Thomas Harrison in 1733 to provide free education for indigent boys from the parish of St Michael, but the number of students was not to exceed 25. The school occupied these premises until 1870 when the Freemasons bought the building to use as a lodge.

Towering above the cathedral, the Freemason's Lodge and indeed over all of Bridgetown, is the **Central Bank** headquarters. At 11 stories high, it is the tallest building on the island. It cost more than $60 million of public money, which raised quite a stir among taxpayers. One of the island's most important cultural centers is housed in a side building of the Central Bank. The Frank Collymore Hall can seat 491 and has the latest stage equipment for theater performances, concerts and conferences. Every November as part of the Independence Day celebrations, the National Independence Festival of Creative Arts (NIFCA) is held here.

Roebuck hucksters: The Central Bank is bounded on its north by **Roebuck Street**, named after a tavern called the Roebuck, established by Thomas Noell, a London merchant, who sold the establishment in 1659. It continued to flourish for many years, and was once the favorite meeting place of the Barbados Council and the General Assembly. It has been claimed that the street was named in honor of the *HMS Roebuck,* a ship of the Royal Navy whose crew allegedly saved the neighborhood from destruction by fire in 1766. But Mayo's plan of Bridgetown, published in 1722, proves otherwise, as it definitely identifies the street as "Roe Buck" more than 50 years before the fire.

Roebuck Street today holds a lively concentration of shops, both wholesale and retail. But well before the mid-18th century, the area was noted for its many "huckster shops" – streetside produce stands. Selling everything from pineapples to plastics, these stands are a

Left, St Michael's Cathedral, interior. **Below**, Cheapside market vendor.

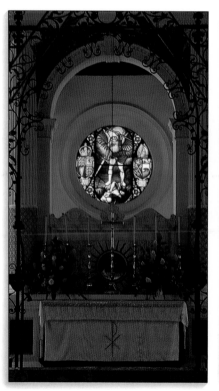

200-year-old tradition that remains an integral part of Bridgetown life.

From the lower end of Roebuck Street to the upper Careenage, including the area around the Charles Duncan O'Neale Bridge, is a district once called Marl Hill or Gravel Hill. It acquired these names because of the nature of the ground. One street in the area retains a part of the name – Marhill Street.

A short walk west of Roebuck Street is **James Street** and its environs. Like many others in and around Bridgetown, James Street has important Quaker connections. Early in Bridgetown's history, the Quaker community purchased a plot in this area for use as a burial ground. They were cheated of the property by those who held it in trust, and it was sold to the Wesleyans in 1861. It remained in their possession until shortly after World War II, when the Barbados Telephone Company bought it.

Swan Street and the synagogue: A side street running from James Street to Magazine Lane leads to the site of the old Jewish synagogue. Tradition held that the Dutchmen who introduced sugarcane to the island were Jews, but other researchers say that Jews did not settle in Barbados until 1654. In any case, the Jews in Barbados became particularly noted for two things: success in business and the dedicated practice of their faith. They became so entrenched in trade that Swan Street, where most of them had set up business, became known as "Jew Street."

The first synagogue in Barbados, built before 1654, was seriously damaged by the hurricane of 1831, and a new one was built on the same site in 1833. As the old building was starting to decay and the valuable furnishings were disappearing into museums, the National Trust decided to completely renovate the synagogue at the end of the 1980s. It now gleams brightly and is once again used by the Barbadian Jewish community. The interior can be viewed on weekdays between 9am and 4pm.

Particularly impressive are the four brass chandeliers hanging above the carved prayer benches. The oldest grave-

"Hucksters" selling vegetables in Cheapside area.

stones in the Jewish cemetery date from the 1630s.

Another reminder of the Jews is the old drinking fountain in the green triangle before the **Public Library**, presented to the city of Bridgetown by John Montefiore in memory of his father. The fountain was set up in Beckwith Place in 1865, but in 1940 it was moved to its present site in Coleridge Street.

On this street you will find the **High Court**. The site on which it stands is believed to be the first piece of land owned by the Barbadian government. It was purchased on December 5, 1682, by the Governor, Sir Richard Dutton, for the building of a new public warehouse. The warehouse was constructed in 1683 but demolished in 1728 to make room for a single structure to house the Legislature, the Law Courts and the jail. The Town Hall Gaol, as it was called, was not only used to detain criminals but also prisoners of war. An American sea captain named John Manley and his crew were imprisoned there in 1779 and escaped with the aid of a rope ladder.

Placing a Town Hall in the same compound as a jail was an anomaly, and the source of many wry comments from visitors to the island. The prison was finally closed in 1878 by order of the Governor, Sir John Pope Hennessy. Today the buildings house the Law Courts, the Magistrates' Courts, the Public Library and the Police Station.

Behind this complex is one of the city's oldest roads, **Tudor Street**. It was here that the island's first Quaker meeting house was built in 1670. Because it was illegal for this religious body to meet, this place was closed, the seats torn out, the furniture pulled down and the windows and doors nailed shut no less than four times within the three years from 1680 to 1683.

All night long: The upper end of Tudor Street leads into Broad Street, but its other end leads into a narrow road known as the "Street That Never Sleeps"– **Baxter's Road**. Every night, it becomes an ongoing party, the tiny rum shops and restaurants open their doors, and the air fills with music and an aroma as

At the Careenage after a day at sea.

tempting as anything you have ever imagined. The smell is delicious, but it's nothing compared to the succulent flavor of the spicy Bajan fish or chicken. This is the prime spot for locals and visitors alike to stop at any hour of the night. In tiny bars the jukeboxes blare and business hops until 4 or 5am. Cooks dish out local food in the one-room, ragged restaurants until the same hour. At one end of the street, vendors stand over "buck pots," old cast-iron pots, deep-frying fish, chicken and pork – Bajan style – over bright coal fires.

Leading from Tudor Street into the western section of Bridgetown is **Suttle Street** and **St Mary's Row**. Until about 1827, these two streets formed what was called Back Church Street, so named because it ran beside **St Mary's Church**. Suttle Street was once a respectable neighborhood, until the late 19th century. Now it is nothing more than a back alley devoted mainly to trading in small shops and doorways. Surrounded by gardens, St Mary's Church remains the neighborhood's most dignified figure.

The church was completed on July 15, 1827, to accommodate the overflow from St Michael's Cathedral. Actually, this was the site of the old St Michael's Church, later abandoned for a more central location in St Michael's Row.

Continuing from St Mary's Row is the street and district called **Lake's Folly**, named after an 18th-century landowner. This area has a violent history; on the night of March 5, 1773, a gang of 12 armed men ventured forth from the neighborhood and went on a rampage through the town, killing two people and seriously wounding another. The night before they set out on the warpath, they formed an "Association," swearing to stand by each other until death. To seal this bond, each man punctured his arm with a shoemaker's awl and let three drops of blood fall into a mixture of rum, gunpowder and brimstone, which they all drank.

Rasta-Mall: Across from St Mary's Church is another bus terminal, the **Lower Green Station**, which services the northern section of the island. This

terminal is supplemented by another public transport system on the Princess Alice Highway and the privately owned mini-buses which are stationed a few yards west of the Lower Green terminal, at Temple Yard. This area acquired its name from a temple of the Ancient Masons who converted an old naval hospital into a lodge.

Behind the mini-bus station, a group of Rastafarians set up their own outdoor "shopping mall." The wooden stalls were joined together crudely, and it was from here that these artistic and talented people sold their goods, mainly handcrafted leather products. The stalls were originally put there by the government because the vendors had erected stalls all over the city, often on busy sidewalks where they caused congestion.

West of the mini-bus station is the **Cheapside Market**, the second of the city's two public markets. Farther along this street is the **General Post Office**. Originally, the postal services were housed in the Public Buildings, with the Senate and the House of Assembly. For more than 40 years plans were hatching to construct a separate building, and the task was finally completed in 1984.

Behind the Post Office the **Princess Alice Highway** runs parallel to the coast. On the seaward side of this highway, you'll see a small park and then the stunning blue of Carlisle Bay. The Rotary Club of Barbados undertook to beautify this area, right up to the gates of the Deep Water Harbour. The National Conservation Commission took over the upkeep of the park, **Trevor's Way**, named after a young man who was killed in an accident nearby.

Sweet cargo: Opposite the park is the **Pelican Village**, an amalgam of art galleries, a restaurant and curio shops selling local handmade items including clothing, pottery, paintings, baskets and straw mats. The land here is reclaimed from the sea. Until the 1950s, there was a little island off the shores of Barbados called Pelican Island. The island was joined to the land on the construction of the **Deep Water Harbour**.

After more than 60 years of debate, the new harbor was officially opened in 1961. The debate centered on the method of shipping sugar. As competing sugar producing countries began shipping in bulk, Barbados's sugar magnates debated doing away with shipping in bags. Finally, a new bulk sugar store with a capacity of 81,280 tons was built on reclaimed land. Sugar arrives at the bulk store from the island's factories and is carried via conveyor belts and underground channels to loading towers. There it is discharged into ships' hatches at the rate of 508 tons an hour.

The harbor provides 1,700 feet (518 meters) of quay space and about 2,700 feet (822 meters) of protective backwater for ships. It has four groups of berthing areas, can take in eight ocean-going ships, and can easily provide simultaneous bunkering for five vessels.

Cruise liners dock here too, as you can always tell when one is in port. From early in the morning, a stream of taxis stretches from the harbor gates down Princess Alice Highway, ready to carry visitors into the lively hustle and bustle that is Bridgetown.

Left, an entrepreneur on every corner.

THE STORY OF RACHEL PRINGLE

Bridgetown's history has its lighter moments. One of them involves an infamous Barbadian hotel owner of the 1700s named Rachel Pringle.

Rachel was the mulatto daughter of a Scottish schoolmaster, William Lauder, and his African slave mistress. According to legend, Rachel became a beautiful young woman who was badly treated by her dissolute father. She was able to escape his cruel hand, however, with the aid of one Captain Thomas Pringle, a British naval officer. Pringle paid an exorbitant price to Lauder for Rachel, and set her up in a house in lower Bridgetown. In gratitude, Rachel adopted Pringle's surname.

Much to Pringle's dismay, his liason with Rachel was barren. In order to maintain Pringle's affections, Rachel "borrowed" a baby while Pringle was away at sea and presented it to him as their own upon their return. Her ruse was revealed, however, when the rightful mother arrived to claim her baby. Pringle left the scheming Rachel in disgust, but she quickly found herself another wealthy "protector" named Polgreen.

At some time in 1780, Rachel managed to open the island's first modest hotel, starting a Bridgetown tradition of taverns run by black or mulatto women who were favorite paramours of influential men.

Rachel's hotel (on what is now St George Street) quickly became popular with the British Royal Navy. One night in 1789, a visiting party of Navy officers, led by Prince William Henry (later King William IV), booked in at Rachel's hotel.

The Prince and his companions had their fill of what we might assume was Barbados rum, and in a spree of drunken horseplay, smashed furniture and shattered glassware. When the Prince topped off his merriment by capsizing Rachel's chair and sending her sprawling onto the ground, she remained remarkably quiet.

The next morning, just before the Navy ship sailed, Rachel sent the Prince an itemized bill for 700 British pounds – a princely sum indeed. He paid the bill promptly and Rachel restored her hotel in a more sumptuous style. She renamed it the Royal Naval Hotel.

Regrettably, her hotel was destroyed by fire in 1821. Her story lives on in Bajan folklore and until recently was reenacted at a weekly show at Balls Plantation. ∎

RACHEL PRINGLE of BARBADOES

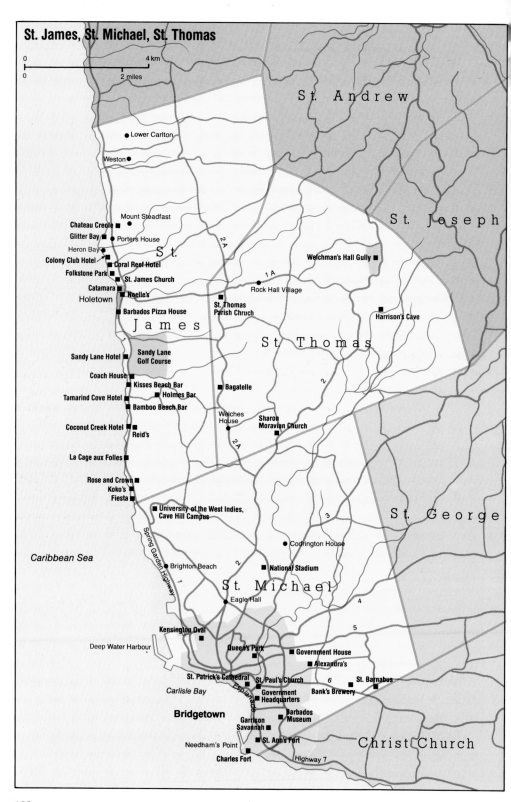

St. James, St. Michael, St. Thomas

0   4 km
0   2 miles

St. Andrew

St. Joseph

Lower Carlton

Weston

Mount Steadfast

Chateau Creole
Glitter Bay
Porters House
Heron Bay
Colony Club Hotel
Coral Reef Hotel
Folkstone Park
St. James Church
Catamara
Noelle's
Holetown
Barbados Pizza House

St.

James

Welchman's Hall Gully

2 A

1 A

Rock Hall Village

St. Thomas
Parish Chruch

St. Thomas

Harrison's Cave

Sandy Lane Hotel
Sandy Lane
Golf Course

Coach House
Kisses Beach Bar
Holmes Bar
Tamarind Cove Hotel
Bamboo Beach Bar
Coconut Creek Hotel
Reid's

Bagatelle

Weiches
House

2

Sharon
Moravian Church

La Cage aux Folles

2 A

Rose and Crown
Koko's
Fiesta

University of the West Indies,
Cave Hill Campus

3

St. George

Codrington House

Caribbean Sea

Brighton Beach

2

National Stadium

St. Michael

Eagle Hall

4

Kensington Oval

5

Deep Water Harbour

Queen's Park

Government House

Alexandra's

St. Patrick's Cathedral

St. Paul's Church

Government
Headquarters

6

Bank's Brewery

St. Barnabus

Carlisle Bay

Bridgetown

Garrison
Savannah

Barbados
Museum

Needham's Point

St. Ann's Fort

Charles Fort

Highway 7

Christ Church

Spring Garden Highway

Esplanade

188

ST MICHAEL

Encompassing the capital city of Bridgetown, the parish of St Michael is a thriving coastal area, the hub of Barbadian culture and commerce. A traveler, writing about the parish in 1672, said it "hath a commodious road for ships, is a place well frequented and traded unto, and is strongly defended by two powerful Forts."

Steeped in a colorful, tumultuous past – from the bloodthirsty Caribs to the colonial pomp of the British West India Regiment – St Michael makes a natural location for the **Barbados Museum**, located just south of the capital. There is no better place to begin a tour of this parish than with a trip to the museum, and back in time. Housed in the old military prisons of the British garrison, the Barbados Museum offers a guided tour of the history of Barbados, from the Amerindians and the Arawaks through the first settlers, the days of slavery, and the development of the island. And the museum's curators have not forgotten the island's natural world; fish of the surrounding seas, and native plants and birds are all represented here.

Most of the galleries are former prison cells. The two wings at the back of the main building were built between 1817 and 1821, and the main block was completed in 1853. Here are amassed artifacts of the native Arawaks, who lived on the island centuries ago and their warlike conquerors, the Caribs; relics of the British colonists, including period rooms, a children's gallery filled with historic dioramas, a collection of toys and games from bygone days, and a fascinating collection of old maps.

The museum is a fine example of Georgian architecture, with a pleasant open-air courtyard used for cultural activities. The popular dinner show, *1627 And All That* was held here before the Sherbourne Centre took over as host. The production portrays the history and social rituals of Barbados through song and dance.

The Barbados Museum and Historical Society was established in 1933 by a group of public spirited individuals, led by E.M. Shilstone, who were interested in the history of the island. A few years ago, the government took steps to update the museum in an effort to have it reflect not only the history of the island but also its people. It is open Monday to Saturday 9am–5pm; Sunday 2–6pm.

Across the street from the museum is the **Garrison Savannah**, described in its heyday as one of the finest parade grounds in the West Indies. After seeing the pictures in the museum, you can stand on this green oval and, in your mind's eye, see the brightly colored regiments parade on these grounds.

Today, the Savannah is more often used for horse racing, for which there

Carlisle Bay, circa 1750.

A Prospect of Bridge-Town in the Island of Barbadoes.

are two seasons each year, and for soccer and rugby. Early mornings and evenings joggers use the track to keep fit. But if you are lucky, you may be visiting Barbados on one of those few occasions when the armed forces are on parade. On November 30, the island's Day of Independence, the Barbados Defense Force, the Royal Coast Guard, the Cadets, Girl Guides, Rangers and other groups gather at the Savannah to march before the Governor General.

Grand homes and ramparts: Among the many fine buildings that surround the Savannah, few can match the stately beauty of the **Savannah Club** which, with its distinctive cupola tower and clock, has been the subject of many paintings and photographs. It was formerly the guard house of the British Regiment and the venue for the grim business of court-martials and subsequent penalties. The clock tower bears the date 1803 and the building itself was probably completed a few years later.

South of the Savannah Club stands the Drill Hall. It was built on the founda-

tion of one of the ramparts of St Anne's Fort, which lies directly behind it.

Construction of **St Anne's Fort** began in 1704, but it was never completed. Only the main ramparts survive from that period, indicating the grand design once envisioned for it. The fort today is of a much simpler style. Its walls range from 4 to 20-feet (1 to 6-meters) thick, and inside are the store rooms, armory and powder magazines as they were at the end of the 18th century.

Today, the Barbados Defense Force is headquartered at the fort, carrying on some of the same drills and duties that were a familiar sight within these walls over one hundred years ago.

It was the threat of French invasion during the American War of Independence that led to the establishment of the first garrison of British troops on Barbados. As the size of the military establishment grew, Barbados became the headquarters of the British forces in the Leeward and Windward islands. But it was tropical diseases, not the French, that killed the British recruits. One report states that of 19,676 soldiers sent to the West Indies from England in 1796, 17,173 died before 1802.

Numerous tombstones and memorials to British soldiers, dated between the years 1800 and 1900, can be found in St Michael's Cathedral, and some from a later period can be seen at St Paul's Church. But most of those who died after 1800 must have been buried in the area behind St Anne's Fort. The earliest burials seem to have been near the shore, roughly where the Hilton International Barbados now has its tennis courts. Sometime in 1820, the garrison discontinued burials in this area, and began to use a new site, farther west on what is today Highway 7. It is this new burial ground that is today known as the **Military Cemetery**. It is still used for the burial of service personnel, active or retired, and their families.

Next to the cemetery is the modern **Barbados Hilton Hotel** which opened in 1966, the year the island gained its independence. Located on Aquatic Gap, the hotel shares lovely Needham's Point with several other hotels, the Mobil Oil

Morning trot at the Garrison Savannah racetrack.

Refinery, one of the island's four lighthouses, and Charles Fort, the largest of the defenses built during the prime of the British Regiment.

The beach at **Needham's Point** is one of the finest on the island, and a favorite with Barbadians, who flock to the area on weekends and public holidays. One bygone attraction of this beach was a hot water pool, called a "pot" by the locals. Situated a few yards out to the sea, the pot was heated courtesy of the nearby Barbados Light and Power Company. People who suffered from arthritis, rheumatism and other ailments used to go for a "bath in the pot." The pot has since been removed, but the beach remains a popular picnic place.

The headquarters of the Light and Power Company in Bay Street has an unusual past; it was once a theater where actors, engaged by the military, entertained the men of the garrison.

G.W. slept here: Along Highway 7 toward the city of Bridgetown is **Crofton House**, at the corner of Bay Street and Chelsea Road. Better known as **George Washington House**, after the first President of the United States. It was said that Washington stayed here while on a visit to Barbados in 1751 – reputedly his only trip to a foreign country. According to his diary, he and his half-brother Lawrence stayed in a house that belonged to Captain Crofton, who was the Commander of James Fort. Lawrence suffered from tuberculosis, and had come to Barbados hoping to be cured by the invigorating climate. George, who accompanied him, had the misfortune to contract smallpox, the scars of which he bore for the rest of his life. Some historians intimate that Washington's illness was not all bad luck. By surviving the disease in Barbados, he developed an immunity which kept him alive and at the head of the rebel forces throughout the American Revolution, while smallpox ravaged his troops.

Along Bay Street, you will see the **Government Headquarters**, which house the offices of the Prime Minister. At the front of the circular driveway, bordered on all sides by poinsettias,

Heraldry and pomp; clock tower in background.

begonias and hibiscus flowers, stands a bust of the first Premier of Barbados, Sir Grantley Adams.

Across the street, along the seaside, extends the **Esplanade**, with a splendid view of the calm waters of **Carlisle Bay**. This small park, maintained by the National Conservation Commission, is an ideal place to watch the spectacular Barbadian sunsets.

Facing **Bay Street**, with its two storey facade and parking lot , is the **Carlisle Bay Centre**. Designed mainly for cruise passengers who want to spend time at a beach with all the facilities of a resort, the centre has changing rooms, shops, watersports and a pleasant, breezy restaurant called Young Roy's.

Two churches and a baobab: Along this way, two churches soon come into view. The first is **St Paul's Church**. Built in 1830, the very next year it was destroyed by a hurricane. Rebuilt in 1832, it was used as a garrison church, and its nave is still decorated with marble tablets bearing the names of many British soldiers formerly stationed on the island.

The other church, at the corner of Jemmotts Lane and Bay Street, is **St Patrick's Cathedral**. This Roman Catholic church was rebuilt in 1897 in early-Gothic style after the earlier church was completely destroyed by fire. For many years no Catholic priest was allowed to reside on the island, a situation which did not change until 1839 when the Connaught Rangers, one of the British regiments stationed on the island, demanded the services of a chaplain. When St Patrick's was built, the Irish soldiers attended services there; and to this day their flags and traditional crests adorn the cathedral's walls.

Lower Bay Street leads into Bridgetown, but if you travel along Jemmotts Lane, you will pass the old General Hospital, now the Ministry of Health, and the modern **Queen Elizabeth Hospital**, opened by the Queen in 1964.

At the northern end of the hospital and across Constitution Road is **Queen's Park**, where a giant baobab tree, its girth measuring over 61½ feet (18½ meters) has stood for more than 1,000

Left, St Patrick's Church. **Below**, street in Eagle Hall area.

years. A children's playground has been built beneath the protective branches of this ancient tree.

Queen's Park is notable for **Queen's House**, the former official residence of the Commanding General of the Imperial Troops. These troops were stationed in Barbados until 1906. The General lived here in stately grandeur, with Nelson Gate pointing in the direction of Nelson's statue in Trafalgar Square, and the Governor's Gate, through which the Governor entered when he came to call. The park is under the maintenance of the National Commission, which restored Queen's House and converted it for public use without altering the character of the building. The ground floor is now an exhibition hall, and the floor above houses a small modern theater (Daphne Joseph-Hackett) which puts on some fine productions. The Steel Shed and bandstand, once part of the official residence, have also been renovated.

Opposite Queen's Park stands the Ministry of Education building. The site was once home to one of the leading secondary schools on the island, **Queen's College**, but has since relocated to St James. The land was said to have been "a barren common" back in 1818, but the following year the Boys' Central School, later to be known as Combermere School, was founded on the site.

Beautiful Belleville: Traveling eastward along Constitution Road and into Belmont, you will come to Belleville District. This picturesque suburban area was designed in the 1880s, and the houses retain a 19th-century grace. Many of the wooden structures have been renovated, maintaining their original architectural lines. The designer of this elegant neighborhood, Sam Manning, owned a residence called **Erdiston**, which is now the Teachers' Training College, and overlooks the 11 avenues that form Belleville.

North of Erdiston is **Government House**, official residence of the Governor General of Barbados. Originally called Pilgrim House, it was purchased by the Government in 1736 from John

Carlisle beach.

Pilgrim, a Quaker. This sturdy mansion, which survived several hurricanes over the centuries, incorporates the typical features of Barbadian plantation "great houses," with its shady verandahs, arched porticoes, jalousied windows, parapet roof and circular driveway. Its beautiful gardens have been praised by many distinguished visitors.

Bordering the southern side of Government House is Pine Road and the surrounding area of **Pine Garden**, one of the first residential areas in Barbados. In this locality are the houses of various High Commissioners and embassy officials. At the far end of this area, on Highway 4, is **Bishop's Court Hill**, named for Bishop's Court, the home of the Anglican Bishop of Barbados.

Famous brew: Moving away from the city, Highway 4 leads along Collymore Rock to a commercial district. The first commercial enterprise you will see is **Bank's Breweries**, where the famous Bank's Beer is brewed. Over the years, this beer has won numerous awards and medals for its fine taste and quality. It soon becomes the hands-down favorite with many visitors to the island. A tour of the distillery, with tasting, can be arranged by telephoning in advance.

Behind Bank's Breweries is the **Wildey Industrial Park**, a new industrial development where a number of factories are located. Further along Highway 4, you will find the **Barbados Institute of Management and Productivity**, where Barbadians take short courses in specialized areas such as management and computer technology. You will also notice several commercial banks, car dealers and a shopping center. In 1992 Barbados acquired its first completely covered sports hall with space for 4,000 spectators. The Garfield Sobers Sporting Complex is used for basketball, boxing and volleyball.

The Barbados External Telecommunications, Ltd. (BET) is situated on the **Errol Barrow Highway**, the access highway connecting the Grantley Adams International Airport in the south with Speightstown, the island's second largest town, in the north. This part of the

Milk-dish, St Michael.

highway is also known as the ABC Highway; A for Adams; B for Barrow and C for Cummins, all former premiers.

Along the highway modern technological facilities contrast sharply with the quaint, centuries-old villages. Two institutions in this area have encouraged modernization throughout Barbados – the Caribbean Development Bank, and the Caribbean Broadcasting Corporation, the only TV station on the island.

To the west of the highway is **Pinelands**, built in the 1960s, the first housing project developed by the government for low income families. At times subject to heavy criticism, the 1980s have seen it become the object of several beautification projects.

At the northern end of the St Barnabas Highway, in the center of the traffic circle, stands a statue called **"The Freed Slave,"** which was erected in 1986. Standing defiantly, his head raised slightly towards the heavens, his hands still carrying the broken chains of slavery, he faces the fertile fields of the St George Valley, as if to say, "It was through toil and sweat in yonder land that I was able to free myself from this bondage." He represents a plantation slave, Bussa, who purportedly led the slave rebellion of 1816. The statue is the masterpiece of Karl Broodhagen, one of Barbados's best known sculptors.

Coralstone and columns: A turn west at the roundabout will take you along Two Mile Hill, where you will find the official residence of the Prime Minister of Barbados, **Ilaro Court**. This house was designed in 1919 by Lady Gilbert Carter, the American wife of Sir Gilbert Carter who was the Governor of Barbados from 1904 to 1911. Built mainly with coralstone, it combines many luxurious and varied architectural features, including Ionic columns and an enclosed swimming pool. It was purchased by the government in 1976.

Two Mile Hill extends to Government Hill, which passes the northern boundary of Government House. A right turn at the junction will take you through Welches to Tudor Bridge and Bank Hall. One more right turn at the Tudor Bridge

Rasta selling coconut water on a typical Bajan street.

traffic lights, and you will make your way past **Glendairy Prison**, the only adult correctional facility on the island, erected in 1855.

This route leads to the **National Stadium**, which was opened in 1970. In addition to track and field events, soccer and cycling, concerts and other cultural events are held here each year. With a seating capacity of 5,000 and standing room for 2,000 more, it is the largest gathering place on the island. Its only drawback is that occasionally events must be cancelled due to rain.

Passing the stadium, proceed down Highway 2, away from the outskirts of Bridgetown, and you are bound for the parish of St Thomas, traveling into the heart of the island. The road into Bridgetown will take you past the 300-year-old **Codrington House**, once the residence of Christopher Codrington, an enterprising colonist who arrived in Barbados in 1628 and amassed a large fortune. A little further along Spooner's Hill, as this road is called, you will see **Tyrol Cot**, home of the late Sir Grantley Adams, the first Premier of Barbados.

When you reach the junction of Eagle Hall, Bank Hall and Black Rock, you will find a densely populated neighborhood, packed with a mixture of small stores offering a wide variety of goods. Rum shops, tiny gardens, chickens, sheep and children compete for space and attention along the crowded streets.

Turn right at this corner onto the street known as Black Rock. On this route, traveling northward, you will see the **Psychiatric Hospital**. Black Rock ends at the junction of the new Spring Garden Highway and Cave Hill. A trip up this hill brings you to the Cave Hill Campus of the University of the West Indies, one of three campuses in the Caribbean.

Continuing northward on the main road, you will pass the **Lazaretto**, which was once a leprosarium. It is now the **Barbados National Archives**, which keeps some of the most valuable documents on the history of the island.

Back to the junction, and heading south on the **Spring Garden Highway**, pass the **Mount Gay Rum Distillery**

and Visitor Center, which is open for guided tours Monday–Friday 9am–4pm and Saturday 10am–1pm. You will also pass the popular **Brighton Beach**, a local favorite.

Near Brighton Beach, on the inland side, is an area called **Indian Ground**, where a monument was erected to commemorate the tercentenary of the first landing of the English on Barbados. The monument bears the date 1605, but the event really occurred in 1625, when he English landed at Holetown, walked up the beach and erected a sign to mark their presence. Since the mid-1980s, this area has developed as an industrial park, with new manufacturing plants, including branches of overseas firms, lining the highway.

Continuing down the highway, at the junction of Holborn Circle, a turn takes you to the **Deep Water Harbour** with its sugar warehouses and molasses terminal. Nearby is the **Kensington Oval**, which dates from 1882, where white-clad teams compete in the wildly popular cricket matches.

Below, inside the West Indian Rum Refinery; and right, kids out on school vacation at Brighton Beach.

SOPHISTICATED ST JAMES

Stretching along Highway 1 in St James is the area known as "the gold coast" or the "platinum coast" of Barbados because of the abundance of wealth along this strip. Almost all the luxurious hotels on the island are in St James – most of them right on the edge of the clear, glittering Caribbean Sea with its white sand beaches. Here, luxurious homes, many hidden behind long, tree-lined driveways, rival stately plantation great houses and plush hotels. These establishments exist side by side with their more humble neighbors, the gaily-painted Barbadian chattel houses.

Beachcomber's paradise: St James is the place for those who like to walk along miles of uninterrupted white sand beach. You can stroll along just to take in the natural beauty of the coastline and gentle azure sea, or check out the other sights of the St James beach: a vacationing movie star, local craftsmen selling their wares, fishermen drying their nets, a lively game of beach cricket, people roasting breadfruit and flying fish over an open fire, a family picnic.

Besides the luxury hotels, there are also many reasonably-priced apartment hotels here, like the comfortable **Na-Diesie Resort** in Holetown. The more expensive hotels such as the Colony Club, Coconut Creek, Tamarind Cove, Coral Reef, Sandy Lane, Treasure Beach, Almond Beach, the Sandpiper Inn, Glitter Bay and Royal Pavilion have earned world-wide reputations for excellence. All these hotels are on Highway 1.

The **Colony Club**, for example, has an atmosphere of casual elegance; it has a lovely beach shaded by graceful casuarina trees and a seaside terrace for lunch or a rum punch at sunset. **Coral Reef**, right next door, is delightfully English in its tradition of serving afternoon tea and thoroughly Caribbean with its open-air dining by a moonlit sea. **Coconut Creek**, a little farther south on Highway 1, is a charming hotel perched on top of a coral cliff.

The rich and famous: But it is **Sandy Lane** that has welcomed many of the world's rich and famous in the quarter-century of its existence. It was built by the late Ronald Tree, an Anglo-American who settled in Barbados and wanted a place where his friends could vacation in luxuriant tropical surroundings, while maintaining the habits and standards of English upper class life.

He spared no expense in the construction of the hotel, traveling far and wide to ensure that only the finest materials and workmanship would go into Sandy Lane. Portuguese masons were brought in to do the bathrooms – and many of the original tiles are still there. Tree designed much of the original furniture himself. Sandy Lane opened its doors in 1961 to great fanfare and a magnificent first winter. Its fame grew, and people such as Princess Margaret, Claudette Colbert, Jacqueline Kennedy Onassis, David Niven, Tom Jones and Mick Jagger have passed through the porticoes of this grand hotel.

Many of Tree's friends purchased

property and built houses around the hotel and its golf club. Now, the exclusive 380-acre (154-hectare) Sandy Estates has more than 100 luxury homes on its ground.

Sandy Lane's golf course, nine holes of which were built in 1962 and another nine added 10 years later, an 18-hole championship golf course on the island. Sandy Lane faces competition from the similarly exclusive **Royal Westmoreland**. In the winter of 1994 the first nine holes of the new course opened 2 miles (3 km) inland. Opened more recently the golf course designed by Robert Trent Jones Jnr has 27 greens – and will be surrounded by 350 luxury villas.

Not far away from Sandy Lane, also off Highway 1, is **Sunset Crest**, a sprawling complex of villas, apartment buildings, shopping centers and nightclubs. Especially vibrant are the grocery stores and shops – always bustling with both visitors and residents.

First settlers: Sunset Crest stretches into **Holetown**, the site of the first settlement in Barbados. This was where Captain John Powell of the *Olive Blossom* and his crew landed on May 14, 1625, and claimed the island in the name of King James of England. They named the area St. James' Town, but it was later changed to Holetown because the shallow-draft ships could enter the river at this point, reminding sailors of The Hole on the River Thames.

Two years later, on February 17, 1627, the *William and John* landed with 80 settlers and 10 Negro slaves captured from other ships on the way over from England. A monument in the heart of Holetown commemorates the event. Mid-February, every year, the Holetown festival celebrates the discovery of Barbados: streets are filled with stalls selling local food and crafts, music is heard everywhere, and you can see dance performances and a waterski show.

Behind the Holetown community center – which contains a post office, police station and small museum – is the **James Fort**, which once protected this coastal area. Not much of it is left today, except for part of a wall and one gun.

On the beach at the Colony Club Hotel.

Nearby is **Folkstone House**, also a former fort. This area was landscaped by the Rotary Club, which built a playground and tennis courts.

Underwater park: At Folkstone there is a museum which displays the marine life of the island. In the water is a marked "recreational zone" where snorkelers can follow an underwater trail around **Dottin's Reef**, a 7-mile (11-km) long reef located about a half mile offshore. Scuba divers can hire boats to go to the many diving spots on the reef, a habitat for sea anemones, man-sized fans, soft corals and sea lilies. Less adventurous visitors can view the active marine life from a glass-bottomed boat. A small marine life museum is also open to visitors on weekdays.

The St James coast is also a haven for waterskiing, parasailing, windsurfing, jet-skiing and hobie cat sailing. Swimmers and snorkelers should beware of the loud and fast jet skis. Although it is illegal for them to come within 150 feet (45 meters) of the shore, this rule has proved difficult to enforce and several injuries have resulted. Snorkelers should mark their location with bright colored floats tied to the waist or foot.

Next to the Folkstone is the **Belairs Research Institute** which studies the marine biology of the island. Set up in 1954 as an affiliate of McGill University, Canada, its goals are to improve the agriculture and fisheries of Barbados, as well as to investigate and cultivate new sources of food from the sea.

Also in Holetown is the **St James Church**, erected on the same site 200 years after the original church was built. The first St James Church was probably built just a few decades after the first settlers arrived, and legend has it that the first 10 feet (3 meters) from the foundation are part of the original church. An old bell, dated 1899, with the inscription "God Bless King William" has survived to this day.

Ronald and Nancy Reagan worshipped in this church at Easter during a 1982 vacation in Barbados.

In the church is a mural of Sir John Gay Alleyne, the Speaker of the House

Below, waterski instructor at Coconut Creek Hotel. Right, Dale Yearwood at Sandy Lane beach.

of Assembly in the late 1700s. He was called an aristocrat and a radical, but undeterred by criticism, he succeeded in making the Barbados Parliament a much more effective instrument of government. At the opening of every session, he claimed for society members the privileges claimed by the English Parliament: freedom of speech, freedom from arrest and free access to their representative in government.

Sir John owned one of the plantation great houses in St James – **Porters House**, north of Holetown, opposite the Colony Club Hotel. Porters is one of the few remaining plantation houses constructed in the early period of the island's history. The oldest part of the house dates back to the 1700s, but it has not been preserved entirely in its original form. Sections were added in the 1800s. The house is furnished with Barbadian antiques, including a large mahogany dining room table and mahogany four poster beds.

Stately mansion: Nearby is the stately **Heron Bay**, a house designed along the lines of an Italian palazzo. Heron Bay was built in 1947 by Ronald Tree. Set on 20 acres (8 hectares) of parkland, the Palladian mansion includes in its grounds a small lake filled with mullet, a coconut grove and a citrus orchard.

Leaving Holetown and continuing along Highway 1, you'll pass the villages of Mount Steadfast, Weston and Carlton. In St James, the built-up areas are all along the coast. Traveling inland, you'll see only cane fields interspersed with small villages, mostly situated around plantations such as Orange Hill, Westmoreland and Bakers.

St James is one of the smallest parishes on the island, but it has many restaurants. The **Inn on the Beach** is a small hotel that serves flying fish sandwiches right on the beach every day the sun is shining. You can stroll along the shore and eat your sandwiches right by the sea. But beware of the hot sauce. Its one of the spiciest you'll find anywhere.

Across the street from the Inn is a

Sinking the *Stavronikita* to make a new coral reef.

small **farmer's market** (at Sunset Crest) where Bajan ladies sell locally grown fruits and vegetables – good for snacks. Depending on the season, they sell avocados, which Bajans call "pears," papayas, which they call "paw-paws," mangoes, soursop, passion fruit and a great variety of vegetables.

Local feasts: Most of the restaurants in St James serve simple, "continental" food adorned with a few local touches. The **Bamboo Beach Bar** offers simple fare accompanied by the sound of waves lapping the shore. A bit more elegant is **Nico's**, where you can eat in a tropical garden, and fancier still is **Champagne and Wine Bar** for gourmet French food.

Along Highway 1 there are many restaurants with terraces overlooking the sea, and also further north on the border between St James and St Peter. At **Carambola**, tables nestle along a cliff directly above the waves.

The **Rose's**, a simple and unadorned restaurant on Highway 1, serves lobster. **Neptunes** in the luxurious **Tamarind Cove Hotel** is, as its name suggests, known for its seafood.

There is a wide range of restaurants in Holetown. Choose between top-class **Mews**; eat fast food at **Chefette** or **Fish and Chips**.

Holmes Bar is rum shop in St James, which serves food late into the night. At the top of Holder's Hill (off Highway 1 just across Tamarind Cove), it is a good place for a nighttime snack of spicy Bajan chicken. This bar, with its blaring jukebox, is a fairly typical rural hangout.

There's more nightlife in St James than meets the eye. The popular **Coach House** has live music weekly – by the best bands in Barbados – and draws a big crowd of locals and visitors. Most of the other hotels on the west coast have nightly entertainment, ranging from polished dance performances to the ubiquitous flaming limbo dancers, or music by a steel band.

St James is a place to relax and have fun: bask in the sun, explore the beach, and savor the world's best rum punch.

Heron Bay estate.

ST THOMAS

Situated in the heart of the island is the parish of St Thomas, one of only two parishes not bounded by the sea. Whether you're exploring its limestone caves, walking through a ravine, or traveling over its rich plantation farmland on horseback, you'll find St Thomas a region of unique beauty.

To tour the parish, follow these three highways: Routes 2 and 2A from St Michael; and Route 1A from St James, which meets 2A. Highway 2 begins at the junction near Eagle Hall in St Michael, and passes **Warrens**, an old plantation house built in 1686. It is a fine example of what the wealth of sugar harvests could bring planters in the 17th century. Just beyond the plantation house stands one of two surviving baobab trees on the island. This massive-trunked tree is about 250 years old. The only other example of this African species remaining on the island is an even larger version, on the grounds of Queen's Park in Bridgetown.

A few miles further along Highway 2 is **Sharon Moravian Church**, built in 1799 by the Moravians, who settled on the island in 1765. Arriving from Germany, they were the first missionaries to bring Christianity and education to the slaves, and the first in Barbados to admit slaves to their congregation. Sharon Church is one of the few 18th-century buildings unspoiled by alterations and additions. Its stately tower and handcrafted windows reflect the staunch faith and hard work of the Moravians. Admired by visitors, the church shows a marked architectural influence from the Low Countries of Europe, the birthplace of Moravianism.

Natural wonder: Next along this route, is the exotic **Welchman Hall Gully**, where tropical plants and trees abound, highlighting the lush natural wonder of this three-quarter-mile (1¼-km) ravine. The gully is actually a crack in the coral

Preceding pages: cotton field in St Thomas. **Left,** Harrison's Cave.

limestone cap which covers most of the island. The area got its name from the Welshman, General Williams, an early settler and the original owner of the land.

Around 1860, one of his descendants cleared a portion of the gully and planted fruit and spice-bearing trees, adding to the already plentiful native growth there. But the gully was allowed to grow wild again soon after, and became a tangled overgrowth of trees, interlaced with a profusion of fruits and flowering plants. For over 50 years this gully remained private property and was visited by only a few curious and adventurous souls. In 1962, the Barbados National Trust turned it into a delightful place to stroll through and enjoy a cool respite from the tropical sun.

The Trust left much of the gully in its natural state, adding only a few flowering plants and visitor facilities. Winding paths lead you through the dense green shade of palms and ferns, past colorful flowering plants, exotic herbal treasures, like cinnamon and nutmeg, and breathtaking natural landscape. Par-ticularly in the morning, you may sometimes meet chattering groups of wild Barbados green monkeys (*Cercopithecus aethiops sabacus*).

In the second section of the gully, note the many stalactites, one of which forms a massive pillar, and appears to support the rock cliff above. This large pillar – the result of a stalactite and a stalagmite having joined over the centuries – has a diameter of over 4 feet (over 1 meter), making it one of the largest in the world. At the northern end of the gully don't miss the gazebo, which looks out to the Atlantic Ocean, and offers a most spectacular view across the hilly section of the island.

In the vicinity of Welchman Hall is a road which bears the name Vault Road, named after the burial vault of the Williams family, the only remaining building from the original estate. General Williams was a devoted Protestant and, when one of his sons married a Roman Catholic, the General was grievously offended. When the woman died, she was buried in the family vault, but the

Welchman Hall Gully.

210

next time the vault was opened, the coffins were found in disarray, and the old General's was upright, as if in indignant protest. The vault was rearranged, with the General returned to his original resting place. But the next time the vault was opened, his coffin was again upright. The woman's body was then removed, and the General's coffin has remained in place ever since.

Subterranean splendor: Just a few yards further along Highway 2 is **Harrison's Cave**, a subsurface phenomenon said to be the only one of its kind in the Caribbean. A special tram takes you through the amazing limestone caverns, where you can witness nature's work of art , carved by the slow but steady work of underground streams over the centuries.

This site was known for many years, but it wasn't until 1970 that a Danish speleologist (cave specialist) named Ole Sorenson discovered a new and interesting section of the caves, the Crystal Caverns. Heavy rains had caused severe flooding in several areas of the island, and a large quantity of ground water found its way into the underground system where its force eroded a small entrance into this, unknown and parallel cave. Through this opening, Sorenson found other small passages leading to a large room about 250 feet (75 meters) long by 100 feet (30 meters) wide, and 100 feet (30 meters) high.

The government, encouraged by the National Trust, opened the caves to the public, and today a tour through the underground system is a breathtaking experience. Indirect lighting enhances the magnificent scene, adding a special aura to the thousands of gleaming, actively growing stalagmites and stalactites. Near the lowest point of the cave is a 40-foot (12-meter) waterfall which plunges into a large blue-green lake.

Best of Barbados: Continuing on Highway 2 from Harrison's Cave will lead to the east coast parishes of St Joseph and St Andrew. Backtrack to Warrens, where Highway 2A turns off from the main highway, and come to **Welches House and Plantation**. Owned by Jill Walker, a local artist, the plantation buildings

St Thomas Church on a Sunday morning.

have now been converted into the administrative offices, screen-printing studios and stockroom for the Best of Barbados, a company that produces beautiful crafts and gifts that depict the culture of the island. The plantation started soon after the first settlement in 1627, but the present plantation house dates from the mid-1800s, probably following the great hurricane of 1831, when most of the buildings on the island were either damaged or totally destroyed.

Leave Welches and continue north along Route 2A and you come upon **Bagatelle Great House**, now a restaurant which has earned a worldwide reputation for its gourmet dinners. This plantation great house goes as far back in time as St Nicholas Abbey and Drax Hall, the two oldest houses on the island. The original owner, the first Earl of Carlisle, was once the proprietor of the entire island. In 1651, the property was handed over to Lord Francis Willoughby of Parham and its name was changed to Parham Park House. In 1877, the property left the Willoughby family's hands, lost as part of a gambling debt, and its name was changed to Bagatelle. It was then owned by Nicholas Hudson, who displayed a picture of Lord Willoughby on the souvenir menus he presented to his guests, and is now owned by Richie Richings and his wife Val.

Further down the highway is the indomitable **St Thomas Parish Church**, which can boast of having suffered more hurricanes than any other institution on the island. Destroyed by the hurricane of 1675, it was rebuilt five years later. Damaged in 1731, it was completely demolished again by the great hurricanes of 1780 and 1831.

First free village: Turning off the main highway and traveling inland, you will come to **Rock Hall Village**, an old settlement of great significance to Barbadians. This was the first black freehold village in the country, and possibly the first in the entire West Indies. The Rock Hall story unfolded in the pre-emancipation year of 1820, when the area was part of Mount Wilton Plantation owned by Reynold Alleyne Elcock.

Roadside poinsettias.

This young white planter, a man with moral values well ahead of his time, recognized the plight of the slaves and was determined to improve the lot of those who depended on him. In a will he made in 1820, he bequeathed £5 sterling per year to each of his 120 adult male slaves, making additional provision for the repairs of their quarters. Somehow, news of the will and its contents leaked out, with tragic consequences. Unwilling to wait for his master to die a natural death before reaping the rewards, Elcock's valet, Godfrey, took fate into his own hands. It is not clear if he acted alone or was part of a conspiracy, but he slashed the throat of the sleeping 32-year-old Elcock one night in 1821.

Godfrey was apprehended at nearby Hangman's Hill and subsequently paid the ultimate penalty for his crime. Because of the murder, the slaves at Mount Wilton had to wait a further 17 years, until the Emancipation Act came about in 1838, to reap the fruits of their generous master's will. They used the money to purchase plots of land at the Mount

Wilton Estate and the village so formed became known as Cut-Throat Village. We know it today as Rock Hall.

Other white planters in this parish followed Elcock's example and willed their plantations to their colored (mulatto) children, born to slave mothers. Among these were William Ellis, Henry Simmons and George Hewitt. Ellis's son, Thomas, one of the first colored men to be elected to the House of Assembly, inherited Canefield Plantation; Hewitt left Cane Garden and Bloomsbury to his colored son, who also won a seat in the House; and Simmons' three mixed race descendants inherited Vaucluse Plantation, where Simmons's gravestone can still be seen.

St Thomas is one of the major agricultural districts on the island and therefore, on your trip through this parish, you will pass fields and fields of sugarcane and other crops. A beautiful way to view this land is on horseback, especially in the early morning, just at sunrise, when the freshness of the earth saturates the air and envelops you.

Fertile fields and plantation house.

THE SOUTHERN PARISHES

They say that the parish of St George "has no sea," that St John is "behind God's back," that people in St Philip are clannish, and that anyone well-educated who lives in Christ Church must be sophisticated and wealthy. Though the four parishes that comprise the southern half of Barbados are considered to be more alike than they are different, some of the startling contrasts between them explain why a small, relatively insular society can be exciting, and full of pleasant surprises.

If you look beyond the familiar attractions in these four parishes, you'll find areas full of unique features that reflect the historical, geographical and social heritage of the island. One of St George's familiar attractions is the old Gun Hill signal station and the panoramic view of the south that it affords; but don't overlook St George Church which boasts a hoard of treasures dating back to the 17th century. And there's Drax Hall plantation, the only estate that has remained in the hands of a single family since the time of the island's settlement.

In St John you'll find treats like the historic Codrington (Theological) College and the cool eastern retreat of Bath on the coast. Christ Church features the nightlife in St Lawrence Gap, the folk heritage of Oistins Town and the popular surf of Rockley Beach. But those who like curious tales will be drawn to the graveyard in Christ Church's Dover Woods, the site of one of the island's greatest mysteries.

St Philip is home to the world-famous luxury resort, Sam Lord's Castle and the "wicked" waves at Crane Beach. But one is less likely to hear about the Woodbourne oil fields of St Philip, or the changing nature of the land surrounding the Ragged Point Lighthouse – once forgotten and barren. These are but a few of the subtleties of the four parishes. The southern half is a rich area of fertile plantations, resorts and industrial centers, pregnant with contrast, waiting to be explored.

Preceding pages: windsurfer Trevor Hunte at South Point. **Left,** cane fields of St George.

ST GEORGE

A drive on Highway 3 allows you to explore some hilly areas of St George, for the most part a flat parish. This road offers one of the best chances of experiencing Barbados's "sugarcane country," which extends for miles through sugarcane estates, and bisects countless tiny villages whose histories are linked to the area's plantation tradition.

Highway 3 starts (as do all the highways of the southern half) in Bridgetown. It is the road that branches off Roebuck Street by the Globe Cinema roundabout and passes through Station Hill, Waterford, cuts through a limestone cliff, and continues on to Hothersal Turning where it swings to the east into St George.

At Market Hill, the route through St George splits into three: Highway 3 heads northeast into St Joseph; a secondary road ahead takes the traveler into the St George districts of Sweet Vale, Golden Ridge and Redland; and Highway 3B is the third branch, leading east toward St John.

Highway 4 proper begins at Welches Post Office which is set in a triangle of land bordered by three roads on the outskirts of the city. All the way out of St Michael, Highway 4 is lined with houses. Some of these form such working-class neighborhoods as My Lord's Hill, the Ivy, Rouen and Salters. The Salters area is actually what Bajans call "but an' boun'," meaning that it straddles two parishes: part of it is in St Michael and the rest is in St George.

At Salters, a road which branches off the highway takes you north, to St George Church and Gun Hill. If you stay on

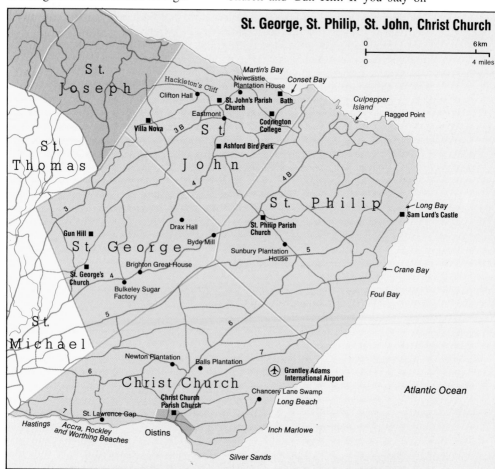

Highway 4, you'll continue east into the heart of the fertile **St George Valley**.

Fertile valley: Understanding the sugar industry's impact on the character of Barbados is a prerequisite to appreciating the earthly charm of the southern parishes.

Though the days when sugar production rose to over 200,000 tons – 1957 and 1967 were the record years – are long gone, thousands of Barbadians still depend on the sugar industry for their livelihood. Across the entire island, cane is grown both by small farmers and on the island's large sugar estates, more than half of which are found in the southern parishes. Together, the small farmers and large plantations produced the cane for the 50,000 tons of sugar that Barbados manufactured in 1993. The island has over 160 sugar estates. The worldwide sugar market is suffering from overproduction, so Barbadian producers depend on EU import quotas. At the moment, almost all of the Barbados crop is exported to Europe at fixed prices, while domestic consumption is met by the import of cheaper sugar from central

America. The tourist industry overtook sugar production as a source of income many years ago.

Although Barbados is often described as a flat garden, the mainly limestone island rises in a series of gentle terraces, from west to east, to the 1,100-foot (330-meter) peak of Mount Hillaby, the highest point on the island. In the Scotland district, the chalk and clay have made farming difficult and sometimes impossible. But the fertile St George Valley is ideal for agriculture.

The Drax Hall estate, set in the valley on Highway 4, was the first spot on the island where sugarcane was cultivated. The 878-acre (355-hectare) estate is the only plantation on the island to belong to the same family since the 17th century.

Portable dwellings: Large estates in the valley, such as Drax Hall, have been major centers of employment and settlement for as long as sugar has been cultivated in Barbados. Through the tenantry system, peasant families rented the land on which they built their houses, sometimes for generations. Recent legisla-

Revelers at "village meet" in Market Hill.

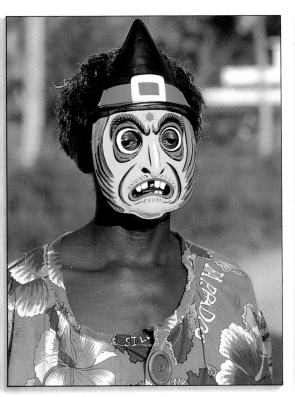

tion, which forces landlords to offer tenants the right to buy, has brought significant improvements to the peasants' quality of life. Now that they have land to call their own, families can build more permanent stone houses to replace the traditional wooden, chattel houses which were always built so that they could be dismantled and moved if necessary.

The names of many villages in Barbados are the names of the plantations they were once a part of. For example, in St George, Boarded Hall is a plantation and a village with its own police station; Drax Hall estate includes the large Drax Hall tenantry where the descendants of the plantation workers now live; Bushy Park, in St Philip, is better known as a dilapidated car racing arena than as a plantation. It once was Mangrove plantation in St Philip, now better known as the home of the Barbados Workers' Union Labour College. In Christ Church, Wotton, now a government housing estate, has become synonymous with vivid TV scenes of flooding during the rainy season rather than as a plantation where sugarcane is grown; and Newton plantation now has to take second place in the public eye to Newton Industrial Park, which has supplanted former sugarcane fields.

Valley Plantation is the first large estate on Highway 4 after Salters. Spanning 254 acres (103 hectares), it is the property of Clarence Shepherd who, for several years, managed Drax Hall for the Drax family, who lived in England.

A few miles after Valley Plantation there is the **Bulkeley Sugar Factory**, the only one in St George remaining in operation. Unlike most of the island's six sugar factories, Bulkeley is on a major route and therefore accessible.

Sweet nights: It is a great joy for locals and visitors alike to visit a sugar factory at night and watch the sugar and molasses being made. Anyone who wants to visit a factory during harvesting – between February and May – can arrange a nighttime tour; just call and make arrangements with the supervisor so he can show you the operation and answer your questions. A comprehensive tour of a factory takes at least an hour. After-

Cane fields and sugar mill.

wards, your guide is sure to offer you some aromatic "liquid," the brown, hot sugarcane juice that is removed from the mixture just before it crystallizes to sugar. The juice is hot enough to crack a glass container. Bring a plastic bottle with you so that you can take some of the delicious liquid home.

To manufacture sugar efficiently, the island's plantations are grouped into zones, with each plantation sending its cane to the factory in its particular zone to be refined into sugar. Bulkeley produces sugar from cane grown in St George. During harvesting (February to May) Bulkeley and the other five factories collectively grind over 530 tons of cane an hour. They are capable of grinding an average crop of 1 million tons in 16 weeks.

As recently as 1944, there were over 60 sugar factories in Barbados, but the number gradually declined because of increased production efficiency. Bulkeley is one of the oldest factories still in operation, while the newest (Portvale) was built in 1981 on the St James–St Thomas border. Informal visitor tours can be arranged at any time.

Half a mile past Bulkeley, there is a turnpike by a little village where Highway 4 branches into Highway 4B. The latter heads southeast towards St Philip while Highway 4 northeast, deeper into the parish. Highway 4B leads from the turnpike to two historic plantation houses.

House with a history: The first, **Brighton Great House**, ranks with St Nicholas Abbey and Drax Hall as one of the oldest houses on the island. It also has the distinction of remaining in the hands of one family (the Piles) for over 100 years. The first owners were the Wiltshires, who had the property from 1638 to about 1800. Arthur Oughterson bought it in 1802 and sold it to John Gittens Archer two years later. Archer, the first white Bajan to be convicted for the murder of a slave, sold Brighton to Conrad Pile in the first quarter of the 19th century. Dr Henry Fraser and historian Ronnie Hughes, in their book *Historic Houses of Barbados*, explain how a marble slab in the outer wall of the south wing helped determine the age of the house. On the slab is the name "Wilsheir" and the date 1652. Brighton's roof is

"Snow on the mountain" tree in front of chattel house.

As you drive up to one of the sugar factories in Barbados, you'll see tons of freshly cut sugarcane piled up at the front, with a high, overhead crane slowly feeding it into the mill. At the back of the factory are mounds of the golden "bagasses" – what is left of the cane after it has been chopped into pieces and pressed several times by rollers to extract all the juice.

Inside the factory, the cane is chopped and ground mechanically, under a steady flow of water. There, "milk of lime" (a mixture of calcium hydroxide and water) is added to the diluted juice, and the liquid then passes through a rotating clarifier that removes its impurities.

The milk of lime and the rotation causes the large impurities to settle. The clean juice is then channeled to a series of evaporators, which remove much of the water from the sweet solution and leave a thick, brown syrup that is ready to form crystals in the factory's vacuum pan.

The goal at the vacuum pan stage is to produce sugar with crystals as large as possible. One of the most important workers in a sugar factory – the sugar boiler – controls this very intricate process. He checks the pans often, because when the first crystals start to form he must let in more syrup so that the crystals grow larger and new crystals do not start to form. He also decides when to let the thick, syrupy mixture of crystals and molasses pass on to the centrifugals.

A centrifugal is a metal basket that spins at very high speeds, throwing the molasses through the holes in its sides while the mixture is sprayed with water to make the crystals as clean as possible. The crystals fall out at the bottom of the basket and are stored in large bins before being taken to warehouses to await export or distribution to shops.

None of the by-products created in the making of sugar go to waste. The bagasses can make chicken feed and hardboard; it is also burnt in the factory as fuel. The mud that is produced when all the impurities are washed away at the chopping and grinding stage is returned to the sugarcane fields as fertilizer because it is rich in phosphate. The molasses is good feed for cattle, horses and other stock. It also makes industrial alcohol and carbon dioxide, not to mention the island's world-famous rum.

The sugar industry has been in decline – only a handful of factories remain – and there were Government plans to bump up production. However, many producers have other plans for the land, which center around the flourishing tourist industry. ∎

supported by mastic columns and 20-feet (6-meter) beams, while its walls are made of a mixture of rubble and corn husks.

Several miles further east on Highway 4B, actually on the eastern tip of the parish where it borders St John and St Philip, is the entrance to another of the island's historic plantation houses, **Byde Mill**.

Although no one knows exactly when Byde Mill was built, it is believed that Joshua Steele, who is credited with starting a Barbados Society of Arts and Crafts, initiated construction on the site. Steele, a fellow of the Royal Society, London, leased the estate in 1777. He also owned the adjoining Kendal plantation in St John where Richard Ligon – one of the most quoted historians of the island – spent his three years in exile (1647–1650). Ligon's book, *A True And Exact History of Barbados*, was the earliest recorded history of the island.

Don't take Highway 4, but the northern route, 4B, at the turnpike. The road will take you to what is perhaps the most revered and renowned great house in St George, **Drax Hall**. From the turnpike, the road gently climbs, passing through the large village of Ellerton and alongside the new housing development of The Mount, perched on a pleasant, breezy ridge commanding one of the most spectacular views of the valley.

Jacobean gem: A long, narrow driveway goes from the road to the Drax Hall great house which is completely hidden by trees. James Drax, and his brother William built the estate in the mid-1600s. No one knows the exact date – but in *Historic Houses of Barbados*, Fraser and Hughes write: "There is a length of copper guttering at Drax Hall that bears the date 1653, but this does not prove the date of the present house. The copper drain pipe may have been used originally on an older house and reused on a later house if rebuilding occurred. Architecturally, however, Drax Hall is typically Jacobean, a stately English manor house in a tropical setting. It has steep gables, corner finials, casement gable windows, and an exceptionally fine Jacobean staircase and ornately carved hall archway of mastic wood. These all firmly suggest a pre-1700 date. Although a much plainer house

than St Nicholas, it is equally dramatic."

The massive Drax Hall estate dominates a great deal of the eastern section of St George, and its influence is reflected in the names of some of the villages and surrounding areas. Within a 4-mile (6½-km) radius, you'll find Drax Hall Jump, Drax Hall Woods, and Drax Hall Green. Drax Hall, Brighton House and Byde Mill can only be visited either by special arrangement or as part of the Open House Scheme operated by the National Trust.

Middle class on the move: The influence of the plantations is somewhat less evident in the parish's western section which is reached by the secondary road that branches off Highway 4 at Salters. Like its neighboring parishes – St Philip and Christ Church – St George is rapidly becoming a desirable area for residential development in Barbados, and hence a home for the island's middle class.

Some areas of recent middle-class residential development in St George are Rowans, Fairview and Walker's Terrace. Interestingly, all these areas are on elevated parts of the parish, and some house

Right, amber waves of cane.

owners are lucky enough to enjoy magnificent views of the St George Valley.

The western parts of the parish were tagged in the island's physical development plan as areas of "significant population increase" during the 1970s. St George's population grew an average of 23 percent every year for those 10 years. In comparison, St Michael's population grew only 0.06 percent, and St John's grew by 0.4 percent.

However, in certain areas of the parish the population declined. This was mostly in the sugar belt above the second cliff in the St George Valley. The government attributed this to the increased mechanization of agriculture – jobs on the sugar estates fell from 8,000 to 4,000 during that period.

The secondary road that branches off Highway 4 at Salters leads to **Charles Rowe Bridge**, a heavily populated section of the parish where there is a petrol station. Charles Rowe Bridge leads up a gentle incline to two major attractions in St George: the parish church and Gun Hill.

Hurricane survivor: The **St George**

Church is about half a mile up the road from Charles Rowe Bridge. Built in 1784 for a mere £600, it is the oldest ecclesiastical building in Barbados. It survived the 1831 hurricane; the chancel and the tower were added in 1923 and 1953 respectively.

The church is the site of "The Resurrection," the altar painting by Benjamin West, first American President of the Royal Academy. There is also a sculpture by Richard Westmacott, who created the statue of Lord Nelson in Bridgetown's Trafalgar Square.

After passing the parish church, the road becomes steeper, rising up from the valley toward **Gun Hill**. The milk-white limestone lion on a cliff on the left side of the road is the first part of Gun Hill you'll see. From the lion, you can see the old Gun Hill military signal station above. The Barbados National Trust has preserved it as a historic site. The lion was sculpted in 1868 by Henry Wilkinson, the Adjutant-General of the Imperial Forces stationed in Barbados.

Two inscriptions are carved in the rock of the base. The first includes the name of the sculptor, his rank and the date he completed the project. Then there is the affirmation: "It [the British Lion] shall rule from the rivers to the sea, and from the sea to the ends of the earth." An inscription to the right of the sculpture lists Wilkinson's four military helpers.

Scenic signal station: The signal station itself, which can be reached by car through an entrance further up the road on the left, has been praised by many writers for the incredible view and the healthy quality of the air.

Historian Robert Schomburgk's description of the view from Gun Hill in 1848 holds true today: "The ridge of cliffs, a continuation of those in St John, traverse St George and reach their greatest height near Gun Hill, where there is a signal-post and a convalescent station for the soldiers of the garrison. The air here is considered very salubrious, and the view from the station, over the rich and fertile valley to Bridgetown and Carlyle Bay, is extensive... no stranger who visits Barbados should omit seeing this spot..."

Left, old-time donkey cart. Right, Gun Hill Signal Station.

225

ST JOHN

The sight of expansive sugar plantations, dotted by tiny villages, continues in St John, but the parish has more hills than St George, and its entire northeastern section is dominated by Hackleton's Cliff, which runs north into St Joseph. History buffs, nature enthusiasts and those who like to chat with residents of small fishing villages will find St John a delightful parish.

Hackleton's Cliff is 1,000 feet (300 meters) above the sea and offers one of the most panoramic views of Barbados's east coast, capturing the scenery from Pico Teneriffe in the north to Ragged Point in the south.

It is said that the cliff was formed several million years ago when waves on the island's east coast eroded the limestone cap, leaving the area that is now known as the Scotland District. Hackleton's Cliff, a limestone ridge jutting out above the Scotland District, is said to be the point at which the erosion stopped.

Heading into St. John are two main arteries: Highway 4 and Highway 3B. Highway 4 enters St. John at Woodland Plantation.

The bird and animal sanctuary is part of the **Ayshford Plantation**, which was a working estate of 197 acres (80 hectares). The present owner is but the most recent of a long list of people who have owned the estate over the years. The most famous owner of Ashford was Ferdinando Paleologus, a descendant of the imperial line of the last Christian Emperors of Greece, who held the plantation from 1649 to 1670. Paleologus' tomb is in the graveyard of St. John's Church, not far away.

The bird and animal cages are arranged along a paved track that goes around the great house. Visitors thus walk through the yard of the plantation house. A small admission fee is charged. Among the birds are an African Grey Parrot, a parrot found on the nearby island of St. Vincent called Vin, the Plumheaded Parakeet, White Doves, a Cockatiel and a flock of pigeons that fly freely about the yard.

Ayshford also offers a rare opportunity to see much of the island's plant life in one place. The extensive list includes grapefruit, orange, shaddock, mandarin, passion fruit, mango, paw-paw, golden apple, banana, sugar-apple, soursop, breadfruit, mahogany, royal palms and bay-leaf. You'll find many flowering plants as well, such as hibiscus, orchids, ixora, stephanotis and the Honolulu Wood Rose.

Ayshford, near the center of the parish, is a good point from which to survey the surrounding scenery. The road that leads off Highway 4 to Ashford Bird Park meets junction at the northern end of the plantation yard. One road leads east through miles of plantation land to eastern St. John, the other is a northerly route to Highway 3B.

Magnificent view: Highway 3B takes you towards the historic **St John's Parish Church** which is nestled by a little road that leads off the highway. The church is set upon a splendid cliff that

overlooks both coastal St John and the Atlantic Ocean.

Although a stone version of St John's Church was built as early as 1660, the present building was constructed in 1836 after the earlier church was totally destroyed by the hurricane of 1831.

St John's pulpit is made up from six different kinds of beautiful wood: ebony, locust, Barbados mahogany, manchineel, oak and pine. The church also contains an interesting sculpture depicting the Madonna and Child with the infant St John.

Ferdinando Paleologus' tomb in the graveyard at the back of the church has an intriguing history. Ferdinando was a descendant of the Byzantine Imperial family and thus was buried according to Greek custom. His coffin was therefore placed in the vault with his head pointing to the west and his feet to the east. In 1844, nearly 200 years after Paleologus died, the rector of the parish (apparently curious to find out whether the story about the coffin's arrangement was true) ordered the lead coffin to be opened. All skepticism about the nature of Paleologus' burial was put to rest when his skeleton was found inside imbedded in quicklime according to the Greek funeral custom.

The view of the rugged St John coast from behind the parish church is guaranteed to instill in anyone the urge to explore this beautiful area. The road from the church goes north, and at the T-junction, you swing left onto a road that leads directly into the fishing village of **Martin's Bay**.

Before that, you'll pass a wooded area by the side of the road, the ruined **Newcastle Plantation House**, one of the many historic great houses that dot the landscape of St John.

Norma Nicholls, who once lived at Newcastle in the days when it was a private home, paid stirring tribute to her former residence in an article that appeared in the August 1977, edition of *The Bajan*, Barbados's sole monthly magazine: "Memories of Newcastle where I spent most of my holidays as a child, come flooding back. Newcastle

Unusual Anglican church.

in the morning, the smell of almonds – West Indian almonds – of roses and the sea. Blowing up from Martin's Bay, the sea breeze brought with it the aroma of burst almonds in the driveway and my aunt's roses which grew in a small bed just below the drawing-room window. Pungent, refreshing, exhilarating, I would take deep breaths and drink it all, as I sat on the window-sill of the front bedroom, looking down at the horses as they nuzzled away at their oats and corn in the long concrete trough which stood nearby, the sunshine rippling on their flanks, their tails swishing in contentment."

In the same article Ms Nicholls referred to a gardener at Newcastle named Thomas, who was "a descendant of the Scottish political prisoners who had been banished to the West Indies in the 17th century: his eyes were as blue as the seas and he always had a tale to tell."

Red Legs: Legend has it that the term "Red Leg" was used by the English to describe the Scotsmen because the kilts they wore exposed their legs to the sun. But for generations in Barbados it has been a term for the poor whites who settled "below the cliff." The "Red Legs" have lived mainly in the area below the cliff northward into St Andrew. Their presence is linked to the many caves below the cliff where white indentured servants and escaped prisoners successfully hid themselves away from the advancing authorities in the early days of the island's settlement.

Toward the end of the 1800s and until it ceased operation in 1930, the old Barbados railway passed through Martin's Bay. The road at Martin's Bay, which runs along the coast, today basically follows the train's path. A hiker can follow the path from the bay along the coast and into the parish of St Joseph. Aside from the abandoned train tracks, this region, known as **Glen Burnie**, remains a wild and rugged place, unspoiled by civilization. Glen Burnie is regarded by the local naturalists as one of the last areas on the island with original tropical fauna. When Tom Adams was Prime Minister he designated the whole of the east coast between

Villa Nova.

Ragged Point, St Philip and North Point, St Lucy as a nature conservation area. There were plans to establish a Tom Adams Memorial Park in memory of the late Prime Minister who died suddenly in the 1980s

A group called the Barbados Outdoor Club organized to ensure that Glen Burnie's natural beauty was preserved. They even made a formal proposal which stated that: "Through this village, locals and visitors would be able to really experience and understand the true way of life of our people – both past and present – and many local people would also be able to find employment by operationg their own stalls or houses within the village. In addition, and flowing out of the village, would be other recreational and educational activities, such as sporting events, nature walks and hikes through the surrounding area and camping facilities for visitors and Barbadians alike, so that the breathtaking beauty of our country may be enjoyed to the fullest."

The rich plant life that flourishes be-

low Hackleton's Cliff also captured the Outdoor Club's watchful eye. Dubbing this area the "Forgotten Forest," they sang its praise: "It is the last surviving piece of tropical jungle to be found in Barbados...

"The size and shapes of the trees, the profusion of tropical fruits, the beautiful butterflies, the birds, bees, pawn flies, lizards, and the now deserted homes of early settlers, the deep caves of the ancient Caribs, the upside-down bats which now live in these caves, the winding foot paths, cut out of the rock so ...by some hardened hands, all serve to remind us of the people who lived amongst these trees for so many years – black and white, in perfect harmony."

More recent plans to establish picnic sites, nature trails and a museum village in colonial style have not yet been put into practice. Thankfully, however, because the area is officially a national park, Glen Burnie will remain a hiker's paradise, even if it will not become an "historical village."

Picnic spot and satellite dish: The road into Martin's Bay also takes you out. There is a four-cross road at the top of a hill by the exit and a southward turn leads towards the popular picnic spot of Bath as well as the historic Codrington Theological College.

Two miles (3 km) past the junction, a road branches off at the left and meanders down a hill to **Bath**. Although Bath was a thriving plantation in the days when "sugar was king," it is now better known as the site of the massive satellite dish which links the island to the outside world, and as a park where Bajans come to picnic on public holidays.

At the junction on the hilltop, the road which continues from Martin's Bay goes south, up a steep hill, and on to **Codrington Theological College**, 2 miles (3 km) away.

Christopher Codrington III, who was responsible for the establishment of St John's Lodge School and Codrington College, came from a long line of Codringtons who owned land in St John. The first Christopher Codrington came to St John from England and bought

Cutting up the catch at Martin's Bay.

232

land there in 1642. Codrington's son, Christopher, went on to become Deputy Governor of Barbados in 1668. The Codrington of Codrington College fame was *his* son, who served a stint as Governor of the Leeward Islands.

Born in 1668, the third Christopher Codrington died a bachelor in 1710. He had attended All Souls College, Oxford, and later studied law at the Middle Temple in London. He was made a fellow of All Souls College because of his outstanding intellect.

Poverty and chastity: In his will Codrington left £10,000 for the "Society for the Propagation of the Gospel in Foreign Parts" to establish an educational institution on the island. His will stipulated: "a convenient number of Professors and scholars maintained there, all of them to be under vows of poverty and chastity and obedience, who shall be obliged to study and practice Physics and Chirurgery as well as Divinity, that by the apparent usefulness offered to all mankind they may both endear themselves to the people and have the better

opportunities of doing good to men's souls, whilst they are taking care of their bodies."

Despite Codrington's best and most pious intentions, his will was contested by his family in England. The court case laboriously dragged on for several years until the society eventually won. The college, however, was not started until 1748, nearly 40 years after his death. Then there was the problem of finding men of the right calibre who would be willing to live under monastic vows. However, by 1760 the first deacon of Codrington College, Philip Harris, had been ordained.

The college has a beautiful campus with lush and peaceful grounds and can be visited daily between 10am and 4pm. The nature walk to the northwest of the buildings has only recently been opened. The waymarked path 1,149 feet (350 meters) long passes through primeval vegetation with imposing cabbage palms and kapok trees. The complex of coralstone buildings stands on a cliff 360 feet (110 meters) above the sea,

Abandoned sugar factory and working satellite dish at Bath.

looking out over a magnificent view of **Consett Bay**.

Bajan safari: If you take the road that passes by the front of Codrington College and follow it south, you'll go down a steep hill. At the bottom of the hill you will find the entrance to Consett Bay on the left. The road 1 mile (2 km) down to the bay is notoriously winding. Prepare yourself for an adventure, something like a safari. The trees that crowd the roadside are home to a number of wild green monkeys, one or two of which are likely to bound across the road in front of any automobile that drives through their territory.

Apart from Codrington College, most of St John's historical buildings are plantation houses, the most well-known of which is **Villa Nova** situated north of Four Cross Roads. First opened in 1834 by the Moravian priest John Gottlieb Zippel, Villa Nova was the center of Edward Haynes' 109-acre (44-hectare) sugar plantation. It was acquired by the Barbados government in 1907, who made the premises available to the local doctor.

In 1965 the former British Prime Minister, Sir Anthony Eden, bought the estate as his winter residence and in 1966 Elizabeth II and Prince Philip were luncheon guests at Villa Nova. Ownership of the house has changed hands more than once and on each occasion valuable treasures from the colonial period have been added to complement the antique mahogany furniture.

In May 1995 this idyllic, historic mansion was closed to the public. A Swiss company, Horizon Resorts, converted the villa into a five-star country hotel with swimming pool, tennis court, fitness center, conference facilities and four gourmet restaurants. Some suites even have their own adjoining butler accommodation. The structure of the original house has not been drastically altered. The old woodland in the grounds will be integrated into the new hotel complex. Building costs have been estimated at around 25 million BDS$.

Two other beautiful and stately great houses worth a visit lie east of Villa Nova: Clifton Hall and Eastmont.

To get to **Clifton Hall**, take a right from Villa Nova, go to the bottom of the hill and then swing left, heading east. Clifton Hall is just off this rambling road, 2 miles (3 km) away. With an arcaded verandah on three sides and a double staircase leading to a central porch, Clifton Hall is a prime example of Georgian architecture. Unlike Villa Nova, it is not open to the public and any tour of the inside of the house has to be arranged privately with the owners.

Eastmont, another private house, can be reached by following the road from Clifton Hall as it heads south into St John. This great house is significant architecturally as the prototypical 19th-century great house, and it has symbolic importance. Miller Austin, a mulatto blacksmith, broke the monopoly of the white plantocracy when he bought Eastmont in 1895, and it has remained in his family since. His daughter, Lucy Deane, inherited the estate. Her son, the Hon. H. Bernard St John, QC, MP, became the third Prime Minister of Barbados in 1985.

THE STANDPIPE

Today, almost all island homes have running water. But modern plumbing is a relative Johnny-come-lately: a generation ago most Bajans trekked to the village standpipe to fill their buckets with water.

Because daily trips to the standpipe were part of every villager's daily routine, it became a community center of sorts – the place where people gathered to gossip and exchange news, where young men and women flirted, and where children played marbles and pat-a-cake.

Almost everyone had to use the standpipe; friends and foes alike would meet there. It was practically impossible for people "who didn't nuse to 'gree" to avoid one another at the standpipe. It was probably the venue for more fights than any other place in the village, as rivals exchanged insults and sometimes even blows. Tempers shortened, too, as the queue for water grew longer. Trying to jump the line would be met with the indignant question, "You in know that you come and find me?"

If those who went to fetch water at the "pipe" did not want an unscheduled bath, they had little choice but to assume a finely poised carriage, for water buckets were carried on the head. Some women can still transport them long distances without spilling a drop. Men often brought water home in washpans, carrying the 70 or 80 pounds on their heads. Some held a bucket filled with water in one hand while riding a bicycle down rough cart roads.

Another standpipe tradition was the pipe cleaner, who would arrive on occasion with official-looking brooms and scrapers. He would often demonstrate his authority by taking his cool time at his job.

Today, the standpipes are still there and sometimes you'll see a passer-by stop for a drink of the pure, fresh water that flows from any of them. But gone are the days when they were the center of the vibrant village life. ∎

Although St Philip is the largest parish on the island, it is one of the least celebrated. This has stemmed partly from its distance from Bridgetown, and from the fact that in the past it was not an agriculturally productive .

"Philipians," who are distinctive even in their manner of speech, have developed an unusual homogeneity because of their parish's isolation. This communal feeling among the people of St Philip is especially strong during the Crop Over calypso competition, when they support their homegrown calypsonians, particularly the champion, "Red Plastic Bag."

Now that St Philip has emerged as one of the most productive and fastest growing parishes, it is also less isolated. It has some of the finest hotels on the island. The government's Physical Development Plan for the 1980s identified St Philip as an area of "significant population increase." This increase, according to the government, is due to the availability of low-cost lands not required for intensive agricultural production. St Philip's population of 18,500 now logs in at third behind Christ Church (40,300) and the most crowded parish, St Michael (99,000).

Highways 4B and 5 are two of the main roads into St Philip. Highway 6 also leads to the parish, entering it from Christ Church and running through St Philip's oil fields.

Tales of treachery: St Philip is perhaps best known for **Sam Lord's Castle**, one of the island's major attractions. The castle, which is located on a cliff above **Long Bay**, can be reached by Highway 5. For the traveler driving through the parish, Sam Lord's Castle is always easy to find since signs pointing the way pop up at almost every turn.

Sam Lord's is now a luxury resort, but it is steeped in history and folklore, and the "castle" is the main part of the

Preceding pages: Ragged Point. <u>Left</u>, a "Philipian" checks out what's happening.

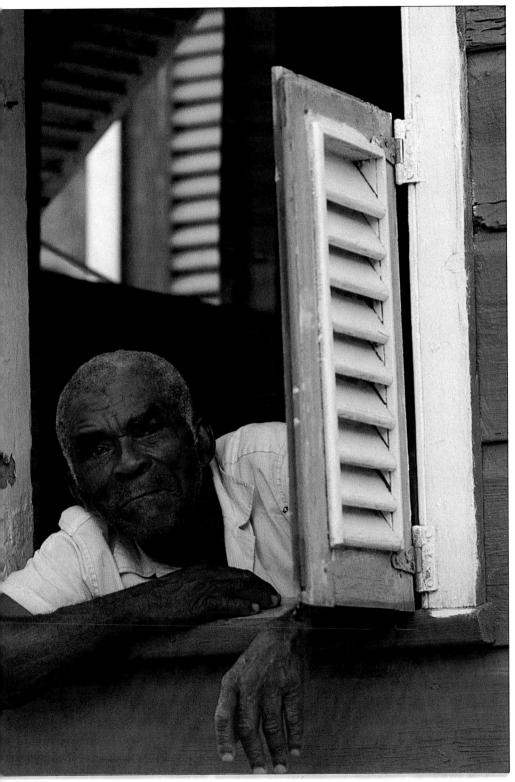

hotel. One of the most well-known characters of Bajan folklore, Sam Lord, has been the subject of at least one book (*The Regency Rascal* by Lt. Col. Drury) and a record produced by Barbados's world-famous old-time calypso group, The Merrymen. He imported craftsmen from Europe to build his regency mansion around 1820. The construction took three full years.

As the castle shows, Sam was a man of lavish tastes who apparently felt no qualms about spending money he often did not have. He died with a debt of £18,000. But Sam Lord is best remembered for his treachery. He apparently put lanterns in the trees at Long Bay to trick ship's captains into thinking that the harbor was safe. When the ships were wrecked on the rocks, he would plunder them. It is said that Sam Lord's treasure is buried somewhere in the grounds of his castle, but whether this is actually the case is anybody's guess.

James H. Stark, in a guide to Barbados published in 1903, described the mansion before it was changed into a hotel and commercialized. Stark wrote: "Within a hundred yards from the sea, stands a large house known as "Long Bay Castle", or as "Lord's Castle". The building is of a pretentious style, the rooms are large and lofty, and the tall mahogany pillars of the dining room have a fine effect. The house is too large, and its situations too remote for the wants of most Barbadian families, therefore, it has been unoccupied for years and is slowly going to decay."

Some time after Stark's visit, the property was bought by the Cooke family, and in 1942, a consortium of Bajan businessmen bought the castle from Mrs George Cooke and turned it into a hotel. They converted the north and south open porches into castellated wings and terraced the gardens to the east. Since then the castle has changed hands twice and now, as a Marriott resort, offers lodgings that are among the most expensive in Barbados.

Two outstanding architectural features of Sam Lord's Castle's are the classical mahogany columns and the **Ragged Point.**

beautiful ceilings. Inside the old building you get to see some of the furniture Lord had imported for the mansion, as well as his own four-poster bed, mahogany wardrobe and mahogany sofa. The castle is said to be haunted, of course. Castle and hotel are open daily from 8.30am–5pm. Admission price includes use of the swimming pool and the superb beach.

Pink sand: Another elegant and picturesque hotel, **The Crane**, is about 2½ miles (4 km) southwest of Sam Lord's Castle. It is perched above St Philip's rugged coastline. Stairs built into the bluff lead to a beach of very fine, pinkish sand and a surf that provides excellent waves for riding.

Rusticity and ruins: Today, luxriant trade winds still caress the Crane Hotel. For generations, **Crane Beach**, north of the bluff, has been a popular site for picnics. In recent years, erosion has come to the Crane, but on holidays one still finds many swimmers riding the waves, enjoying the rustic nature of the place and exploring the ruins on the northern end of the beach. If you are interested in the island's past then do not miss the opportunity to look at the old photographs under the hotel arcades. And no one should miss the sunset from the hotel's picturesque terrace.

There was once a wharf at what is now called **Crane Bay**. Boats plied daily between Bridgetown and the bay to deliver goods. It got its name from the massive crane used to unload the boats.

A mile south of Crane Bay is **Foul Bay**. The bay earned its name because it was a "foul" or bad anchorage for sailboats from Bristol and London. It has traditionally been a popular picnic spot for Bajans. You'll find a species of plant called sea grape (*Cocoloba uvifera*) in abundance there. A number of other bays line the St Philip coast from Ragged Point in the east to Salt Cave Point in the south, including **Palmetto Bay, Bottom Bay** and **Cave Bay**. The coastline north of Ragged Point is an area of cliffs and battering surf that does not have such friendly bays.

Ragged beauty: Just off the coast about 1½ miles (2 km) to the north of the

Crane Beach Hotel.

lighthouse at Ragged Point is Barbados's only colony – **Culpepper Island**. No more than 7,875 sq. feet (732 sq. meters) in area, it's about 20 feet (6 meters) above sea level. A channel about 35 yards (32 meters) wide separates the island from the coast. But the channel's depth makes it impossible to wade to the island: one has to swim.

In *Exploring Historic Barbados,* Maurice Hutt wrote: "On the island one has that sensation of being in a small world of one's own, reached by one's own physical efforts, not by some mechanical contrivance, which is always rewarding. And as in all intimate contact with wild nature, one feels a close kinship with the natural forces of the earth which is beyond the price of rubies."

The most easterly part of Barbados, the spectacular **Ragged Point**, is known for its high limestone cliffs and pounding surf. A lighthouse there was once open to visitors but is now closed. However, the cliff on which the lighthouse stands is an popular spot for those in search of solitude and a pretty view.

Following the road from Ragged Point north, taking all left turns and therefore keeping to the west, brings you to the more fertile and agricultural regions of the parish.

After passing through the tiny villages of Marley Vale and Bayfield, the road leads back to Highway 4B at Thicket. The highway then runs through plantation land below a steep ridge to its north for about 4 miles (6 km) until it reaches **St Philip's Parish Church**.

Plantation relics: A road at the western end of the church's graveyard leads to another place worth visiting in St Philip, **Sunbury Plantation House and Museum**. About 1½ miles (2 km) down the road and amongst the cane fields.

Sunbury House was opened as a museum in 1983. It was almost completely destroyed by fire in 1995, but some original features remain. It is the only plantation house completely on view, including the owners' living quarters. The 2½ feet (76 cm) thick walls of the house date back to the late 17th century. Flint and other hard stone not indige-

Left, hoops on a hot day. **Below**, beach near Sam Lord's Castle.

nous to Barbados was used on the walls, brought over from England as ballast for schooners.

Original architectural features of Sunbury include old fashioned jalousies, frame sash windows with storm shutters and a turned mahogany staircase.

Here, you'll see tools, kitchen equipment, and other relics from the plantation era, such as restored buggies and ox carts. Sunbury has a courtyard bar and restaurant. On Tuesday and Thursday evenings, 14 guests may dine at the old dining room table, by reservation. The house is open daily.

Sunbury has its own rocky driveway that runs into Highway 5. A drive across the highway leads directly to a secondary road that is a straight route to Highway 6, 1 mile (1½ km) away. Turn right at the junction with Highway 6, leading to the Woodbourne oil fields in the western corner of the parish, where it borders Christ Church. Highway 6 pierces through Woodbourne, and the small blue and yellow pumps are collected on what once used to be agricultural land.

Black gold: Production of petroleum started at Woodbourne in 1972 when the General Crude Company struck oil. The discovery marked a new phase in the search for petroleum in Barbados which dates from the 1970s. Before the success in St Philip, other parishes had been explored with few or no rewards.

The oil fields at Woodbourne were nationalized by the Barbados government in 1982, and a National Petroleum Corporation (NPC) was set up to implement public policy on crude oil and natural gas production. The Barbados National Oil Company, a subsidiary of the NPC, was also started to manage production at the Woodbourne oil fields. In a typical year, the 107 wells produce 480,000 barrels of crude oil.

Nationalization of the oil field was an important economic step. It came amidst severe world recession and was among measures taken by successive Barbados governments, to reduce the island's oil import bill. It also confirmed the public sector's confidence in the island's fledgling petroleum industry.

Playing dominoes.

CHRIST CHURCH

By the year 1652, Barbados was neatly divided into 11 parishes. Since then the country has seen two attempts to further subdivide the island. The first was to create a new parish named All Saints. The second was to split Christ Church in two. Neither plan met with success, but those who wanted to divide Christ Church must now be turning in their graves, declaring "I told you so!"

Because of its beautiful southern coastline, with its string of sandy beaches and wonderful surf, **Christ Church** was the first parish to develop in the early days of Barbados's tourist industry. Its population grew at such a steady pace that the Christ Church coast is now the most built-up on the island – with enough people, money and action for any parish.

In the 1970s, real estate developers inevitably discovered Christ Church too, as they rushed to meet the demands of people eager to escape the urbanization of Bridgetown and the congestion of St Michael. It rapidly became dotted with a number of middle- and upper-class housing areas, particularly along the coast. Because of the sudden boost in population, a number of businesses found it profitable to set up shop, making the parish a commercial center.

The entire Christ Church tourist belt is serviced by Highway 7, which runs almost parallel to the sea from Hastings to Oistins, at which point it swerves up Thornbury Hill and heads northeast toward the Grantley Adams International Airport. The other major artery through Christ Church is Highway 6, which passes through the middle of the parish and across the farmlands that dominate the parish's northern half. At the roundabout at Graeme Hall, you can also pick up the Tom Adams highway directly to the airport.

Because the Christ Church coast has gained a reputation as the island's premier tourist playground, many forget that, like most other parishes, it also has many sugar plantations. These estates, with names like Bentleys, Grove and Newton, dominate the north of the parish as much as hotels, apartments and guesthouses do the south.

Chic battle for Hastings: On the way from Bridgetown via Highway 7, the first part of Christ Church you will reach is **Hastings**, an area that, as its name suggests, is steeped in military history. A number of old red buildings line the left side of the road as you enter Hastings. These were once barracks for St Anne's Fort, just off Highway 7 to the north. (Read about the fort in the chapter on St Michael parish.) Once humble soldiers' quarters, they are now the chic residences of private tenants – and the envy of many, since the waiting list for these apartments is very long. A military hospital and surgeons' quarters also graced Hastings in the fort's glory days; and the residential areas Marine Gardens and Navy Gardens, off Highway 7 to the south of Hastings, were the sites of a naval hospital and quarters for the Admiral and his staff.

The coastal stretch from Hastings to Oistins at one time featured some of the

island's finest beaches. Regrettably, the pollution of the seas that has accompanied the development of Christ Church's coast has all but killed the reefs of the south coast, thus leaving the beaches exposed to the ravages of erosion. With the loss of tons of sand, beaches like **Accra, Worthing**, and **Dover** are now but a shadow of what they used to be.

Yet, here in the Eastern Caribbean, where few islands are blessed with many white sand beaches, vacationeers still find the Christ Church beaches a delight. The government is also making efforts to preserve the beaches and protect the marine habitat through a program of laying artificial reefs.

To top off a day of surf and sand, many people enjoy the south coast's lively and varied nightlife. The action heats up at the major night spots clustered along **St Lawrence Gap**, which branches off Highway 7 by the Worthing Police Station. Each club is unique, with its own ambience and following. Some of the names to know are the **Ship Inn**, **After Dark**, **Tapp's on the Bay** and **B4 Blues**. US Country and Western bands often play at Tapp's, while B4 Blues is about the only place on this calypso-crazy island where you can hear Barbados blues bands live.

After Dark, on the other hand, is Barbados's answer to a North American club for young urban professionals and it's popular with locals and tourists alike. On weekends it's jammed with men and women in their late 20s and early 30s.

If you work up a big appetite with all that swimming and dancing, you're in luck. St Lawrence Gap is also where you will find many of the island's better restaurants – from the American cuisine of **Boomers** to the Mexican treats in **Café Sol** to the Caribbean variety of **Witch Doctor**. **Pisces**, located at the water's edge in the St Lawrence Gap, features seafood and drinks in a romantic setting. Another venue off Highway 7 that offers some nightlife and good dining is the **Maxwell Coast Road**. A residential area with a more restrained character, the restaurants here include **Mermaid**, **The Lobster Restaurant**,

the **Sea Breeze** and the **Welcome Inn**, which also serves meals.

Austin's Oistins: Half a mile east of Maxwell Coast Road on Highway 7, you will come upon the fishing town of Oistins. It got its name from an early settler, Austin (which people pronounced *Oistins*) and is of importance not only for its large fishing fleet but for its historic past.

It was at Oistins in 1652 that the so-called "charter" of Barbados, or articles between the Royalist supporters in Barbados and the Commonwealth naval forces anchored in the bay, were signed in the Mermaid Tavern. Onerous to the Royalists, these articles pledged the islanders to loyal obedience to Cromwell and his Commonwealth Parliament. Unfortunately, the historic tavern no longer exists.

Oistins is better known as a fishing capital. For generations, Bajans have traveled to Oistins Bay, on foot or by bus, to buy all types of fish caught offshore. The town was also the focus of social activity for the south coast. But

Fishing boats at Oistins Bay.

the face of Oistins had undergone quite a sea change in the past 25 years.

The transformation began in the early 1970s when the cinema at Oistins was torn down to make way for a shopping plaza built at the eastern end of the town, on the corner where Highway 7 swings northeast up Thornbury Hill. Over the years, the modern **Oistins Shopping Plaza**, has housed a launderette, Barclays Bank, a supermarket, disco, boutique, video club and electronics shop. Then competition, in the form of **Southern Plaza**, sprang up at the west end of town. Its lure for one-stop shoppers has always been a branch of **Super Centre**, one of Barbados's largest supermarket chains.

The government got in on the act by building a $10 million fisheries terminal to facilitate Oistins' traditional industry – the capture and sale of fish. The terminal occupies over 4 acres (2 hectares) of land, most of which was reclaimed from the sea. By providing facilities for fishermen and vendors, the government has encouraged the mod-

Fishing boats at Oistins Bay.

ernization of the industry. For example, ice machines have now been installed at Oistins, vital to the growing number of long-distance fishing boats that have replaced the smaller launches.

But the sea somehow remains the center of life in Oistins, and the catch the same: dolphin, shark, barracuda, snapper and, of course, the ubiquitous flying fish. At times, shoppers can find Old Wives, a succulent fish that is not as large as a shark or barracuda but can be prepared the same way. In the old days, before the fish terminal, women selling fish stood at the roadsides calling out "Fish! Fish!" and the day's prices.

Going to Oistins for fish is not unlike a trip to the supermarket, except that the vendors may well approach you in the parking lot, even before you leave your car, to entice you to their stalls. In times of plenty, flying fish sell as cheaply as eight for a dollar. Out of season (during the months that don't end in 'r'), you might be asked to pay as much as two dollars for four fish. The area has also become a lively Friday night hot spot.

The great coffin mystery: On the ridge overlooking Oistins is the **Christ Church Parish Church**, which has gained international notoriety as the site of the "great coffin mystery." The strange happenings, which occurred in the Chase Vault in the church's graveyard, are regarded by some people as among the great unsolved mysteries of the world.

George Hunte, in his book on Barbados, described the strange happenings. He wrote: "The trouble at the Chase Vault began on 9 August, 1812. When it was opened for the interment of Colonel Thomas Chase, two leaden coffins inside were discovered by workmen to be in an unusual position, while the coffin of an infant, Mary Ann Chase, had been moved from one corner of the vault to another.

"Twice in 1816 and again in 1817 a state of confusion was found when the vault was opened for burial of other members of the family. The Governor of Barbados, Viscount Combermere, was present on 7 July 1819 when the coffins had been restored to order after the interment of Thomasin Clarke. He

South coast sport.

made impressions with his seal on the cement which masons had put on the outside of the entrance to the vault.

"On 20 April, 1820, Viscount Combermere visited the vault. The cement was unbroken, the seal intact. The Governor then commanded the entrance to the vault to be broken and sent a man inside. The man discovered one huge leaden coffin standing up and resting against the middle of the stone door. He also noticed the infant's coffin lying at the far end of the vault where it had been thrown with so much force that it had damaged the wall of the vault. The publicity associated with this official discovery caused the family to remove the coffins and to bury their dead elsewhere. The vault remains unused to this day."

Clues to slave life: To the northeast of Oistins, farther inland, you will find another of the treasures of Christ Church – **Newton Plantation**. You can reach it by following Lodge Road east for 1½ miles (2.5 km) until you reach a four-way crossing. A left turn onto the road heading north, and then a right turn into a white marl gap a few yards away leads directly into Newton Plantation yard. This reveals a pattern similar to that used in the days of slavery, with the manager's house on an incline overlooking the rest of the yard.

In the 1970s, the excavation of a large slave burial ground at Newton revealed valuable information on slave life and conditions in early Barbados. Professor Jerome Handler, the American who supervised the expedition, and Dr Fred Lange, reported their findings in the book *Plantation Slavery and Slave Life in Barbados: An Archaeological and Historical Investigation*.

They wrote: "Newton and its slave population typified medium to large-size Barbados sugar plantations. Because Newton, as a plantation, so well reflected island-wide characteristics, and because its slave community also seems to have typified the Barbadian pattern, we assume that in their mortuary beliefs and practices Newton's slaves also displayed characteristics that were found elsewhere. In general, we believe that

South coast sports fans.

the findings of the archaeological investigations at Newton's slave cemetery can be extended to indicate patterns that also existed in other Barbadian communities."

The National Cultural Foundation recognized Newton's historic value by making it the venue of the ceremonial delivery of the last canes, so launching the Crop Over Festival.

Inch Marlowe Swamp: If you ignore Highway 7 at the junction on the eastern end of Oistins (where the highway goes up a hill to the northeast) and take the road going straight ahead, you will be heading towards the southernmost tip of the island. This area of land, which bulges out on the bottom of the island, contains a number of large middle- and upper-class housing developments beginning on the coast and spreading further inland.

After leaving Oistins, the first right off the road leads to Enterprise Coast Road, which runs parallel to the shoreline for a while before shifting inland, where it becomes enveloped by houses on both sides. The road extends southeast through a number of residential districts – **Atlantic Shores**, **Silver Sands**, **Ealing Park** and **Inch Marlowe** among them – that have sprung up within the last 20 to 30 years. There are two hotels within this area, **Silver Sands**, which nestles on the coast below a cliff, and **Silver Rock Hotel** with Beach Bar Restaurant, popular with visiting windsurfers.

By taking all right turns after passing the road that leads down the cliff to the hotel, you will soon come to Inch Marlowe. Many years ago Inch Marlowe was swampland, connected to the Chancery Lane Swamp beside it. The Inch Marlowe Swamp was drained to make way for tourist development, which many felt was ideal for the area because of sandy **Long Beach** that runs along the edge of the swamps.

Long Beach stretches for 1½ miles (2.5 km) from the cliffs below Paragon (an area to the south of Grantley Adams International Airport) to Inch Marlowe Point. A desolate spot, often forgotten by the populace at large, the entire beach

Left, local talent. **Below**, enjoying a cold Banks at the Ship Inn, St Lawrence Gap.

and swamp once belonged to the Chancery Lane Plantation.

In the early 1970s, ambitious plans were brewed for Long Beach. But more than two decades later, the only tourist-oriented activities here are the Surf View Condominiums, owned by expatriates who use them as winter homes, and a few hotels which are mainly involved in the time share business.

Long Beach and Inch Marlowe are generally perceived as out of the way, the "outback" of Barbados. Until recently, they were used as a shooting range by hunters. (The only other spot for this sport in Barbados is Graeme Hall Swamp, along the Christ Church coast, between Worthing and Lawrence.)

In 1966 archaeologists unearthed the remnants of Arawak and Carib settlements near Chancery Lane Swamp. It was an exciting discovery, for the pottery they found was very different from any seen before on the island. It indicated that the first inhabitants of Barbados were agricultural people, and that they settled on the island in about AD 600.

Wandering cricketers: No description of Christ Church would be complete without a word about Barbados's national sport, cricket. It so happens that Christ Church is home to the island's oldest cricket team, the Wanderers. The club's field is at **Dayrell's Road**, to the north of Hastings, east of the Garrison Savannah. Any weekend during the latter half of the year, a visitor can stop by and savor the sound of ball against willow and participate in a unique Bajan experience. The Wanderers started in June 1877, at a time when only the soldiers at the Garrison, and the Lodge School, St John, had proper pitches. In the beginning, the club was elitist, but it had to adapt and admit blacks as society gradually changed.

Bruce Hamilton wrote in *Cricket in Barbados*: "If the soldiers may be called the missionaries of modern cricket in Barbados, and Lodge the pioneers among the local people, to Wanderers must certainly be given the credit of setting the game on a permanent footing and keeping it there."

Twilight stroll.

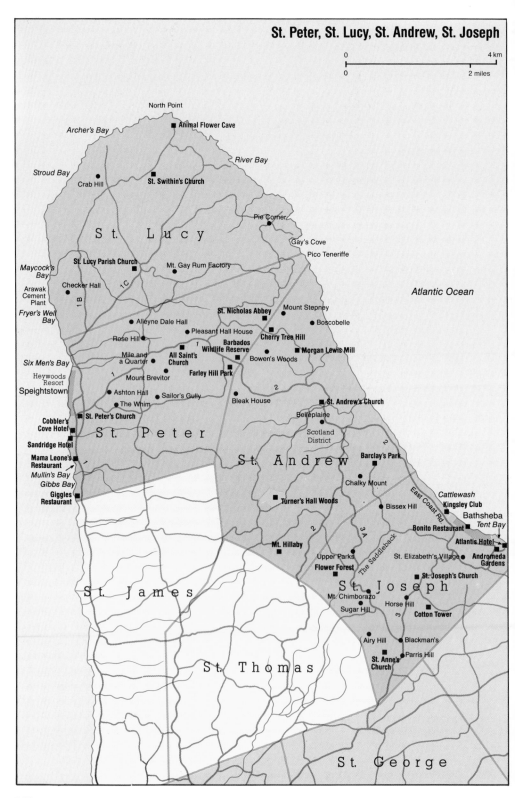

St. Peter, St. Lucy, St. Andrew, St. Joseph

0   4 km

0   2 miles

North Point
■ Animal Flower Cave

Archer's Bay

River Bay

Stroud Bay

Crab Hill ●
■ St. Swithin's Church

Pie Corner ■

S t.   L u c y

Gay's Cove
Pico Teneriffe

Maycock's Bay
■ St. Lucy Parish Church
● Mt. Gay Rum Factory

Arawak Cement Plant
Checker Hall ●

1 C

Fryer's Well Bay

Alleyne Dale Hall ●
■ St. Nicholas Abbey   Mount Stepney

1 B

● Boscobelle

Pleasant Hall House ●
Barbados
Wildlife Reserve ■   ■ Cherry Tree Hill

Rose Hill ●●

Six Men's Bay

Mile and
a Quarter ●
■ All Saint's Church
● Bowen's Woods
■ Morgan Lewis Mill

Heywoods Resort
Speightstown
Mount Brevitor ●
■ Farley Hill Park

1

Ashton Hall ●
● Sailor's Gully
Bleak House ●

The Whim ●

Cobbler's Cove Hotel ■
■ St. Peter's Church

S t.   P e t e r

■ St. Andrew's Church

Belleplaine

Sandridge Hotel ■

Scotland District

Mama Leone's Restaurant
1

S t.   A n d r e w

Mullin's Bay
Gibbs Bay

● Barclay's Park

2

Giggles Restaurant ■

2

Chalky Mount ●

Atlantic Ocean

Cattlewash
Kingsley Club ●

■ Turner's Hall Woods
● Bissex Hill

Bathsheba
Tent Bay

2

■ Bonito Restaurant ■
Atlantis Hotel ■

S t.   J a m e s

3 A

■ Mt. Hillaby

Upper Parks ●
St. Elizabeth's Village ●
● Andromeda Gardens

Flower Forest ●
■ St. Joseph's Church

S t.   J o s e p h

Mt. Chimborazo ●
Horse Hill ●

Sugar Hill ●
■ Cotton Tower

3

S t.   T h o m a s

Airy Hill ●
● Blackman's

■ St. Anne's Church
Parris Hill ●

S t.   G e o r g e

East Coast Rd.
The Saddleback

THE NORTH AND EAST

It is to the north and east coasts that both Bajans and visitors go for escape. Here, the scenery is stunning and the people are among the friendliest on the island. Rugged hills and gentle slopes are bordered by a stretch of narrow coastline with sweeping bays and some postcard-spectacular views. The Atlantic crests over treacherous reefs and pounds over the shore, mangling the huge rock formations on the beaches – in dramatic contrast to the turquoise calm of the island's western side.

The countryside lies like a patchwork quilt, decorated at intervals with tenantries, small clusters of houses on the peripheries of plantations. The occasional great house, flanked by graceful cabbage palm avenues, stands like a sentinel.

Relics of the past spring like surprises from all corners of the landscape: the ruined walls of mills that once ground sugarcane, overgrown gullies, once the beds of flowing rivers, and picturesque bridges that crossed those rivers.

In this beckoning region, you'll see the colorful chattel houses of St Lucy, the green rolling hills of the Scotland District in St Andrew and St Joseph, the fishing villages of St Peter. And along the coasts of all these parishes, you will find some of the world's prettiest picnic spots.

Hotels, fast-food restaurants and other markers of modern living are few and far between in the north, but a well-developed network of good roads make exploring easy. The rural northern parishes are for those in search of wild places and open spaces.

ST JOSEPH

The smallest parish in Barbados, St Joseph is bedecked with old plantation houses and cabbage palm avenues. Along its meandering coastline, sculptured rocks jut from the foaming Atlantic and wind-eroded sea grape vines hug the deserted sandy beaches.

Highway 3 leads into St Joseph from St George. On its way to Joe's River Plantation, Highway 3 descends from **Horse Hill**, one of the steepest roads in Barbados. Here the traveler will find banana, mango and soursop trees in abundance: the overhanging greenery creates a welcome coolness on hot days.

From Horse Hill and Joe's River, there is a magnificent view of the **Scotland District**, a rustic roll of hills and valleys, rural villages and grazing sheep. The district reminded early British settlers so much of Scottish scenery that they gave it this name. The area is completely different from the mainly flat limestone cap that occupies the rest of Barbados. This rugged region, with steep and uneven roads, consists of folded and faulted sedimentary rocks – sands, clay, shale and conglomerates. These rocks were probably formed 60 to 70 million years ago when the area that is now Barbados was just a muddy sea. Earth movements then caused the rocks that were to become the bottom layer of Barbados to sink deep beneath this sea. A second layer of white, clay-like rock built up over the original rock. A final layer, this of coral, then grew on top of the second layer. The island emerged from the sea. Over the years, tidal waves which beat upon the eastern side of the island gradually removed the coral cap there, exposing the sands, clays and shale of the Scotland District.

At **Joe's River Plantation**, a Bajan legend finds its home. According to local historian Edward Stoute: "The legend is that at some period during the eighteenth century, the owner of the property died leaving an infant son as heir. He left the child's uncle to see after the estate and to take care of the child.

The uncle was a schemer and desired to possess the estate for himself…One fine day the child and his nurse disappeared and could not be traced.

"In due course the wicked uncle died, and it is claimed that two pairs of horses which were put in succession to the hearse refused to draw it, and that he was eventually buried on the estate. After the death of the uncle, this mansion became known as a 'haunted house,' for it was claimed that the ghost of the nurse and child were frequently seen walking around.

"It is also claimed that during alterations to the house a very thick wall was removed, and to the surprise of everyone, two skeletons, one of a child and the other of an adult were discovered. These were given a decent burial and the ghosts were never seen again…this old mansion was demolished around the turn of this century."

The National Conservation Commission is currently marking out footpaths in the Joe's River woods.

Panoramic views: Horse Hill is on the

Preceding pages: view of Atlantic coast. **Left,** waiting for the bus to Bridgetown. **Right,** on the road to St Joseph.

northwestern tip of **Hackleton's Cliff**. This is where the waves stopped their erosion: it is a ridge of limestone jutting above the sedimentary rocks of the Scotland District. From the **Malvern Plantation**, there is a panoramic view of hills and dales.

After Highway 3 descends from Horse Hill it leads to **Bathsheba**, a fishing village on the east coast where many families have lived for generations, and a number of wealthy folk from other parts of the island own beach houses. Bathsheba's **Soup Bowl** – so named because the surf there is very foamy – is a good place to surf. Soup Bowl's surfing competitions, generally held in September, always draw large crowds.

Before Highway 3 reaches Horse Hill, it turns into Highway 3A which goes west into a remote rural area of St Joseph that is almost virgin in character. The adventurous traveler who is willing to seek out the sights and talk to the villagers will not be disappointed. Highway 3A leads to rural villages like **Sugar Hill, Chimborazo, Spa Hill, Fruitful Hill** and **Cane Garden**, on St Joseph's northern border.

Highway 3A also leads to the **Flower Forest**, a beautifully landscaped area of exquisite plants and tropical trees, with winding paths and spectacular views. The Flower Forest is open daily, there is a modest admission fee, and a snack bar, gift shop and rest rooms.

A right turn at Horse Hill off Highway 3 leads to **Cotton Tower**, another site that offers a panoramic view of the Scotland District. The tower, at the end of Hackleton's Cliff, was one of many old military signal stations used by the British during the colonial days when communication was difficult. It was restored by the Barbados National Trust and is now open to visitors.

Cotton Tower is set among rolling cane fields and from its balcony there is a clear view of the Parks Road Saddle Back to the north and Buckden Gully to the south. To the east, a few yards away from the tower, are the ruins of Buckden Plantation House. The tower's caretaker is Mr Cespert Mayers, who is responsi-

Sugarcane fields dominate the St Joseph region.

ble for the beautiful gardens at the base. A tailor by profession, he has a wide knowledge of the area.

Above Horse Hill is the **St Joseph Anglican Church**, rebuilt in 1839 after the original was destroyed in the 1831 hurricane. Fraser and Hughes in *Historic Churches of Barbados*, relate an amusing tidbit about its history: "The story goes that the Vaughn family and the Blackman family were competing to donate land for the new church. The Vaughn family won because they demanded only a single family pew, rent free, in perpetuity, while the Blackman family had demanded two pews!"

Mythological treasures: After the road winds down Horse Hill, the signboards name almost every nook and cranny of this rugged region. South of Bathsheba are two of Barbados's most alluring treasures, and both have taken their names from mythology.

Andromeda Gardens is named after the maiden in Greek mythology who was chained to a rock. The island's foremost horticulturist, the late Mrs Iris Bannochie started the gardens in 1954 and named them after Andromeda because they are situated on a cliff. Currently, the gardens are leased by the Barbados National Trust. A stream bisects the 6-acre (2-hectare) profusion of exotic flowers and plants, which include many varieties of orchids, bougainvilleas, hibiscus, heliconias, cacti, succulents, ferns and shade-loving ornaments. Mrs Bannochie acquired plants for the Andromeda from all over the world. The gardens are open daily.

Below Andromeda is **Tent Bay** – the only place along the rugged St Joseph–St Andrew Coast where fish is landed. Barbados has 25 landing areas in all – so it's unusual to see such a long stretch of coastline with only one.

Overlooking Tent Bay, down what must be the world's steepest driveway, is the famous **Atlantis Hotel**. A simple, very pleasant place, with a reputation for the best local food on the island, it took its name from the legendary continent of Atlantis, said to have occupied what is now the entire North Atlantic.

Black belly sheep.

Atlantis is one of the oldest hotels on Barbados, with balconies and sunlit rooms looking onto the dazzling blue ocean. The island's best known novelist, George Lamming, lives here for part of the year. Lunch on the terrace is a memorable experience: cool winds caress you as you savor delicious Bajan fish or chicken and gaze out at the colorful fishing boats and the vast Atlantic. Be sure to try the coconut pie – a real island delight. Every morning at dawn, guests can watch one of the oldest island rituals: the communal launching of the fishing boats, which have to maneuver through a dangerous S-shaped channel before going out to sea.

Breathtaking beauty: The road north from Andromeda Gardens and Atlantis Hotel is winding, hilly and leads to the **East Coast Road**. This road goes from St Joseph into St Andrew and follows the exact path of the old railroad to Belleplaine. At the St Joseph end there are quaint beach cottages which can be rented by vacationers. At the small **Bonito Restaurant** you can get fresh local seafood and crab.

The road goes through an area called **Cattlewash**, where you'll see sea grape vines and windblown coconut groves, **Kingsley Club** is a delightful old world hotel, known for its fish and chicken "cutters" (local sandwiches on buns).

The vigorous trade winds make the surf beating against the East Coast beach particularly violent and hazardous to swimmers. However, at low tide, the beach and coral reefs along the East Coast Road are ideal for exploring. Coral reefs are native to warm, tropical seas like the Caribbean. They are fragile ecosystems that take years to regenerate – brain coral, for example, increases its diameter by 1 or 2 inches (25–50 mm) each year. Over long periods, corals can build up large expanses of rock.

The scenic East Coast is full of many unexplored places and wonderful picnic spots. Barbadians flock here on holidays, but it is enticingly deserted on regular workdays.

<u>Right</u>, the fishing village of Bathsheba, with Atlantis Hotel in center.

ALL ABOARD FOR BATHSHEBA

This is an excerpt from *The Bridge: Barbados* by Patrick Roach

Barbados had a train that operated from 1881 up to 1938 and was a wonderful means of transport, linking many beautiful scenic places such as Bath, Martin's Bay, Atlantis Hotel, Bathsheba, Kingsley, Dan and Belleplaine. In those days the roads left much to be desired, and most of the motor cars in Barbados were incapable of ascending the terrific hills such as Cleavers Hill above Powell Spring Hotel or Round House Hill or even Horse Hill. If one took a chance and drove down to Bathsheba it was essential to leave well before sunset to get over the hills.

Bathsheba and Bath were not then served by buses and when one went on holiday, which many families did, it meant going for a month or two. This necessitated packing up and bringing down by train suitcases with clothes, bed linen and pillows, large quantities of canned goods such as salmon and condensed milk, PY canned salt butter and hundreds of pounds of Wallaba wood in

264

bags to be fed into the old wood and coal cookers. Ice was always brought down 200 pounds [90 kg] at a time and this had to be got up to the house and into the ice box.

Yes, it was quite an undertaking to pack up and go to Bathsheba by train in those days. The train used to leave Bridgetown on afternoons around 4pm and frequently there were heavy landslides in the Consetts cutting or Bath section which meant that a crew had to be summoned to work shoveling the earth from off the train lines. This sometimes took two or three hours and, of course, mothers always had to have emergency rations easily available for the children so that if a serious delay was encountered there would be a picnic meal to keep everyone happy. The train station in Bridgetown was located in what is now the Fairchild Street Market and the journey from there through all of the intervening stations to Bathsheba took around three to four hours. When the train came puffing around the Beachmount Hill corner it always gave three loud hoots of triumph and all the people at Bathsheba would flock to the station to welcome it.

My favorite was No. 3, which was a very powerful engine, and we knew all of the guards by name. Sometimes letters or messages or packages used to be sent down by these guards and they knew who was in every house. Very few people ever shut doors or windows in the houses and stealing was non-existent.

Yes, there was a train in Barbados and it was loved and looked forward to all day. During August Bank Holidays special excursions left Bridgetown about 6 or 7am and fifteen or sixteen carriages would be filled with holidaymakers with their picnic baskets visiting Bathsheba for the day, and, of course, there were always a few people who got rather tipsy and did most amusing things. These excursions were known as "outings" and were very popular with Sunday School excursionists and other groups. Around 4pm the train began to hoot and they would all flock back into the carriages and the train then pulled out puffing loudly. ■

ST ANDREW

St Andrew is not the smallest parish, but its population is small – just over 6,500 – and so it has managed to keep much of its virgin character. Some of the hills and dales of the Scotland District in this parish are relatively unexplored, despite their unmatched beauty. The villagers of St Andrew know one another well, and, because the parish has been isolated for generations, have perfected the art of interdependence and neighborly courtesy.

The East Coast Road enters the parish of St Andrew at **Barclay's Park**. This popular picnic area has shade, tables and benches, a snack bar and rest rooms. Barclay's Bank created the 50-acre (20-hectare) park in 1966 as a gift to Barbados, to commemorate its independence.

From Barclay's Park the road runs along the coast for about a mile before veering west into **Belleplaine**, the quaint community that is one of St Andrew's largest settlements. The village of Belleplaine has a long-standing place in Barbadian history and folklore because it was at the end of the old railway route. In bygone days, Bajans who were uninitiated in the wonders of the Scotland District delighted in going on the lively train excursions from Bridgetown to Belleplaine.

One modern researcher relates that: "A string band consisting of guitar, violin, mandolin and saxophone accompanied the revellers. The excursionists danced to the lively tempo of the band at various sites en route. Two wooden horses (crudely built merry-go-rounds) were operated at Belleplaine and provided a singular attraction at the end of the train journey."

Though the train no longer exists, these rides to Belleplaine have been preserved forever in a popular Bajan folk song about the ever-resourceful Bromley, a government sanitary inspector of the day, who also owned a horse-and-buggy taxi service and operated a brass band. He occasionally sponsred free train rides from Bridgetown to Belleplaine – gala occasions for the laboring class. In the song, Bromley denies a young lady's request for more than one kind of free ride:

> *Yuh hear what Bromley tell de gal,*
> *Yuh never go down Belleplaine*
> *outa me...*
> *Yuh never wear dat gol' ring*
> *outa me ...*

The road from the East Coast meets Highway 2, the major artery through St Andrew, at a T-junction in front of the Alleyne school, one of the oldest and most outstanding high schools in Barbados.

History and adventure: A turn to the right on Highway 2 is the route to the historic St Andrew's Church, Morgan Lewis Mill, Cherry Tree Hill and the rugged, little explored Morgan Lewis Beach. If the visitor heads north by turning left on Highway 2, the road leads to the pottery works at Chalky Mount. Turner's Hall Woods and Mount Hillaby, the island's highest point.

St Andrew's Anglican Church is a mile away from the Alleyne School on Highway 2. It bears a proud place in Barbadian history since it was one of the

Preceding pages, near Mt Hillaby. **Left,** St Andrew's Church. **Right,** Rasta inscription.

few churches to survive the terrible 1831 hurricane. The church was in disrepair by 1842 and the present building was completely re-built in 1846.

The road north from St Andrew's Church winds through **Walker's** – the district that is the source of all the sand used for construction in Barbados.

The Scotland District has a reserve of over 132 million tons of sandstone. The main deposits are in St Andrew and St Joseph. Top quality glass cannot be produced from Barbados sands, but green and amber glass can be made.

The Walker's sand dune, which towers over the roadway, has been extensively mined for several years. It also has a reserve of 16 million cubic meters of sand which would last, at current rate of usage, for another 100 years. Conservationists have recommended that only 10 million cubic meters of sand from the dune should be removed to prevent serious ecological damage to the area.

A turn right by a bridge after passing Walker's leads to **Shorey Village**. It is a quaint little community that is closely knit. Shorey villagers are proud of the fact that their community produced one of the greatest cricketers in the history of the West Indies, Conrad Hunte.

The story of truckloads of supporters from St Andrew going down to Kensington Oval to cheer on Conrad Hunte when he appeared for the West Indies is now a part of Bajan cricket folklore. Today he is still so much revered by the people of Shorey Village that their cricket team in the Barbados Cricket Association's annual competition is named after him. The team is particularly good, too, and it can be seen in action on the village green on any weekend drive through Shorey Village.

Working windmills: On leaving Shorey Village, the road ascends a steep hill to **Morgan Lewis Mill**, open daily to visitors. It is the only intact Barbadian windmill left on the island, and its wheel house and sails are in perfect working order. It is a good example of the Dutch windmills that were introduced to the island by Dutch Jews who came to Barbados from Brazil and pioneered the cultivation and manufacture of sugarcane.

Morgan Lewis Mill.

The working parts of the mill, you'll soon learn from a tour inside, were manufactured by the George Fletcher firm of Derby, England, in 1908. The Fletcher firm has a worldwide reputation for machinery used in sugar manufacture.

The slaves who worked on the sugar mills generations ago were specially trained and did not have to work as hard as the field slaves. The mill gang of about eight men had as one of its chores the task of moving the mill sails into or out of the wind by pulling and pushing the long tail tree. Heavy wind was just as bad for the grinding of sugar as was a light breeze. Squally wind would rotate the mill out of control and the vibrations could make the entire mill collapse.

At one time there were over 500 windmills on Barbados, all grinding sugarcane. Indeed, grinding cane by windmill was practiced well into the 20th century.

The view becomes truly spectacular when one goes up the hill further to **Cherry Tree Hill**, a steep mile away from Morgan Lewis Mill. Visible from here is most of the Scotland District, including Belleplaine, Chalky Mount and Hackleton's Cliff in the far south.

At Cherry Tree Hill the road levels out and leads into the parish of St Peter. The title Cherry Tree Hill is a misnomer for the long avenue that is lined by mahogany (not cherry) trees. The avenue is about 600 yards (550 meters) long, and the mahogany trees are so old and established that they form a cool canopy over the road, the trees from both sides of the road coming together about 20 feet (6 meters) into the air.

The type of mahogany tree found at Cherry Tree Hill was introduced to Barbados sometime in the late 18th and early 19th century. The trees grow slowly, but can now be found in all parishes of Barbados, even though those at Cherry Tree Hill are the most picturesque.

Isolated beach: Before you leave St Andrew for St Peter via Cherry Tree Hill you should take the time to explore the little-known, isolated beach below the cliff. You'll get there by swinging right onto a narrow road after leaving Morgan Lewis Mill and before getting to Cherry Tree Hill. This road leads directly to the large village of Boscobelle, which straddles the parishes of St Andrew and St Peter. Before you reach Boscobelle, turn onto the overgrown road that branches off the route. This leads down a cliff covered by thick foliage to one of the most isolated spots in Barbados – **Morgan Lewis Beach**, a pleasant, white sand beach about 2½ miles (4 km) long. The road leading to it is not indicated on even the most detailed maps of the island.

Morgan Lewis Beach is the best position from which to view the desolate coastline that runs for miles, past Green Pond, Long Pond and Lakes Beach to the East Coast Road. There are no houses or structures of any kind in this untamed region. It is not difficult to imagine the beach as the location for a film about an abandoned island.

Another point in the parish which affords an unusual view of the area's scenery is **Bleak House** which is on a limestone ridge at the western edge of St Andrew, close to the St Peter border. It is reached by following Highway 2 after it passes St Andrew's Church, up Farley

Green Monkey.

Hill in St Peter, and making the first left turn after passing Farley Hill Park.

The view from Bleak House is of the entire Scotland District amphitheater in all its glory, complete with white waves lashing against the east coast beaches.

The house itself was built in 1886 as a kind of "bachelor great house" by an eccentric, Charles Peddar. Richard Goddard, a Barbadian businessman and head of the local Duke of Edinburgh (Exploration) Awards Scheme, now owns the property. The house has 166 acres (67 hectares) of land, and Mr Goddard is trying to make the property as productive as possible by raising pigs, black belly sheep, chickens and cows, and growing plants such as pawpaw.

Highway 2 south from the Alleyne School leads directly to the **Government Agricultural Station** on the old Haggatts estate. The station is the headquarters of the Soil Conservation and Rural Development Scheme in the Scotland District, which was started in 1957. The station is well-known for its research into fruit tree production, the development of forestry, and fish farming. It also plays a key role in the prevention of soil slippage and erosion in the district.

Nutritious cherries: Haggatts is actually in a valley, bordered by the hills of St Simons and Mount All on the west and Chalky Mount on the east. The valley is dominated by Haggatts' extensive orchards that produce such fruits as mango, citrus and the world-famous Barbados cherry (*Malpighia glabra*).

The cherry is famous because of its extremely high Vitamin C content. Just one Barbados cherry supplies a day's requirement for the human body. The cherry also contains fiboflavin, niacin and thiamin. Under ideal conditions, the plant can fruit up to 10 times a year.

At the Haggatts station the road branches into a "Y," the right arm of which leads to the tiny village of **St Simons** and Turner's Hall Woods at the end of the cul-de-sac.

The Caribbean's foremost gospel singer, Joseph Niles, spent his formative years in St Simons. Niles has distinguished himself as a prolific producer of

Outside the Chalky Mount rum shop.

albums (he cut 15 in 14 years, beginning in 1970) and as a gifted interpreter of songs from the Negro spiritual tradition.

Primeval forest: Turner's Hall Woods on the slopes above St Simons is the last remnant of the dense forest that carpeted Barbados before it was settled in the 1600s. Here you can see what those early adventurers must have seen when they first set foot on the island. The area of thick tropical foliage, including cabbage palm up to 130 feet (40 meters) tall, covers 46 acres (19 hectares) and runs in a northeasterly direction from Mount Hillaby, at heights ranging from about 600–800 feet (180–240 meters) above sea level. Thankfully, the woods have not been developed and remain relatively unspoiled, complete with an overhead orchestra of birds and monkeys.

Cutting down trees such as those found today at Turner's Hall Woods (including Spanish oak, beef wood, fustic, candle wood and silk cotton) was the task of the early colonists of Barbados. In those early days any clearing was solely for agricultural purposes. In 1631, Barbados was still "so full of woods and trees" that one Sir Henry Colt was unable to train 40 of his musketeers. Historian Richard Ligon reported in 1657 that the first English settlers found a landscape which was "so grown with wood as there could be found no champions [open spaces] or savannahs for men to dwell in."

A hole in the ground inside the woods which leaks out natural gas and can be lit with a match is an indication that the land at Turner's Hall is also rich in minerals. Back in the valley by the Haggatts orchards, a road leads off Highway 2 on the left up Coggins Hill towards **Chalky Mount Village**. The residents of Chalky Mount live mostly in wooden houses, many of which are built on the sides of hills. A narrow road that should be negotiated carefully meanders along ridges through the village.

Chalky Mount proper is not accessible by road. The traveler must park where the road ends and hike to it. It is 550 feet (170 meters) above sea level and looms over the East Coast.

Chalky Mount Village is home to the

View of Alantic Coast from central St Andrew.

island's best potters. And not surprisingly, it has one of the largest reserves of clay in the island. This scenic area is dominated by a brownish-red soil, evidence of its clay consistency. The main clay deposit of 78 million tons is at Morgan Lewis. However, clay is now mined only at Chalky Mount and Greenland. The clay taken from Greenland is used to manufacture bricks.

The Chalky Mount potters delight in having spectators watch them shape the rough brown or white blobs into handsome objects. Local creations include "connerees," special pots to preserve meats "pepperpots," and "monkeys," which are water jugs that keep drinking water cool and reportedly make it taste better. Much of the local pottery is glazed to a shining red ochre finish. The craft of the Chalky Mount potter, has been handed down for generations. Surnames such as Devonish, Harding, Springer and Cummins are often found on clay pieces.

Soon after passing the Coggins Hill exit, Highway 2 branches in two at Bruce Vale. The left branch leads into the St Joseph village of St Sylvan's, or Dark Hole, as it is more popularly known to Bajans. The right branch is the route through Baxter's towards Mount All, White Hill and Mount Hillaby.

Road on a ridge: The road through **Mount All** and up **White Hill** is the first exit on the right. Like most of the roads in the Scotland District, this is perched on the back of a ridge and offers some spectacular views. The road leads into the village of **Hillaby** after it reaches the top of White Hill. Hillaby is a larger settlement than Belleplaine but it has not yet been blessed with a police station or post office like the village in the valley below. If you're in this area on a Saturday, you'll find a truly local treat for sale at the rum shop in the nearby village of **Gregg Farm** – homemade "pudding and souse," a traditional Bajan dish.

To get to the summit of Mount Hillaby, go left at the T-junction at the top of White Hall. A swing to the right leads down to **Mose Bottom**, a point which offers a splendid view of the deep ravine on the northern side of Mount All, Haggatts in the valley, and the eastern reaches of St Andrew and St Joseph.

Highest point: After you swing left and take the second left off the road, you will soon find yourself on the summit of **Mount Hillaby**, 1,160 feet (350 meters) above sea level. There is no fanfare here, at the highest point on the island – no park benches, no snack bar; in fact "The Mount," as the people of Hillaby call it, is deserted most of the time.

The summit itself is actually a chalk hill with a dirt cap. On top of it is a stump of cement with a metal cap with the simple inscription

Inter-American Geodetic Survey
Do Not Disturb
Hillaby 1953

Here on the summit it is breezy, and quiet. The view to the south includes rolling fields of agricultural land with the telecommunications antennae at Sturges and Mount Misery furthest away. To the north, are the settlements of White Hill and Gregg Farm, and the land slopes up on the west to St Peter's eastern ridge. To the east is the most spectacular view of stunning ravines, gullies and hills.

Left, Kemeta Belgrave in Shorey Village. **Right**, The Potteries at Chalky Mount; the potter is John Springer.

ST LUCY

In St Lucy, which caps the northern end of Barbados, you'll find the island's most dramatic scenery. Adventurous travelers will delight in exploring its untamed terrain. Along its rugged coastline, the powerful, relentless surf of the Atlantic beats against steep, jagged cliffs. Bajans call St Lucy's foaming breakers "white horses."

St Lucy also offers the best opportunity to see the Barbadian chattel house in all its glory. These little cottages are arranged in small villages that dot the vast plain of sugarcane fields that make up most of the parish.

The number of households here is small: just over 9,000. As the population of the parish and its wealth grow, the small wooden chattel houses that so characterize Barbados are being replaced by less interesting concrete block bungalows, locally called "wall houses." The best examples today of chattel houses are in the villages of Greenidge and Connell Town near Archer's Bay.

In the villages of St Lucy several stone ruins of old peasant dwellings are still standing today. Presumably these belonged to folk fortunate enough to own the land on which to build their own homes. In the 1970s it became popular to describe these old houses as slave huts from the 19th century that needed to be preserved.

But writer Norah Francis, contributing to the May 1974 issue of *The Bajan* magazine, made a valuable point to the debate: "In fact, the houses that slaves lived in are not in existence today. They were small and made of organic materials called wattle and daub. Their roofs as well as those of the stone huts of later date were thatched with materials such as trash or plantation leaves. These houses were usually square or rectangular and consisted of only two rooms, occasionally three."

Touring St Lucy: Going north from St Peter along Highway 1, you'll pass **Almond Beach Village** and the new **Port St Charles Marina** on the Speightstown

by-pass, then reconnect with Highway 1 on the edge of the coast at Six Men's Bay. The fishing communities of Six Men's, Half Moon Fort, Fustic and Checker Hall line the coastal road as it enters St Lucy.

The route goes up a steep incline at the village of **Checker Hall**. Here you'll see a typical Bajan "rum shop," where the men of the village gather to drink and socialize. They are likely to be engaged in a heated discussion about politics or cricket, or taking part in a game of dominoes.

At the top of the hill a road on the left leads to the **Arawak Cement Plant**. The factory has its own jetty that extends out into the Caribbean, to the south of the secluded Maycock's Bay. The plant was built on the northwest coast of the island to take advantage of the calm water-loading facilities as well as the close proximity to the raw materials used in the manufacture of Arawak's Portland cement.

From the cement plant the road meets Highway 1B at a cross junction. On the

Preceding pages: St Lucy coastline. Left, cliffs on the north coast. Right, rock fisherman.

left is the route to the northernmost tip of Barbados. A drive straight through the junction leads to St Lucy's Church and the Mount Gay Factory.

Turn left, and you'll see beautiful **Maycock's Bay** stretching for about a mile along the shore. Two steep paths lead down to the beach: one takes you to the ruins of the old **Maycock's Fort**. Treasure is said to be buried under it.

An overgrown track on the eastern limits of the Barbados Defense Force base leads to the **Harrison Point Lighthouse**. A path down a thickly forested cliff leads to the remote coastline below. Here loom large rocks that have been so eroded by the sea that they assume eerie characteristics. Some of St Lucy's sea cliffs are said to be more than 500,000 years old.

Boots, boots and more boots: The Barbados Defense Force base is out-of-bounds to strangers. Armed soldiers regularly patrol its limits. It used to belong to the US military before it was handed back to the Barbados government in the late 1970s.

On the coast, east of Harrison Point, is **Archer's Bay**, a picnic spot very popular with Bajans. The road into Archer's Bay is at the Crab Hill police station. Here the visitor will not find any tables, benches or rest rooms, but will encounter a rocky track that leads to a grassy expanse shaded by a grove of casuarina trees, just a short walk from a cliff which has a magnificent view of the sea. A path winds through the wooded limestone ledge which leads down to a sandy cove.

Surf and spirits: near the village of Crab Hill, over one of the many narrow dirt roads which lead through fields of sugarcane, is the place the island's serious surfers call **Duppies**. In Barbados, "duppies" are ghosts (*see page 76*), and this area is well-named: tales of huge sharks and mysterious happenings abound here.

When the wind is blowing from the north, surfers flock to this isolated area to ride the 15-feet (5 meter) swells. If the surf's up at Duppies, there will be local teenagers sitting on a bench under the almond tree at the edge of the cliff,

Fishing through a hole in overhanging rock.

munching on sugarcane and watching the surfers.

From Crab Hill, another road leads eastwards to the wave-eroded **Animal Flower Cave**, which got its name from the tiny sea anemones (seaworms) growing in its rock pools. Here stalactites and stalagmites grow towards each other from ceilings and floors, and the seaworms indeed look like flowers as they open and close their tentacles.

The cave, which is run by Eva Ward, is open daily to visitors (9am–4pm) for a small fee. The land around the entrance to the cave consists of barren rock, much like a moonscape; it's difficult to imagine that this region produced sugarcane in the past, when it was known as the Animal Flower Plantation.

The owner has the island's largest collection of business cards, stuck on the walls and roof of the refreshment stands near the cave's entrance and has even made it into the *Guinness Book of World Records*. Here you can find delicious sandwiches, locally called "cutters," served on freshly baked salt bread.

They also serve homemade lemonade, as well as other more potent drinks.

The road south from the Animal Flower Cave goes by the **North Point** at Middle Bay, and to on River Bay.

Adjacent to North Point are the remains of what used to be artificial salt lakes. Water was pumped from the sea, then left to settle and then evaporate, leaving the salt. The salt lakes were closed in the 1940s.

Breathtaking bay: South and North Point is the well-known area of **River Bay**, a destination of Bajan bus excursions for generations. The bay gets its name from a stream that meets the sea at the inlet. From the hills above, it is a breathtaking sight.

Visitors enjoy exploring the wind-eroded landscape and dry riverbed, or just relaxing under casuarina trees. The bay is chiseled into the chalk and limestone rock. Close to land, shallow water hugs moss-covered boulders, while further into the ocean waves break in laundry-white surf. Now and then a fountain of spray appears from below, and a salty

The "Swimming Pool" in the Animal Flower Cave.

breeze caresses the face of anyone lucky enough to inhale the pure air transported over 2,000 miles (3,219 km) of ocean seas.

River Bay is full of picnickers on weekends and holidays: but during the week the chances are you'll have this scenic spot all to yourself.

From River Bay a road leads west back into the center of St Lucy and towards the parish church. **St Lucy's Parish Church** is one of the first six churches on the island. The original structure was already in existence by 1629, and was reconstructed after it was damaged by the 1831 hurricane.

A road meanders up a cliff, from the church to **Mount Gay Distillery** in the east, about a mile away. Mount Gay is Barbados's world-famous rum. The distillery has been making the golden spirit for over 100 years. If you would like to tour a distillery, you must go to Mount Gay's other site (*see page 196*).

A Bajan secret: A perfect place to wind up a tour of the north is **Cove Bay** on St Lucy's Atlantic coast. On maps it is shown as Gay's Cove, but it is locally known as Cove Bay. To get there, you will pass through the village of **Pie Corner**, the site of an archaeological dig where artifacts from Carib and Arawak Indian civilizations have been unearthed. Follow the road out of Pie Corner to a field with a horse farm on the left and cliffs to the right. The road to Cove Bay then cuts right through a cow pasture, but stay on it, and you won't be disappointed.

The bay itself is not the visitor's destination, but a beautiful promontory called **Paul's Point**, which some say is the prettiest spot in all of Barbados. The Point overlooks the bay and the length of Barbados's Atlantic coastline. Here under the coconut trees the trade winds are fresh and vigorous. Towering over the south of the bay is the northern side of the jutting Pico Teneriffe, an unusually shaped white cliff which rises from the sea in stark grandeur, guarding the eastern coastline like a sentry and appearing much higher than its 260 feet (80 meters).

Scott McCranels surfing at Duppies.

CHATTEL HOUSES

They are as delightful a part of the Barbadian landscape as the gently undulating fields of cane and bright blue sea: they are "chattel houses," the tiny, gay, makeshift homes traditionally built by rural Bajans.

"Chattel" is movable property: these wooden houses are constructed on a foundation typically of loose stones, making them easy to dismantle and move. This mobility was once very much a virtue, as the original owners of chattel houses were plantation workers who didn't own the land on which their houses stood.

No two of the island's thousands of chattel houses are identical: but they all share a number of architectural and constructional similarities. Their foundations are made of stone, the walls of the house are weathered planks, and corrugated metal is used for roofs as well as backyard fencing for pigs, chickens and goats.

The windows of chattel houses are inventive. Traditionally, each window sports three wooden shutters, two hinged at the sides and one hinged from above, to allow for maximum flexibility in adjusting to sun and wind. Should a storm or hurricane approach, these shutters, called *jalousies*, can be shut tight to keep out the potential torrents. Today, glass and louvers are fast replacing the centuries-old wooden jalousies, but many fine examples still exist.

Other characteristics of the chattel house include the short eaves, a further protection against the destructive power of the hurricane, and its fantastic colors: it is not unusual to find that the siding, molding, windows and doors of chattel houses are painted in different, exuberant hues.

Modern houses are most often made of concrete, and less picturesque than these generations-old houses. But the influence of the chattel house is not forgotten: Bajans incorporate many of its details into modern island dwellings. ∎

ST PETER

St Peter is blessed with western *and* eastern seafronts: it spans the width of Barbados. The calm Caribbean knocks gently against the western rim of the parish, the hills of rural St Andrew dominate its eastern fringe, the sophisticated parish of St James lies to the south, and rugged St Lucy is to the north.

Highway 1, which runs out of St Michael along the coast through St James, is the most popular route into St Peter. Here you'll see hotels, restaurants, some of Barbados' finest privately-owned seaside houses, and a number of beach bars where thirsty travelers can stop for a fruit punch and gaze out at the sparkling sea.

An even more scenic approach to St Peter is from St Andrew, through Cherry Tree Hill or up Farley Hill. The Cherry Tree Hill entrance, with its canopy of mahogany trees, is the most majestic. Immediately after entering the parish by this cool avenue, there is, on the right, one of the most treasured attractions of the north, **St Nicholas Abbey**.

It is the oldest house on the island, and one of three remaining examples of Jacobean-style architecture in the Americas. A visit to the stone and wood mansion affords a revealing view of aristocratic plantation life. The house is said to have been built around 1650 by Colonel Benjamin Berringer, a white landowner and member of one of the aristocratic families that dominated the social and political life of the island at that time. Soon after his house was built, Berringer was killed in a duel by Sir John Yeamans who later married Mrs Berringer. Sir John and his bride were among the pioneers who left Barbados in 1669 to settle in South Carolina in the United States. Sir John became Governor of South Carolina in 1672.

The abbey was named after one of Colonel Berringer's descendants, according to local historian Maurice Hutt. Berringer's son John left the house to his daughter, Susanna, who married a

Preceding pages: Market women grow the crops they sell. Below, St Nicholas Abbey.

man named George Nicholas. It was his name that became attached to the property. No one seems to know how the "Saint" and "Abbey" in the mansion's name came about.

North of the abbey are ruins of the sugar factory that once ground the cane produced on the estate. The factory was closed in 1947. However, the present (English) owner, Stephen Cave, has some old film footage which shows life at Nicholas Abbey early in the 20th century, including black laborers at work in the factory. This intriguing footage is shown to visitors on request in a room that used to be the stable. The estate is open Monday–Friday 10am–3.30pm.

Farley Hill National Park and its great house ruins are a few miles away from St Nicholas Abbey. To get there, follow the road from the abbey, turn left at Diamond Corner, and make another left onto Highway 1.

The peaceful Farley Hill National Park consists of several beautiful acres of tropical trees and plants on a cliff 900 feet (275 meters) above the sea, and overlooks the entire Scotland District.

Farley Hill mansion was built 200 years after St Nicholas Abbey, on the grand scale of the 19th-century plantation houses. The massive great house was built in sections, beginning in 1818. During the late 1800s, it was owned by Thomas Graham Briggs who lived what can only be described as a high life here. Farley Hill gained a reputation as the most lavish of the old Barbadian merchant palaces, and included a billiard room, library, oversized dining room and several reception rooms.

Hollywood comes to Barbados: After Briggs' death in 1887, Farley Hill had a number of different occupants but it never regained its earlier elegance. It was nevertheless selected for the filming of a Hollywood movie in the 1950s. For many years after, the unbelievable things that happened when Hollywood came to Barbados were the talk of the island. Journalist George Hunte wrote: "The glory that was Farley Hill had faded by the time that Robert Rossen approved it as Bellfontaine, the Fleury

Another roadside attraction.

home in the 20th Century Fox film of Alex Waugh's novel *Island In The Sun* (starring Harry Belafonte).

"Then for two months in 1956 the crumbling old "palace" experienced a transformation as 300 persons worked under the supervision of art director John de Cuir from Hollywood and his assistant, Walter Simmons, to convert it into a mansion suitable for a sugar baron. A complete new gallery and stairway was constructed to face the lawn. An open veranda was added in front of the main entrance, where a huge *porte cochère* with overhanging roof bordered an artificial lake. The water-works of Barbados had to pump hundreds of thousands of gallons of water into this lake daily for weeks because its bottom was porous. Special paints were flown in from the United States and used to transform ordinary green leaves until they looked through the camera lenses like scarlet flamboyant flowers and magenta bougainvillea blooms.

"One flamboyant tree was delicately cut into numbered pieces at Crystal Springs on the St James coast, transported to Farley Hill and there stuck back carefully together as a single tree growing alongside the *porte cochère*."

The large quantities of wool and other flammable materials that were used in the restoration were a danger, however, and a few years later, a fire destroyed everything at the mansion except the walls. In 1965 the Barbados Government bought the Farley Hill property and declared it a National Park. It was officially opened by Her Majesty Queen Elizabeth II, on February 15, 1966.

Over the years the park has been a popular recreation area for Bajans and visitors. The beautifully landscaped grounds have dozens of different fruit trees such as mango, soursop, mannee apple and tamarind. There are benches on the edge of the cliff where visitors can sit and savor the view, one of the nicest in Barbados. It is open daily from 7am–6pm for a small entry fee.

Highway I west from Farley Hill leads into the most densely populated part of the parish, down sloping hills into set-

Sea-bath for man and beast.

tlements such as Mile and a Quarter, Ashton Hall, The Whim and the city of Speightstown on the coast.

Haunted house: A right turn off the highway at Mile and a Quarter leads to **Alleynedale Hall**, an old Barbadian great house that is said to be haunted. Before proceeding down to the St Peter coast, pay it a visit to savor its architecture and wonder about its secrets. Alleynedale Hall is set in the factory yard of the 315-acre (128-hectare) Alleynedale sugar estate.

The Barbadian historian Edward Stoute has written: "The last male of this family was a clergyman and he committed suicide by cutting his own throat. However, they did not, as was the custom of the day, bury his body where four roads crossed and drive an iron stake through it, but put him in a leaden coffin and buried him in the wall of the cellar. Sir Reynold Alleyne, whose grandmother was a Miss Tyrrill, purchased the place in 1810 and changed the name to Alleynedale Hall. What has become of the leaden coffin and the body of the unfortunate Reverend is not known, but there is, or was, a cavity in the floor of the cellar in the shape of a coffin. It is related that the spirit of the unfortunate Reverend walks around the house at night."

That unfortunate Reverend would have known **All Saints Church**, on Highway 1 to the east of Mile and a Quarter. The original All Saints survived hurricanes in 1675 and 1780 but could not withstand the great hurricane of 1831. A foundation stone was laid in 1839 and the new church was consecrated in 1843. This new church barely lasted 40 years before the walls were found to be shaky and the church had to be demolished to make way for a new building which was completed in 1884. Despite all the rebuilding All Saints Church remains on the original site and a number of the old tombstones are still present, providing a journey into old Barbados with the names of the prominent planter families of centuries ago.

On a whim: South of Mile and a Quarter (so named because it is that distance

Playing "Warri," a game slaves brought from West Africa.

from Speightstown (*see page 291*) is an exit to the left off Highway 1 into the **Whim Gully**. This is one of the most accessible of the many gullies that dot the island since the road passes through its floor. The foliage rises up on both sides, and in the center of the gully the road crosses a bridge where the temperature is very cool. In times of heavy rain, water flows over the rocks of the gully's floor and under this bridge. The Whim is notorious to the residents of Speightstown as the source of much of the water which floods the town after heavy rains. The road from The Whim goes through the other of St Peter's major gullies, Sailor's Gully.

Sailor's Gully is bordered on the south by a cliff about 80 feet (25 meters) high. Hanging from the cliff are festoons of thick vines. And in the limestone is the opening of a cave with mossy stalactites and stalagmites visible from the road. In Sailor's Gully the road branches into two, and both routes lead into miles and miles of St Peter's distinctive sugarcane fields and eventu-ally back to the Farley Hill Park region.

At Orange Hill there is a panoramic view of the land sloping down to the west coast and the scenery of St Lucy, dominated by the Arawak Cement Plant on the Checker Hall coast.

Before leaving this part of the parish for the west coast or St Peter's Atlantic coast the visitor should also take the time to see the **Barbados Wildlife Reserve, Signal Stationa, Forest** and Pleasant Hall Hill.

Shy monkeys: The reserve is a project of the Barbados Primate Research Center in a lush, mahogany woodland with footpaths making it accessible to disabled visitors. It offers a unique opportunity to observe at close range, in their natural habitat, the monkeys of Barbados (*Cercopithecus sabaeus*). You'll see young monkeys at play, mothers caring for their babies and older males keeping watch over their territories as they forage for food. An interesting and well written booklet *The Green Monkey of Barbados* provides information on the behavior of this shy and elusive crea-

Creative advertising at a repair shop.

ture. The booklet, refreshments and gifts are available at a reception center. Opening hours are from 10am–5pm daily and there is an admission fee.

At **Pleasant Hall Hill** there is a cave where it is believed that Carib Indians once worshipped. The entrance is 10 feet (3 meters) above the ground and is hidden by bush. Inside the cave is a small carved piece of rock in the shape of a human head.

Secret picnic spot: The villages of **Boscobelle** and **The Risk** are the communities closest to the desolate and rugged Atlantic coast of St Peter. You can reach them by following the road east from Diamond Corner. Most people go to Boscobelle to see Barbados' best known landmark on the Atlantic coast, **Pico Teneriffe**. This is a tall pillar of rock that can be seen from as far south as St John. Nearby **Cove Bay** (actually in St Lucy), is one of the island's best picnic spots (which most visitors don't know about) and it offers the best view of Pico Teneriffe.

George Hunte wrote in his book on Barbados: "It rises like a large bump on a rugged eroded cliff. Anyone who has seen the towering mountain at Teneriffe in the Canary Islands must wonder at the imagination of the person who first gave Pico Teneriffe its name. Yet, situated where it is on the south side of the deeply indented Gay's Cove, the peak seems higher than its few hundred feet while the figure on its pinnacle may be mistaken on a misty day for a sorrowful Madonna gazing out to sea in anxious care of her beloved fisherfolk."

Full of charm: People who live in the north go to **Speightstown** to do their shopping. The character of Speightstown has not changed much over the past century, even though its face has been revamped. It is unique among the island's four towns because it is the only one to have retained much of its original street system. It is a charming town of small streets lined with simple, two-story shops, many boasting old-fashioned Georgian-style balconies and overhanging galleries propped up on slender wooden pillars.

Church Street, Speightstown.

The construction of a by-pass highway has routed traffic away from the center of the town, making it an ideal place for strolling, especially on Saturday mornings when the "hucksters" sell fresh produce from their trays on the narrow streets, and it seems as if all the north come to Speightstown. In the center of town are remnants of the Denmark and Orange forts, which once mounted 23 cannons between them. Some of the old cannons are still standing on the **Speightstown Esplanade**, which overlooks the sea.

The town was reportedly named after William Speight, who was a white landowner and member of one of the earliest parliaments in Barbados. Speight came from Bristol and owned land in the St Peter area. The town was once called "Little Bristol" since it was a bustling port for the shipment to Bristol, England, of sugar produced in northern Barbados.

Glory days: Speightstown had its greatest glory in the days when there were no motor vehicles, and Bridgetown could only be reached by foot, horse-drawn

carriage, or boat from the northern end of the island.

At the center of the town is **Speightstown Mall**, opened in 1980. It is one of the best shopping areas on the island, with a department store, bank and fast-food restaurant.

Two of Speightstown's most interesting landmarks are Arlington House and St Peter's Parish Church.

St Peter's Parish Church is in the heart of Speightstown, at the corner of Church and Queen streets. It was one of the island's earliest churches, first built in the 1630s. It was rebuilt in 1837, in Georgian style, and then again restored in 1980 after a fire devastated all but its walls and tower. The restoration took three years and cost BDS $750,000.

Nightlife of the north: North of Speightstown, below quaint fishing villages such as Six Men's, is one of Barbados' largest resorts, **Almond Beach Village**. With almost 300 rooms the complex offers some of the best tourist accommodations and facilities on the island. It stands on 30 acres (12 hectares) of beachfront property and was designed around an old sugar plantation. The hotel, formerly known as "Heywoods" was completely renovated and extended for the 1994–95 winter season at a cost of 24 million BDS$. The extravagant complex now boasts nine swimming pools, a fitness center, and a nine-hole golf course. Like its sister company, the **Almond Beach Club** in St James, it is an "all-inclusive" club.

A nice way to absorb an extensive view of the sloping west coast of St Peter and to end a tour of the parish is to stop at **Eastry House**, set in 6 acres (2 hectares) of landscaped gardens on top of a cliff 200 feet (60 meters) above the sea. Owner Gordon Carlstrom is proud of the image of the 34-bedroom hotel which caters to an upscale market. The Queen of Denmark has vacationed here on several occasions.

The view from Eastry House extends as far down the coast as the Deep Water Harbour in Bridgetown and as far north as the Arawak Cement Plant in St Lucy. Below the cliff is the residential district of Mullins Bay.

Left, Pico Teneriffe. **Right**, a solitary moment.

FISHING BOATS OF BARBADOS

BARBADOS

MOTOR POWERED FISHING BOAT

50 c

INSIGHT GUIDES
Travel Tips

Insight Guides portray destinations in depth, providing the complete picture and the top photography

Insight Pocket Guides focus on the best choices for places to see and things to do and include large fold-out maps

Insight Compact Guides' portability makes them the perfect books to carry with you for on-the-spot reference

Three types of guide for all types of travel

INSIGHT GUIDES Different people need different kinds of information. Some want *background information* to help them prepare for the trip. Others seek *personal recommendations* from someone who knows the destination well. And others look for *compactly presented data* for on-the-spot reference. With three carefully designed series, Insight Guides offer readers the perfect choice. Insight Guides will turn your visit into an experience.

The world's largest collection of visual travel guides

Getting Acquainted

Area: 166 sq. miles (430 sq. km)
Capital: Bridgetown
Highest mountain: Mount Hillaby
Population: 260,000
Language: English; Barbadian dialect
Religion: Anglican (40 percent)
Time zone: four hours behind GMT
Currency: Barbados dollar (BDS$); BDS$2 = US$1, fixed rate.
Weights and measures: metric
Electricity: 110 volts A.C. and 50 cycles. Two-pronged US-style plug.
National flower: Pride of Barbados
International dialling code: 246

The easternmost island of the Caribbean, Barbados is 21 miles (34 km) long and 14 miles (22 km) wide. Although it is said that Columbus missed "discovering" Barbados because it was too flat, the landscape in some locales is quite hilly, especially moving toward the north and east along the elevated central plateau. On the windward eastern side, magnificent cliffs rise above the Atlantic waves; on the leeward west coast the sea is calm, lapping against miles of powdery beaches.

The Climate

The climate in Barbados is mild, breezy and sunny all year round. The average temperature is 80°F (27°C), and the warm sunshine – 3000 hours of it per year – is moderated by a steady North East Trade wind. Rain usually comes in quick showers, except occasionally during the hurricane season from June through November. Fortunately, these intense tropical storms usually pass by Barbados to the north.

The Economy

Barbados is one of the most prosperous countries in the Caribbean. The main areas of economic activity are tourism, light manufacturing, a combination of agriculture and fishing, and financial services. Manufacturing contribute roughly equal parts to the economy. Political stability and generous government incentives have made Barbados attractive to foreign investors, a trend which the government continues to encourage.

The Government

Barbados became an independent nation in 1966, after an unbroken relationship with a single colonial power, Britain, stretching back into the early 17th century. In 1989, Barbados achieved 350 years of uninterrupted parliamentary government. The nation retains the British monarch as its official head of state, represented by the Governor-General. A Prime Minister and bicameral legislature, consisting of an elected House of Assembly and a 21-member Senate, govern the country. Twelve senators are appointed on the advice of the Prime Minister, two from the opposition party and the remaining seven are chosen to represent the social, political and religious interests of the country. The Prime Minister is the leader of the majority party in the House of Assembly.

The People

Almost half of Barbadians live in or near Bridgetown, the capital. The population is about 70 percent black, 20 percent mixed black and white, and 7 percent white; another 3 percent are recent immigrants from around the world. Culturally, despite the long political and economic domination of Britain, Barbadians have fashioned a distinctly Bajan point view from their country's complex history.

With such close relations with the USA and Canada, North American influences on the island's day-to-day life are more and more apparent.

Etiquette

Good manners are extremely important in Barbados. Visitors are expected to act like guests: to say "please" and "thank you," and to ask permission before taking anyone's picture. It is considered impolite not greet some-

one with "good morning," "good afternoon," or "good evening," when you pass them on the road, or enter a shop. Always use a greeting before asking a question – like asking for directions – or requesting service.

Planning the Trip

What to Bring

Paperback books, sunscreens, cosmetics, and sporting goods are expensive in Barbados because of import duties; it is probably better to bring them from home. Also, a small radio will open up a world of local sounds.

What to Wear

Light, casual, tropical wear is recommended year-round. Evenings can be slightly more formal. A jacket for men or a long floaty dress or evening ensemble for women is appropriate at elegant restaurants, concerts and the theater.

Modesty in dress should be a general rule, whatever you bring. Barbadians are a stylish but conservative people. Bathing suits are unacceptable except at the water's edge. Skimpy clothes look out of place in town, or at banks and shops.

Maps

Basic maps are available at most hotels and tourist information desks. The free *Barbados Island Guide* lists places of interest and suggests a sight-seeing tour route. A word of caution, though: depend only on the most current maps. Barbados has worked hard on its roads and older maps do not include all the improvements.

Entry Regulations

Visas & Passports

Citizens of the United States, Canada and the United Kingdom should carry a passport to enter Barbados, but no visa is required. Officially visitors must hold valid return tickets. Passports are required to leave and re-enter the USA and United Kingdom.

Visitors from most other countries do not require a visa, for a stay of less than three months, but check with officials in your home country. Citizens of the CIS, Eastern European countries, the People's Republic of China and Cuba are require a visa.

Extension of stay

To stay longer than three months an extension of stay can be obtained for a modest fee, but be prepared for a long wait. Take your passport, airline ticket and details of accommodation along with proof of ability to maintain financial support to the Immigration Office, The Wharf, Bridgetown, tel: 426-9912.

Customs

Passage through customs is usually rapid, if you have nothing to declare. However, all bags are subject to inspection. Agricultural products, firearms, marijuana and narcotic drugs are forbidden. Import duties may be charged for everything except personal belongings including cameras and sports equipment, beyond the following exemptions: 26 ounces (735 grams) of spirits, one half pound (.23 kilos) of tobacco and 50 cigars, or one carton of cigarettes. If you are planning to bring a number of gifts to Barbados, check well in advance with the Customs Department, tel: 427-5940 to determine what charges apply.

United States

US Customs regulations allow each resident to take home purchases totaling US$400 without paying duty, provided the resident has been out of the country at least 48 hours and has not claimed the exemption within the past 30 days. Family members living in the same household can pool their exemptions. Only one customs declaration form per couple or family traveling together is required. You may also mail home an unlimited number of gifts worth up to $50 each, as long as one person doesn't receive more than $50 in one day. However, these gifts may not include cigars, cigarettes, liquor or perfume. For more information, write for the booklet *Know*

Before You Go, which is available from the US Customs Service, Washington, D.C. 20229.

Canada

Returning residents of Canada who have been out of the country over 48 hours may bring back C$200 worth of merchandise without paying duty. The merchandise must accompany the resident, and the exemption, claimed in writing, may be taken no more than once per quarter. Canadians who have been abroad more than seven days may bring home duty-free goods worth up to $300 once each calendar year. These goods may be shipped separately, but must be declared when the traveler reaches Canada. Canadians are eligible to take both the $200 and $300 exemptions on separate trips, but the two cannot be combined, Fifty cigars, 2lbs of tobacco for residents, over 16, 40 ounces of wine or liquor, or 24 cans of beer, if you meet the age regulations of the province where you arrive.

Europe

The total exemption for residents returning to the **United Kingdom** from outside the EU is £32. This may include nine fluid ounces (225 grams) of *eau de toilette*, two fluid ounces of perfume (50 grams), and for persons over 17, 1/2 pound (250 grams) of tobacco, or 200 cigarettes, or 100 cigarillos or 50 cigars. If you live outside Europe, double the tobacco limits. Duty-free alcohol is 2 pints (1 liter) of spirits or 31/2 pints (2 liters) of sparkling wine, plus 31/2 pints (2 liters) of still table wine.

Customs regulations for other countries are regularly listed in the Visitor and other publications for tourists.

Animal Quarantine

Barbados has no rabies; entry regulations for animals and frozen meat products are quite strict. Requirements vary depending on the animal and country of origin. On the whole, it is best to leave pets at home. However, if you plan to bring an animal, find out the pertinent regulations by writing the Senior Veterinary Officer, Ministry of Agriculture, Food and Fisheries, Pine, Plantation Road, Barbados, tel: 427-5073; fax: 420-8444.

Health

Barbados has some of the purest naturally filtered drinking water in the world. Tropical diseases were wiped out long ago, The sun is perhaps the greatest hazard to visitors, when they underestimate its near equator intensity. Regardless of your skin color, wear a strong sunscreen, preferably at all times, but especially near water. To avoid serious sunburn, build up a tan gradually, starting with no more than 15 minutes exposure in the early morning or late afternoon.

Other hazards include coconut trees – do not sit or leave a child beneath one of these trees because the nuts can fall at any time – and manchineel apples, which resemble crabapples. These poisonous trees grow by the seas; merely touching the fruit or foliage can cause blisters. In the water watch out for sea-urchins; if you step on one, let the spines dissolve on their own rather than trying to pull them out.

Finally, snorkeling without a marker can be fatal. Always tie a brightly colored float such as a bleach bottle to your waist or ankle to alert jet skis and other water traffic of your position.

Money

Visitors may bring as much foreign currency as they can carry. It is simpler to use Barbadian currency, but both US and Canadian dollars are accepted at most major stores and hotels, and by many taxi drivers. Exchange rates are listed in the newspaper.

Barbadian paper notes come in denominations of $2, (blue), $5 (green), $10 (brown), $20 (mauve), $50 (orange) and $100 (grey). Coins come in 1, 5, 10 and 25-cent pieces. There is also a silver dollar.

Besides the many banks in Bridgetown and branches on the southern and western sides of the island, there are Barbados National Bank currency exchange booths in Grantley Adams International Airport, open from 9am until the last flight of the day arrives or departs and also at the harbor. Major credit cards and international brands of travelers' checks (not Eurocheques) are accepted at most (but not all) hotels, restaurants and shops.

ATMs allow visitors with cards that

are part of the Visa and Plus system 24 hour-a-day, seven day-a-week banking. Money can be withdrawn – in Barbados dollars – from the cash machines located at Bridgetown banks and throughout the island. There are also facilities at larger supermarkets such as Julie 'N', on the Highway, near Six Roads.

Public Holidays

Banks, public agencies and most businesses close on the following holidays:
New Year's Day – January 1
Errol Barrow Day – January 21
Good Friday
Easter Monday
Labour Day – May 1
Whit Monday – eighth Monday after Easter
Kadooment Day – first Monday in August
United Nations Day – first Monday in October
Independence Day – November 30
Christmas Day – December 25
Boxing Day – December 26

Festivals

Holetown Festival – February
Holder's Opera Season – Easter
Oistins Fish Festival – April
Congaline – April/May
Gospelfest – May
Crop Over – July/August
For more information *see* page 305.

Getting There

By Air

There are close to a dozen carriers offering flights to and from Barbados's **Grantley Adams International Airport**, considered to be the Caribbean's largest and most efficient facility.

Air Canada flies direct to Barbados from Montreal and Toronto, with connections from all other major Canadian cities. Wardair flies direct from Montreal and Toronto weekly. British Airways offers daily flights from London and a seasonal service on Concorde.

British West Indian Airways (BWIA) has service direct from Miami seven days a week, New York five days a week, Toronto two days and from Baltimore on Friday, Saturday and Sunday. BWIA also runs regular direct flights from London Heathrow. American Air-

lines makes connections with all major US cities via San Juan daily.

Leeward Island Air Transport (LIAT), Cubana Airlines, Air Martinique, BWIA, Cruziero and Guyana Airways link Barbados with the rest of the Caribbean region and South America.
Air Canada, tel: 800-422-6232; (Grantley Adams Intl. Airport) tel: 428-5077.
Air Martinique, Bridgetown, tel: 431-0540.
American Airlines, tel: 800-433-7300; (Grantley Adams Intl. Airport) tel: 428-4170.
British Airways, tel: 800-247-9297; (Grantley Adams Intl. Airport) 428-1660.
BWIA, tel: 800-327-7401, (Bridgetown) 426-2111; (Grantley Adams Intl. Airport) 428-1650.
Canadian Airlines and **Wardair**, Canadian Holidays Ltd., Salem St Lawrence Gap, Christ Church, tel: 428-9324.
Cubana Airlines, tel: 426-2111 (through BWIA sales agents).
Cruziero Brazilian Airways (St Michael) 427-3456.
Guyana Airways, (Bridgetown) tel: 431-0575.
LIAT, (Bridgetown) tel: 434-5428; (Grantley Adams Intl. Airport) tel: 428-0986.
Mustique Airways, (Hastings, Christ Church) tel: 435-7009; (Grantley Adams Intl. Airport) tel: 428 1638/9.

By Sea

Nearly 500,000 cruise ship passengers visit Barbados every year, part of a pattern of growth that seems likely to continue. Bridgetown's Deep Water Harbour is within easy reach of the center (half a mile) and has a vast cruise ship passenger terminal, with duty free shopping, banking and a variety of facilities for travelers. Unfortunately, most seafaring visitors remain only for a day or less. The following cruise lines include the island on their schedules; the '800' telephone numbers are toll free in the country of origin only.
Carnival Cruise Lines, tel: 800-327-9501
Chandris Cruises, tel: 800-223-0848
Costa Cruises, tel: 800-462-6782
Cundard Cruise Lines, tel: 800-221-4770
Epirotiki Lines (World Renaissance), tel: 800-221-2470

Holland American Lines, tel: 800-426-0327
Norwegian Cruise Lines, tel: 800-237-7030
Ocean Cruise Lines, tel: 800-556-8850
Regency Cruises, tel: 212-922-4774
Royal Caribbean Lines, tel: 800-327-6700
Royal Cruise Lines, tel: 405-956-7200
Sun Line, tel: 800-872-6400
Wind Star Cruise, tel: 305-592-8008

Special Facilities

Foreign Investment

In recent years, Barbados has campaigned to attract foreign investors. The government – via the **Barbados Industrial Development Corporation** – is seeking to capitalize on its reputation for political stability in order to capture a greater share of overseas investment market.

Advantages for would-be manufacturers include full exemption from corporate taxes for ten years, exemption on all import duties for parts, materials and production machinery, and unrestricted repatriation of capital profits. Under the International Business Companies Act, overseas firms that do not engage in local trade or investment enjoy between one and two and a half percent annual taxation rate. Local regulations regarding offshore banking, foreign ship representation, exempt insurance, and foreign sales corporations have been eased. Low office and industrial space rental rates also contribute to the government's incentives. Information, tel: 427-5350; fax: 426-7802.

For further information, call or write the Barbados Industrial Development Corporation, 800 Second Avenue, New York, NY 10017, tel: (212) 867-6420.

Traveling with Children

Most hotels give substantial discounts for children, and often children under 12 stay free in their parents' room. Many hotels have baby sitters or can provide one on request. Some resorts also offer lessons in watersports that children will enjoy. Still, if you are traveling with children, you may find that an apartment or villa with its own cooking facilities is more convenient than a hotel.

The **National Conservation Commission** administers all parks in Barbados, and has developed children's play parks throughout the country. **Oughterson Zoo** in St Philip is set in beautiful gardens and has a nature education center. If you are touring by car, children can let off steam on the swings and slides of **Errol Barrow** play park in Wildey, St Michael or at the **Claybury** park on Highway 5 in St John. A playground and miniature golf course in St James will supervise children's play while you enjoy dinner elsewhere. Call 425-1200 for more information. And of course the beach is always a great place for the whole family to enjoy the sunshine and sea.

Caribbean weddings

Visitors can combine a wedding and honeymoon in Barbados. Tour companies offer complete packages, or you can organise it yourself through a wedding co-ordinator, usually on staff at the larger hotels.

No residential qualification is required to marry on the island and so you can, if you wish, marry on the day or within days of your arrival. As long as both parties are neither divorced nor widowed all that is needed are a valid passport, or birth certificate and a marriage licence for which you will be charged a modest fee (BDS$100 plus BDS$25 stamp fee). Apply for a marriage license at the Ministry of Home Affairs in the General Post Office Building, Cheapside, Bridgetown (tel: 431-7600).

Ceremonies can take place in a church, hotel, on the beach or any number of venues. Couples have been known to say "I do" on the Atlantis submarine and in the beautiful Flower Forest. For more information contact the **BTA** office in your home country, *see* Tourist Information.

On Departure

If you are leaving by plane, be at the airport two hours before your scheduled flight. Last minute flight changes are not unheard of, so reconfirm your reservation at least 48 hours in advance, and make sure the flight is on time before leaving for the airport.

On leaving Barbados, you will be required to pay a BDS$25 departure tax, if traveling on a package, check with the tour company, the tax may have been included in the price of the holiday. You will also be asked to surrender the carbon copy of the Immigration Card you filled out on arrival. Beyond the customs and immigration checkpoint, the airport departure area has duty-free shops and several refreshment stands. But once you have entered this area, you will not be permitted to leave until your flight is called.

Useful Addresses

Tourist Information

Close to a half million people visit Barbados annually. The **Barbados Tourism Authority (BTA)** can help you plan your visit by providing brochures and information about festivals, tour packages and accommodations.

CANADA

5160 Yonge Street, Suite 1800, North York, Ontario M2N GL 19, tel: (800) 268-9122 (toll-free in Canada); (416) 512-6569/6570/6571; fax: (416) 512-6581.

UK

263 Tottenham Court Road, London W1P 9AA, tel: (0171) 636-9448/9449; fax: (0171) 637-1496.

USA

800 Second Avenue, New York, New York 10017, tel: (212) 986-6516/6518; (800) 221-9831 (toll free in US); fax: (212) 573-9850, telex: 023-666-387; 3440 Wilshire Blvd., Suite 1215, Los Angeles, California 90010, tel: (213) 380-2198/2199; fax: (213) 384-2763.

Practical Tips

Business Hours

Hours for most banks are 8am–2pm Monday through Thursday; 8am–1pm, 3–5pm on Friday. A number of banks may also be open 9am–noon on Saturday. The Barbados Bank at Grantley Adams International Airport is open every day from 8am until the last plane arrives or departs. Cash machines (ATMs) also offer bank facilities any time of the day throughout the week.

Supermarkets open at 8am and close at 6pm from Monday through Wednesday, but stay open an hour later on Thursday and Friday On Saturday all but a few of the larger supermarkets close at 1pm. With some exceptions, department stores and shops are open from 8am until 4pm on weekdays and until 1pm on Saturday. A number of small convenience stores stay open 9am–9pm, Monday through Saturday.

Weights & Measures

Officially, Barbados uses the metric system, though spoken directions and descriptions of quantities are often phrased in miles and pounds. Given below are some standard equivalents of metric units:
1 inch = 2.54 cms
1 foot = 0.305 meters
1 mile = 1.609 km
1 sq. mile = 2.69 sq. km
1 gallon = 3.785 liters
1 ounce = 28.35 grams
1 pound = 0.434 kg

Tipping

A 10 percent tip is standard. But make sure you don't pay twice. Many restaurants automatically add it to your bill.

Religious Services

Traditionally, the Anglican Church has claimed the most members in Barbados, but over 100 religious groups are represented on the island. Most welcome visitors (and prefer to see them properly dressed). The Yellow Pages of the telephone book has a list. There are also religious radio broadcasts on Sunday, and throughout the week.

A few of the many religious services include the following:

African Methodist Episcopal Church, Upper Collymore Rock, St Michael, tel: 427-1046. Sunday, 11am and 6.30pm.

Anglican: St Michael's Cathedral, Bridgetown, tel: 427-0790. Sunday, 6.30am; 7.45am, 9am, 11am, and 6pm. **St Mathias**, Hastings, Christ Church, tel: 429-5733. Sunday, 8am and 9.30am.

Barbados Baptist Convention: The Emmanuel Baptist Church, President Kennedy Drive, Eagle Hall, St Michael, tel: 426-2697. Sunday 10.00am and 6.30pm.

Church of the Nazarene, St Christopher, near Silver Sands, tel: 425-1067. Sunday, 11am and 7pm.

Bethel Methodist Church, Bay Street, Bridgetown, tel: 426-2223. Sunday, 9am and 6pm.

Jewish: The Schaare Tzedeck Synagogue, Rockley New Road, Christ Church, tel: 428-8414. Friday 7.30pm.

Muslim: Juma Mosque, Kensington, New Road, Bridgetown, tel: 436-2764. Service five times daily and special service 12.30pm on Friday.

Pentacostal Assemblies of the West Indies: The People's Cathedral, Bishop Court Hill, Collymore Rock, St Michael, tel: 429-2145. Sunday, 7.30am and 10am, 5 pm and 7pm.

Roman Catholic: St Patrick's Cathedral, Bridgetown, tel: 426-2325. Sunday, 7am and 8.30am, and 6pm; Monday, Wednesday and Friday, noon and 6pm; Tuesday, Thursday and Saturday, 6am and 6pm.

Media

Barbadians are kept informed by two daily newspapers and various magazines. The state-owned TV station and six radio stations also provide news on current events and entertainment.

Newspapers & Magazines

There are two daily papers *The Advocate*, established in 1895, which also produces *The Sunday Advocate*, the *Investigator* a weekly tabloid and *The*

Barbados SunSeeker a free bi-monthly for visitors. The *Nation*, established in 1973, also publishes a weekend edition, the *Sun on Saturday*, *Sunday Sun*, and the *Visitor* a giveaway weekly paper for tourists.

The *Visitor* provides current information and a calendar of events. Free from hotels, restaurants and shops.

Television & Radio

Television is broadcast on Channel 8 by the Caribbean Broadcasting Corporation (CBC). CBC-TV also broadcasts pay-TV which includes USA-based Cable News Network (CNN) news from 6am – 10am daily. Satellite dishes are also a popular route to US and other foreign TV channels and programs.

There are seven radio stations. CBC broadcasts news and popular music programmes on MW (AM) 900 KHZ and FM, Radio Liberty (98.1MHz), (BBS) Barbados Broadcasting Service (90.7MHz) and Yess Ten Four FM (104MHz) and (VOB) Voice of Barbados (790KHz).

Internet Services

There are many information services for the Caribbean region and several specific Barbados sites.

Barbados Tourism Authority:
http://www.barbados.org/bta
CPSCaribNet:
http://www.cpscaribnet.com
Fleet House: Barbados:
http://www.fleethouse.com/barbados/barb-hom.htm
Miller Publishing Co.:
http://www.insandouts-barbados.com

Wire service

CANA (the Caribbean News Agency) is based in Barbados serving print and electronic media throughout the Caribbean region and the rest of the world. CANA also operates a radio service.

Postal Services

There are post offices in all 11 parishes, as well as the large, modern **General Post Office** in Cheapside, Bridgetown (tel: 436-4800), which houses the island's main post office, parcel post, philatelic and registration/money order departments, open 7.30am–5pm. Most other branches are open daily 8am–3.15pm; closing at 3pm on Monday. Closed on Saturday and Sunday.

Telephone

The Barbados Telephone Company, Ltd. (tel: 434-2273) operates a dependable island-wide service. Overseas calls may be made in conjunction with Barbados External Telecommunication, Ltd, (BET, tel: 427-5200). Check the telephone directory or dial **0** for current overseas rate information.

Calls from hotel rooms can be considerably more expensive than from a domestic or public phone. Phone cards, with a value of between BDS\$10 and BDS\$60, are available from many of the larger shops in Bridgetown and from hotels.

Telegrams and faxes can be sent through hotel operators and post offices. BET also provides telex and cable service. Subscribers to Facsimile (Fax) services are listed in the telephone directory.

Tourist Offices in Barbados

The main office of the Barbados Tourism Authority (BTA) is in Bridgetown at Harbour Road, (tel: 427-2623; fax: 426-4080), there is another one at the cruise ship terminal (tel: 426-1718) and information booths for visitors at Grantley Adams International Airport (tel: 428-0937) and Cave Shepherd department store, Bridgetown.

Embassies & Consulates

CANADA

Canadian High Commission/High Commissariat du Canada, Bishops Court Hill, Pine Road, St Michael, tel: 429-3550.

COSTA RICA

Garden Gap Number 1, Worthing, Christ Church, tel: 435-7864.

DOMINICAN REPUBLIC

c/o Hilton Hotel, St Michael, tel: 426-0200.

HAITI

Sugarlands Farm, Salters, St George, tel: 436-6144.

JAMAICA

Six Cross Roads, St Philip, tel: 423-6706.

MEXICO

Suite 205, Kay's House, Roebuck Street, Bridgetown, tel: 429-5320.

NETHERLANDS

5-6 Ocean Spray, Inch Marlow, Christ Church, tel: 428-0034.

TRINIDAD & TOBAGO

Cockspur House, Nile Street, Bridgetown, tel: 429-9600.

UNITED KINGDOM

Lower Collymore Street, St Michael, tel: 436-6694.; fax: 436-5398.

UNITED STATES

Canadian Imperial Bank Building, Broad Street, Bridgetown, tel: 436-4950.

VENEZUELA

Worthing, Christ Church, tel: 435-7619.

Emergencies
Security & Crime

Use common sense in Barbados as you would in any other cosmopolitan area. Place valuables in the hotel safe; do not leave them unattended in your room or at the beach. Leave your key at the hotel reception desk before going out. Avoid walking alone after dark on deserted streets and beaches. Take heed of any hurricane warnings.

Emergency numbers:

Police	Tel: **112**
Fire	Tel: **113**
Ambulance	Tel: **115**
Coast Guard	Tel: **427-8819**

Medical Services

There are a number of physicians and dentists in Barbados, particularly in and around Bridgetown. The general hospital, Queen Elizabeth Hospital (tel: 436-6450) is in St Michael, it operates a 24-hour accident and emergency department. A modern, private facility, Bay View Hospital (tel: 436-5446), is also in St Michael. The Barbados Defence Force has a decompression chamber for divers.

The Samaritans staff a phone line for people in despair or suffering other extremities, tel: 429-9999, 8–11pm Monday through Thursday; 5–11pm Friday; 1–11pm Saturday and Sunday.

Alcoholics Anonymous can be reached on tel: 426-1600.

Getting Around

On Arrival

Just prior to arriving by land or sea, you will be asked to fill out an immigration form. Save the duplicate. You will need it for departure. Also be prepared to show your return ticket and tell the Immigration Officer your address in Barbados. If you arrive at the airport without a hotel reservation, there are telephones and information on accommodations in the arrival area. You may make arrangements and report back to Immigration.

Airport baggage handlers assist arriving and departing passengers at a charge of BDS$1.00 per item.

From the Airport

Unless your package vacation includes airport transfers, or you have arranged to pick up a rental car, you will probably take a taxi to and from the airport. Approximate fares are: BDS$55 to North Point, St Lucy; BDS$22 to Sam Lord's Castle, St Philip; BDS$20 to the Hilton, St Michael; BDS$30 to Bridgetown Harbour and BDS$55 to Almond Beach Village in St Peter.

Public Transportation

You can travel to any part of Barbados by bus – either the larger Transport Board buses, smaller privately operated minibuses, or ZR vans. All cost BDS$1.50 for any journey. Get aboard at numerous bus stops on most major thoroughfares. Bus stops will be marked 'In to City' or 'Out of City'. In Bridgetown, the main Transport Board terminals are on Fairchild Street for south-bound commuters, or Lower Green and Princess Alice Highway for coastal routes. A few route numbers are 12 to Sam Lord's Castle, 13a to St Christopher via the south coast, 6 to Bathsheba and 4 to Harrison's Cave. Minibus terminals are at Temple Yard, Probyn Street and River Road.

The Barbados Transport Board (tel: 436-6820) will provide additional information upon request.

Private Transportation
Car Rental

Driving is the best way to appreciate the distinct character of Barbados's parishes, and the only way to reach a good share of attractions in a reasonable amount of time. In order to drive, you must present a driver's license from your home country along with a fee. Driving licenses for visitors are available at the airport, police stations throughout the country, and almost all car rental companies. Some will deliver your license along with your car.

Car rental in Barbados is handled by local fleets and garages. Charges vary for an open-top Mini Moke, cross-country four-wheel-drive vehicles and saloon cars. Additional collision damage waivers cost about $10 per day. Some companies rent cars only for two days or more, and most require a substantial refundable deposit which usually can be paid by credit card.

Some of the larger car rental companies are:

Auto Rentals, Ltd., Top Rock, Christ Church, tel: 428-9085/9830; fax: 420 6844.

Corbin's Car Rentals, Upper Collymore Rock, St Michael, tel: 427-9531; fax: 427-7975; email: corbin's@ndl.net.

Courtesy Car Rentals, Wildey, St Michael, tel: 431-4160; fax: 429-6387. Grantley Adams International Airport, tel: 420-7153.

Dear's Garage Car Rentals, Browne's Gap Hastings, tel: 427-7853.

Jones Garage, Ltd., Bridgetown, tel: 426-5030; 432-0843 (after hours); fax: 426-7896.

Sunny Isle Motors, Worthing, Christ Church, tel: 435-7979; fax: 435-9277; email: sunisle@caribsurf.com.

Sunset Crest, St James, tel: 432-2222; fax: 432-1619.

Williams L.E. Tours, Hastings, Christ Church, tel: 427-1043/427-6006; fax: 427-6007.

Two-wheel rental

Motor scooters can be rented for about BDS$30 to BDS$60 per day, or $160 to $298 per week. Usually there is an additional $100 deposit to pay. Helmets are required by law and come with the rental. Also required is a motorcycle license or driver's license including a motorcycle endorsement. **Bicycles** can be hired for around BDS$17 per day, or $65 per week.

Motor scooter and bicycle rentals: **Fun Seekers, Inc.**, Rockley Main Road, Christ Church, tel: 435-6852.

William M.A. Bicycle Rentals, Hastings, Christ Church, tel: 427-3955.

Caution: Remember in Barbados you drive on the left. The vehicle on your right has the right of way.

Taxis

In Barbados, taxis do not have meters, but charge pre-determined fares, based on location and mileage. In general, the fare should not be greater than BDS$2.25 per mile or $1.50 per kilometer. Hourly rates should not be greater than $32 for the first hour and $24 for every additional hour. Many taxi cab companies offer tour services as well.

On Foot

Every Sunday at 6am sharp (and occasionally at 3pm), the Barbados National Trust, The Duke of Edinburgh award scheme and the Heart Foundation sponsor a hike. They are popular with both locals and visitors. You can choose among three speed groups; guides provide interesting background on the hike site. Wear comfortable clothing and walking shoes. Each week's site is announced in the newspapers, or call the National Trust, tel: 436-9033; fax: 429-9055 for more detailed information.

The National Conservation Commission (tel: 425-1200) organizes a number of nature walks – mainly in the east of the island.

Highland Outdoor Tours (Canefield, St Thomas, tel: 438-8069) arrange excursions to destinations well away from the beach hotels. Participants can travel on foot, on horse-back or in tractor-hauled wagons.

Where to Stay

Accommodation

With more than 140 hotels, guest houses, apartments and cottages registered with the Barbados Tourism, Authority (BTA) the island's accommodation are diverse in amenities, atmosphere, location and cost. Based on winter season rates – and subject to change – in the listings below **inexpensive** generally means costing less than US$70 (or BDS$140) per night, **reasonable** US$70 to US$100, **moderate** US$100 to US$150, **expensive** US$150 to US$250, and **deluxe** over US$250. In addition to the room price, a 10 percent service charge is usually added plus another 5 percent for tax.

Summer season rates, which usually stay in force from mid-April to mid-December, can sometimes be half as much as winter rates. Twice a year the BTA prints listings of facilities and rates for hotels and apartments. Also supplied are lists of reasonably-priced guesthouses and private houses offering bed and breakfast. See *Useful Addresses* page 299 for the office nearest to you.

The Barbados Hotel and Tourism Association also publishes brochures on accommodations. Contact them at 4th Avenue, Belleville, St Michael, Barbados, tel: 426-5041; fax: 429-7113.

In the slower summer season, hotel reservations are not always necessary, though you may not get your first choice in accommodations. An exception to this is the popular Crop Over Festival during the last two weeks in July and early August. It's wise to make arrangements for this period and the winter season as far in advance as possible, at least from December to April. To make a direct reservation, a fax with credit card details will usually suffice.

See *Useful Addresses* page 299 for the office nearest to you.

Hotels & Apartments
Christ Church

Accra Beach Hotel, Rockley, tel: 435-8920; fax: 435-6794. Extension and upgrade of original building. Complex includes comfortable rooms, restaurants, shops, sports and pool. Moderate–Expensive

Cacrabank Beach Apartments, Worthing, tel: 435-8057; fax: 429-7267. Apartments with sea views. Some air-conditioned rooms with kitchen. Pool, a short stroll to the beach. Moderate

Carib Blue Apartment Hotel, Dover Terrace, Christ Church, tel: 428-2290; fax: 428-5140. Simple accommodation overlooking the beach and close to local shops. Inexpensive

Casuarina Beach Club, Dover, tel: 428-3600; fax: 428-1970. Tropical beachfront hotel with tennis courts and swimming pool. Expensive

Club Mistral, Maxwell, tel: 428-7277; fax: 428-2878. Reasonable

Club Rockley Barbados, Golf Club Road, Rockley, tel: 435-7880; fax: 435-8015. All-inclusive resort with sister hotels in other parts of the Caribbean. Deluxe

Divi Southwinds Hotel and Beach Club, St Lawrence, tel: 428-7181; fax: 428-4674. Luxury complex set in tropical gardens, with pool, tennis courts and a shop . Close to south coast's nightlife. Expensive

Dover Beach Apartment Hotel, St Lawrence Gap, tel: 428-8076; fax: 428-2122. Apartments in a modern block in St Lawrence. Suites and studios with kitchenettes, air-conditioning, bathroom, balconies and terraces. Pool, easy access to the beach and restaurant. Moderate

Golden Sands Apartment Hotel, Maxwell, tel: 428-8051; fax: 428-3897. Modern block, basic apartments. To be refurbished. Five miles (8.5 km) from the airport. Moderate

Howard Johnson Hotel, Maxwell, tel: 428-9112; fax: 428-3428. Former Shangri-La Apartments, now a franchise of the US hotel chain. All apartments refurbished and upgraded some with air-conditioning, telephone and cable TV. Moderate–Expensive

Rio Guest House, St Lawrence Gap, tel: 428-1546; fax: 428-1546. Small guest house in the Gap about 6 miles (10 km) from the airport. Inexpensive

San Remo Hotel, Maxwell, tel: 428-2816/2822; fax: 428-8826. Casual, ocean facing hotel. Reasonable

Sandy Beach Island Resort, Worthing, tel: 435-8000; fax: 435-8053. Modern hotel on the south coast with kitchenettes, air-conditioned rooms, pool and near the beach. Expensive

Silver Sands Resort, Christ Church, tel: 428-6001; fax: 428-3758. Comfortable resort less than five miles (7.5 km) from the airport. Studios and rooms, some with air-conditioning. Tennis courts, watersports, pool , restaurants and beach bar. Moderate

St Lawrence East & West Apartments, St Lawrence Gap, tel: 435-6950; fax: 428-1970. Basic studios with kitchenettes close to the beach and in the heart of lively nightlife. Reasonable

White Sands Apartments, St Lawrence Gap, tel: 428-7484; fax: 428-2641. Basic self-contained units near the beach. Inexpensive

Woodville Beach Apartments, Hastings, tel: 435-6693; fax: 435-9211. Air-conditioned accommodation near to Bridgetown. Pool. Moderate

St James

Almond Beach Club, Vauxhall, tel: 432-7840; fax: 432-2115. All-inclusive resort with excellent watersports, fitness center, tennis courts and pools. Sister resort a few miles up the road in St Peter. Deluxe

Coconut Creek Club Hotel, Derricks, tel: 432-0803; fax: 422-1726. Intimate hotel with good watersports. Part of the St James Beach Hotels group. Expensive

Colony Club, Porters, tel: 422-2335; fax: 422-0667. Elegant resort in seven acres of tropical gardens. Part of the St James Beach Hotels group. Watersports, fitness center, tennis and restaurants and bars. Deluxe

Coral Reef Club, Holetown , tel: 422-2372; fax: 422-1726. Cottages and luxury accommodation away from the road, set in beautiful gardens and on St James Beach. Excellent facilities. Expensive

Crystal Cove Hotel, Appleby, tel: 432-2683/438-4680; fax: 432-8290. Luxury hotel, with excellent facilities including a bar under a waterfall. Part of St James Beach Hotels group allowing guests to use facilities at three other upmarket West coast hotels. Expensive

Glitter Bay Resort, Porters, tel: 422-4111; fax: 422-3940. The former home of Sir Edward Cunard. Luxurious accommodation in lush gardens, beside the beach. Deluxe

Na-Diesie Pirates Cove Beach Resort, Holetown, tel: 432-0469; fax: 432-2715. Apartments and studios with kitchenettes and shop on the complex. Reasonable

Mango Bay Hotel, Holetown, tel: 432-1384; fax: 432-5297. All-inclusive resort with white beach, two pools, restaurants, children's area. Deluxe

Sandpiper Inn, tel: 422-2251; fax: 422-1776. Small classy hotel, rooms with pool, garden or ocean view. Award-winning restaurant. Expensive–Deluxe

Sandy Lane Hotel and Golf Club, tel: 432-1311; fax: 432-2954. Exclusive resort with golf course, tennis and watersports. Deluxe

Tamarind Cove Hotel, Paynes Bay, tel: 432-1332; fax: 432-6317. Large luxury complex with several pools and award-winning restaurants and great white sandy beach. Part of the St James Beach Hotels group. Deluxe

Treasure Beach, Paynes Bay, tel: 432-1346; fax: 432-1094. Upmarket hotel in tropical gardens. Restaurant, pool and watersports. Deluxe

St Joseph

Atlantis Hotel, Bathsheba, tel: 433-9445. Family hotel in a dramatic setting. Accommodation quite basic. Wonderful cuisine. Inexpensive

Kingsley Club, Cattlewash, Bathsheba, tel: 433-9422; fax: 433-9226. Hotel on the rugged East coast. A multi-million dollar refurbishment planned. Reasonable

St Michael

Barbados Hilton Hotel, Needham's Point, tel: 426-0200; fax: 436-8946. Modern hotel in 14 acres of gardens and sandy beach. Tennis courts, watersports, conference facilities and excellent cuisine. Expensive

Grand Barbados Beach Resort, Aquatic Gap, tel: 426-0890; fax: 436-9823. Large modern block, rooms with balcony and TV. Pool, restaurant and conference facilities. Expensive

Sandals Barbados, Black Rock, tel: 424-0888. Luxury all-inclusive planned as part of the Sandals Caribbean hotel chain. Within walking distance of

Bridgetown. On the former site of the Paradise Village and Beach Club. Deluxe

St Peter

Cobbler's Cove Hotel, Road View, tel: 422-2291; fax: 422-1460. Small, friendly, luxurious and elegant hotel. Suites with ocean view or opening on to lush gardens. Excellent award-winning restaurant. White sandy beach, tennis and watersports. Deluxe

Almond Beach Village, tel: 422-4900; fax: 422-0617. Luxury all-inclusive on the former Heywoods Resort site. Set in 30 acres of tropical gardens. Excellent facilities including golf, tennis, watersports, pools, restaurants and bars. The Village has a sister resort 4 miles away in St James. Deluxe

St Philip

Crane Beach Hotel, Crane, tel: 423-6220; fax: 423-5343. Charming, traditional, elegantly decorated hotel. Five miles from the airport. Deluxe

Sam Lord's Castle, Long Bay, tel:423-7350; fax: 423-5918. Legend has it that the castle at the center of the resort was once owned by a pirate. Resort accommodation with pools, rooms and suites with balcony or patio. Large conference room and facilities. Deluxe

Villas

Villas and private houses range in size from one to six bedrooms. Some have tropical gardens, live-in staff and are on the beach; others offer privacy and convenience in modest surroundings. For families and small groups, villa rental can be surprisingly economical. Consult the Tourism Authority, your travel agent or an agency specializing in villa rentals:

Alleyne, Aguilar & Altman, Ltd., St James, tel: 432-0840; fax: 432-2147.

Bajan Services, Ltd., Gibbs, St Peter, tel: 422-2618; fax: 422-5366.

Realtors Limited, St James, tel: 432-6930; fax: 432-6919.

Ronald Stoute & Sons, Ltd., St Philip, tel: 423-6800; fax: 423-9935.

Hibiscus Holiday, tel: (800) 533-7732 (toll-free in the US); 426-3699.

Eating Out

What to Eat

Barbados has restaurants featuring everything from traditional Bajan cuisine to Chinese and Italian. National dishes to try include the delicious (and ubiquitous) flying fish, dolphin fish, red snapper, hot salt fish cakes, pickled breadfruit, cake-like conkies, and pepperpot – a stew so well-seasoned that it literally used to be passed down like an heirloom from generation to generation. As a rule Barbadian food is well seasoned and usually accompanied by rice, macaroni pie, plantain or ground provisions such as cassava and yam.

Barbados also has its share of fast food US-style: pizza, fried chicken, hamburgers of course, and a local specialty *roti* – a savory pocket of chicken, beef, shrimp or potato that originated with Trinidad's East Indian population.

Where to Eat

Some of the grander hotels and restaurants offer international cuisine prepared under the direction of European chefs. Try a homegrown talent, fried fish on a Friday evening at Oistins, or a Saturday night stroll down Baxter's Road, where numerous food stands exude exotic spices. A 10 percent service charge and a 5 percent tax supplement are usually added to the restaurant bill.

Christ Church

Boomers Restaurant & Lounge, St Lawrence Gap, tel: 428-8439. Casual dining, diverse menu including Bajan and American food.
Granny's, Oistins, tel: 428-3838. Steak fish, flying fish, peas and rice; some seating available, but mainly to take out. Also a branch at Freds Plaza, Spry Street, tel: 436-2727.
Ile de France, Settlers Beach, tel: 422-3245 or 422-3052. Relaxed, elegant French dining.

Josef's, St Lawrence Gap, Christ Church, tel: 435-6541; fax: 435-8586. European cuisine. Dinner, also lunch Monday through Friday.
Melting Pot, St Lawrence Main Road, tel: 428-3555. Simple, tasty Bajan food in typical Rum-Shop.
Pisces, St Lawrence Gap, tel: 435-6564. Seafood. Al fresco dining by the sea. Reservations recommended.
The Roti Hut, Worthing, tel: 435-7362. Roti, also chicken and chips.
The Witch Doctor, St Lawrence Gap, tel: 435-6581. Caribbean cuisine but with a touch of Africa.

St James

Bamboo Beach Bar, Paynes Bay, tel: 432-0910. Casual beachside bar and restaurant. Varied and informal menu.
Carambola Restaurant, Derricks. tel: 432-0832; fax: 432-6183. Veal, lamb, steak served at romantic clifftop tables by the sea.
The Coach House, Paynes Bay, tel: 432-1163. *Prix-fixe* dinners, local cuisine in British-style pub often with live music.
Colony Club, St James Beach, tel: 422-2335.
Coral Reef Club, St James Beach, tel: 422-2372. Seafood and beef.
The Fathoms, Paynes Bay, tel: 432-2568. Fish with Caribbean touch, excellent spot by the sea. Canyons bar upstairs.
The Mews, 2nd Street, Holetown, tel: 432-1122; fax: 432-1136. Superb seafood dishes prepared by an Austrian chef. Closed Sunday.
Neptunes Seafood Restaurant, Tamarind Cove Hotel, tel: 432-6999. Seafood with huge decorative aquarium.
The Palm Terrace, The Royal Pavilion Hotel, tel: 422-4444. Continental cuisine and ocean views. Reservations recommended.
Rose & Crown, Prospect, tel: 425-1074. Seafood and steaks.
Settler's Beach Hotel, tel: 422-3052. Tuesday night full Bajan buffet with cou-cou and suckling pig.
Treasure Beach, Paynes Bay, tel: 432-1346. Grand, award-winning, international restaurant.

St Joseph

Atlantis Hotel, Bathsheba, tel: 433-9445. Original West Indian dishes. Reservations essential for their renowned Sunday buffet.

Bonito Restaurant and Bar, Bathsheba, tel: 433-9034. Local specialties and spectacular views from the upstairs porch.

Bridgetown & St Michael

The Boatyard, Lower Bay Street, tel: 436-2622. Mediterranean and Caribbean cuisine. Reasonable prices, lively atmosphere. Views over Carlisle Bay.
Brown Sugar, Aquatic Gap, tel: 426-7684. Local Bajan and Caribbean specialties in a garden patio setting. Excellent buffet lunch Monday through Friday and Planter's lunch on Sunday.
The Rusty Pelican, upstairs at the Bridge House on the Careenage, tel: 436-7778. Seafood and artful appetizers often with live music.
Nelson's Arms, Galleria Mall, Broad Street, tel: 431-0602. Snacks and light lunches, with a fine view over Bridgetown's main street.
The Schooner, Grand Barbados Beach Resort, Carlisle Bay, tel: 426-0890. Lunch and dinner buffets on a restored pier. Also on the pier is the **Boardwalk Cafe**, tel: 426-4000.
The Waterfront Café, The Careenage, tel: 427-0093; fax: 431-0303. Bajan food with live music. Buffet on Tuesday. Closed Sunday.

St Peter

Cobbler's Cove Restaurant, Cobbler's Cove Hotel, tel: 422-2291. Excellent Caribbean and Continental cuisine. Elegant dining by the sea.
Almond Beach Village, tel: 422-4900. All-inclusive complex with a number of restaurants.
Mullins Beach Bar, Mullins Bay, tel: 422-1878. Italian-Continental-Bajan specialties. Relaxed atmosphere and very attractive beachside position.

St Philip

Crane Restaurant and Bar, Crane Beach Hotel, tel: 423-6220. Bajan and seafood dishes by candlelight.
Sam Lord's Castle, tel: 423-7350. Restaurants include **Sea Grille**, **Oceanus Cafe**, **The Wanderer Restaurant**. Reservations recommended.
Sunbury Plantation House, near Six Cross Roads, tel: 423-6270. Courtyard and Bar open 10am–4.30. Refurbished following a fire in 1995. Dinner can be served at a 200-year-old mahogany table, available only by advance reservation.

St Thomas

Bagatelle Great House, tel: 421-6767. International cuisine in romantic colonial-style atmosphere.

Fast Food

Chefette has branches in Bridgetown, Rockley, Oistins, St Michael, Holetown, Six Roads and many others. **KFC** restaurants have appeared in Bridgetown, Hastings, Collymore Rock, Black Rock and Speightstown.

Drinking Notes

Sugar may no longer be king on Barbados, but the island rum is certainly royalty among tropical drinks – and worth taking home. Mount Gay and Cockspur are two of the most popular brands, but don't forget the Doorley's. Falernum, a rum based syrup used in mixed drinks and cooking, is a Barbadian specialty. The local Banks Beer is considered by those who know to be among the best in the Caribbean and some say, the world.

Fresh fruit juices, a Caribbean staple, are available in any cafe or bar and from street vendors.

Attractions

Culture

Be sure to check daily newspapers, *SunSeeker* and the *Visitor* for special performances, concerts and exhibitions happening during your stay. The **National Cultural Foundation's Queen's Park Gallery** (tel: 427-2345) organizes monthly changing exhibitions. At the **Barbados Museum** (tel: 427-0201) there are changing displays of notable local and international work. Venues for dance and theatrical performances throughout the year are the Queen's Park Theater, the Steelshed, Combermere School Hall, the Barbados Museum, the Sherbourne Centre and the National Stadium. Bridgetown's handsome, Frank Collymore

Hall (tel: 436-9083/9084) hosts almost continuous events, from jazz festivals, to ballet, to theater.

A selection of arts and craft galleries are listed under Shopp*ing see* page 307.

Carnival capers

There are four major festivals on the Barbadian calendar. The largest and longest is **Crop Over**, a revival of the traditional celebration of the sugar cane harvest. This is the season for the Decorated Cart Parade, the Calypso Monarch Competition and numerous neighborhood parties, culminating on **Kadooment Day** with costumed revelry and parades from early morning until late at night. For more information, call the **National Cultural Foundation**, tel: 424-0909.

In February, the **Holetown Festival** commemorates the first settlers' landing in 1627. A week of special performances ends with a two-day street fair. The **Oistins Fish Festival** brings a carnival atmosphere to the small coast fishing village over the Easter weekend. Contests in fish boning and other skills test local prowess; stalls sell crafts and home cooked foods. The **National Independence Festival of Creative Arts**, (NIFCA), celebrates Barbadian Independence each November with competitions in dance, drama, song, paintings, writing and other art forms.

Touring the Island

Andromeda Botanic Gardens, St Joseph, tel: 433-9384. Cliffside rock gardens with hundreds of species of plants collected in Barbados and around the world. Open daily 9am–5pm BDS$11.50, children BDS$5.75.
The Animal Flower Cave, St Lucy, tel: 439-8797. A series of caves that are named for the sea anemones that live there. The cave, where the sea anemones can be found, is closed in rough weather, so call ahead. Adults BDS$4, children BDS$2. Open daily 9am–5pm.
Atlantis Submarine, The Wharf, Bridgetown, tel: 436-8929. An underwater trip to see reefs, sponge gardens and other marine life through the portholes. Reservations needed.
The Barbados Flower Forest, Rich-

mond, St Joseph, tel: 433-8152. Flowering trees and plants line a paved forest walk in the Scotland District. Open daily, adults BDS$13.80, children BDS$6.90.
The Barbados Museum and Historical Society, Garrison area, St Michael, tel: 427-0201; fax: 429-5946. Housed in a former military prison, the museum's collections include prints of West Indian life, archaeological finds, maps and a children's gallery. A cafe serves light meals. Open Monday through Saturday 9am–5pm, Sunday 2pm–6pm. Adults BDS$10, children half price.
The Barbados Wildlife Reserve, Farley Hill Wildlife Reserve, St Peter, tel: 422-8826. Project of the Barbados Primate Research Center; uncaged monkeys, otters, hares, raccoons, wallabies and other animals in natural settings. Open daily 10am–5pm. Adults BDS$20, children under 12 half price.
Cockspur Rum Distillery Tour, Brandons, St Michael, tel: 424-3701. Guided tours. Buffet tours available. Open Tuesday through Thursday 9am–4pm. BDS$10.
Francia Plantation, near Gun Hill Signal Station, St George, tel: 429-0474. Open to the public, Still a working plantation. Open Monday through Friday 10am–4pm, adults BDS$8, children half price.
Gun Hill Signal Station and the Lion, St George. A lion carved from one piece of rock; the station was once part of a chain that relayed messages. Good view of the southern part of the island, early evening best time to visit. Open daily 9am–5pm. Adults BDS$9.20, children BDS$4.60, children under 6 free.
Harrison's Cave, south end of the Welchman Hall Gully, St Thomas, tel: 438-6640. Tours of a beautiful limestone crystal cavern with clear streams and stalactites. The first tour is at 9am, the last tour begins at 4pm. Reservations recommended. Adults BDS$15, children BDS$7.50.
Morgan Lewis Mill, St Andrew, tel: 422-9222. Maintained by the National Trust, the working parts of this mill are still intact. Its design comes from the influence of Dutch Jews who came to Barbados via Brazil. Open daily 9am–5pm. Adults BDS$5, children BDS$2.
Mount Gay Rum Visitor's Center, Spring Garden Highway, Bridgetown, tel: 425-9066. Guided tours of the fa-

mous distillery with tasting. Luncheon tours available. Open Monday through Friday 9am–4pm. BDS$12.

Oughterson House and Barbados Zoo Park, St Philip, tel: 423-6203. A Georgian plantation house with rare birds, mammals, caymans, botanical garden and nature education center on the grounds of an historic sugarcane plantation. Open daily 9.30am– 4.30pm. Adults BDS$10, children 2–12 years old half price.

St Nicholas Abbey, St Peter, tel: 422-8725. Probably built prior to 1660, it is the oldest house in Barbados, and one of only two or three Jacobean plantation houses surviving in the Western Hemisphere. Open weekdays 10am– 4pm BDS$5, children under 12 free.

Sir Frank Hutson Sugar Machinery Museum, St James, tel: 432-1100. Route 2a across from the **Portvale Sugar Factory** (432-6748), the most modern in Barbados. Open Monday through Saturday, 9am–4pm. During harvesting (February–May), visitors can watch the modern production methods in progress.

Sunbury Plantation House, near Six Roads, St Philip, tel: 423-6270. An old plantation house in a beautiful setting dating from the 18th century. Elegant furniture. Almost destroyed by fire in 1995. Open 10am–5pm. Small restaurant and bar.

Tyrol Cot, St Michael, tel: 426-2421; 424-2074. Restored by the Barbados National Trust to create a heritage village around the house built in 1854 by William Farnum. In 1929 it became the home of Sir Grantley Adams, first Premier of Barbados. Open Monday to Friday 9am–5pm.

Welchman Hall Gully, St Thomas, tel: 438-6671. A miniature rain forest with caves, monkeys and rare trees; maintained by the National Trust. Open daily 9am–5pm. Adults BDS$12, children half price.

Heritage Passport holders are entitled to considerable reductions in admission prices to Barbados National Trust properties. The passes are available either from most ticket offices or the Barbados National Trust, 10th Avenue, Belleville, St Michael, tel: 426-2421. Full passport BDS$70 and Mini passport about BDS$36, up to two children under 12 years free when accompanied by a passport holder.

Nightlife

Barbados nights are for celebrating, whether you take a "round-the-island-with rum-and-calypso" cruise aboard the **Jolly Roger** or **Harbour Master**, marvel at fire-eaters performing at the **Plantation Restaurant**, or just cruise the late-night eateries. Dance to the beat of local artists and bands such as Gabby, Spice, Jade, Ivory, Private Eye, Syndicate, Kolorblynd and The Merrymen at a wide variety of nightclubs: the **Le Mirage** upstairs on the Careenage, **Harbour Lights** off Bay Street, the **Coach House** in St James, The **Ship Inn** in St Lawrence Gap and **The Boatyard** in Bay Street, to name just a few.

Almost all the resort hotels offer live entertainment, combined with dinner and dancing, including **Sam Lord's Castle**, **Glitter Bay**, the Hilton's **Flambeau Bar**, **The Colony Club**, the **Royal Pavilion** and the **Almond Beach** resort in St James, and **King's Beach** in St Peter.

Dinner shows in Barbados run the gamut from glitz to gala entertainment with superb dancers, cultural and historical content. Below are some of the most popular shows.

Tropical Spectacular, The Plantation Restaurant and Garden Theatre, St Lawrence Road, Christ Church, tel: 428-5048/2986. Admission price includes dinner, drinks and transportation to and from the venue. Reservations are required. Extravagant spectacle with fire-eaters, limbo dancers, steel band and Spice and Co. Wednesday, Thursday and Friday 6.30pm. Complete package BDS$105; drinks and show BDS$50.

1627 and All That, Sherbourne Centre, tel: 428-1627. Thursday. Includes free transportation, open bar, buffet dinner, pre-show minstrel and two-part folkloric show. Reservations recommended. Local and tourist rates.

Bajan Fiesta Night, Sam Lord's Castle, tel: 423-7350. Bajan buffet and dance show, every Monday.

Excursions

The following companies specialize in guided sightseeing and day trips in and around Barbados.

On Land

Barbados Activities Hub, tel: 431-2094. Cave Shepherd department store, ground floor.

L.E. Williams Tour Company, Ltd., Hastings, Christ Church, tel: 427-1043/427-6006.

International Tour Services, Monteray Hotel, St Lawrence Gap, tel: 428-4803.

West Indian International Tours, St Lawrence Gap, tel: 428-1490.

On Water

Bajan Queen Party Cruises, tel: 436-2149/50. Romantic evening cruise and a party atmosphere.

Blue Jay, tel: 437-7490. Charter power boat.

Harbour Master, tel: 430-0900; fax: 430-0901. Day and evening cruises on four decks. Local and tourist rates.

Irish Mist II, tel: 436-9201, 52 ft (17.5 meter) catamaran.

Jolly Roger Pirate Cruises, tel: 436-6424. Party cruises on a pirate ship.

Secret Love Cruises, tel: 432-1972. Romantic cruise on 41 ft (12 meter) yacht.

By Air

Bajan Helicopters, The Wharf, Bridgetown, tel: 431-0069. Helicopter tours.

Skytours, tel: 428-5010.

Island-hopping

There are a number of islands near Barbados that you may want to visit for one of more days, including Mustique, the Grenadines, St Vincent, St Lucia, Antigua, Martinique, Bequia and the Tobago Cays. They can be reached by air charter, scheduled airline service or guided tours.

LIAT (tel: 436-6225) offers special one day fares to a host of island destinations on scheduled flights.

Chartering a plane is a good solution if you are traveling with a small group, but it is not an inexpensive option. With a charter company such as **Trans Island Air** (tel: 428-1654; fax: 428-0946) or **Mustique Airways** (tel:

435-7009; fax: 435-6444), you decide where and when you want to go. Fees range from about BDS$800–$1000 plus per hour, for planes with maximum seating for either five or nine passengers. **Caribbean Safari Tours, Ltd.** (tel: 427-5100) and **Grenadine Tours** (tel: 435-8451), specialize in excursions to one or more islands. Costs are approximately BDS$550 for some of the full day trips, with drinks and lunch included. **Windward Lines** (tel: 431-0449/0937; fax: 431-0452). Principally a cargo shipping line, but the ships can accommodate passengers and cars travelling to St Lucia, St Vincent, Trinidad and Venezuela.

Shopping

What to Buy

Duty-free bargains such as cashmere sweaters, fashions by local designers, artworks and handicrafts: these are three focal points for shoppers in Barbados. Department stores like **Cave Shepherd** and **Harrison's** on Broad Street in Bridgetown feature everything from Liberty print fabric to Scandinavian silver and French perfume. For jewelry there are **Colombian Emeralds**, **Correia's**, **The Royal Shop** and **Louis Bayley**. Da Costa's Mall and Norman Center are the best enclosed malls. Smaller shops cluster along the west and south coastal roads and in the larger hotels – for example, the **Royal Pavilion Courtyard** in Porters, St James, or the **Emerald Boutique** at Glitter Bay.

Visitors shopping in Bridgetown are entitled to buy goods at duty free prices upon production of a passport. Spirits and other goods will be stored in the Customs Office at the airport and returned to you prior to departure.

Local designers fill the racks of two shops on The Wharf along the Careenage. **Origins** stocks Barbadian crafts and accessories as well as fashions by Diane Butcher. **Petticoat Lane Boutique** specializes in the flowing cotton and silk creations of Carol Cadogan. **Intransit** is a local line of stylish casual clothing available in a number of boutiques.

Handicrafts range from handwoven straw work to batik fabric, and smocked or embroidered children's dresses. Barbadian pottery retains a lingering Arawak Indian heritage combined with African and European influences. **Temple Yard** is the center where Rastafarians display their interesting leather work. The best known handicraft outlet in Barbados is **Pelican Village**, a sparse complex of buildings with pyramid roofs near the Princess Alice Bus stand and Bridgetown Port. Small shops in the center often house one artist, like Irica Edward's handsome basketry at **Roots and Grasses**. But there is also a large art gallery with changing exhibitions. Altogether, the village includes 30 shops, all types of crafts, and a comfortable open-air restaurant.

For general reading and hard-to-get editions of West Indian authors, the **Cloister Bookstore** is one of the best in the whole Caribbean region. **Cave Shepherd** also has a good selection.

Where to Buy

Art & Crafts

The shops and centers listed below specialize in fine arts and handicrafts made by Barbadians, sold exclusively or alongside work from other regions.
The Barbados Gift Shop, Sandy Lane Hotel, gifts all made locally.
Best of Barbados, 11 branches specializing the work of Jill Walker, as well as gifts and souvenirs. Head office and information, tel: 421-6900.
Chalky Mount Pottery, St Andrew, tel: 422-9613. Traditional pottery – hot from the kiln.
Chattelhouse Shopping Village, St Lawrence Gap, tel: 428-4289. Souvenirs and locally-produced crafts.
Coffee and Cream Gallery, St Lawrence Gap, tel: 428-2708. Combined restaurant and gallery. Paintings and jewelry produced by local artists. Closed Monday.

Earthworks Pottery, St Thomas, tel/fax: 425-0223. Next door to Potter's House Gallery, features the work of Goldie Spieler. Open Monday through Friday 9am–5pm, Saturday 9am–1pm.
Industrial Development Corporation (IDC), tel: 426-2494, sponsors Pride Craft Shops at The Emporium, Pelican Park; Pelican Village, Harbour Road; Carlisle Bay Centre; Sam Lord's Castle; Harrison's Cave; and Grantley Adams International Airport.
Medford Mahogany Craft Village, Lower Barabees Hills, St Michael, tel: 427-3179. Carved wooden sculptures and functional objects.
Origins, on the Wharf, Bridgetown, tel: 436-8522, Barbadian-made jewelry, accessories, and a small selection of paintings.
The Potter's House Gallery, Edgehill, St Thomas, tel: 425-0223. Showplace for Barbadian pottery, as well as batik and painted fabrics.

Outdoor Activities

Sport

An abundance of sports draws visitors to Barbados: golf, tennis, horseback riding, and the whole array of watersports from windsurfing and scuba diving to parasailing and deep sea fishing. Bajans themselves are sports-mad. Cricket is a kind of national religion. Eager spectators (and gamblers) flock to the Barbados Turf Club races at the Garrison Savannah in St Michael. A game of dominoes under the trees, road tennis – played with wooden paddles and goat racing on the beach: these local pastimes can be enjoyed as spectator or participant. The Barbados Board of Tourism provides information on competitive events like the 10K Run Barbados at the beginning of December (from the airport to Almond Beach Village), Barbados Open Independence Surfing Championship and the Barbados Open Golf Tournament.

Golf

Almond Beach Village, St Peter.
Club Rockley, Christ Church.
Sandy Lane Hotel Golf Club, St James.
Royal Westmoreland, St James.

Tennis

Casuarina Beach Club, Christ Church.
Ginger Bay Hotel and Beach Club, St Philip.
Almond Beach Village, St Peter.
Paragon Tennis Club, Brittons Hill, St Michael.
Club Rockley, Christ Church.
Sandy Lane Hotel Resort Hotel, St James.
Divi Southwinds, Christ Church.
Sunset Crest Club, St James.

Hiking

The Barbados National Trust, St Michael.
Highland Outdoor Tours, St Thomas.

Horseback Riding

Wilcox Riding Stables, Christ Church
Beau Geste Farm, St George.
Caribbean International Riding Center, St Andrew.
Brighton Stables, St Michael.

Squash

Barbados Squash Club, Christ Church.
Almond Beach Village, St Peter.
Club Rockley, Christ Church.

Polo

Barbados Polo Club, St James.

Water Skiing

Jolly Roger Water Sports, St James.
Willie's Water Sports, Paradise Beach Hotel, St Michael.

Scuba Diving & Snorkelling

Blue Reef Watersports, Royal Pavilion Hotel, St James.
Willie's Watersports, St James.

Sailing

Dive Boat Safari, Hilton Hotel, St Michael.
The Dive Shop, near Hotel Grand Barbados, St Michael.
Exploresub Barbados, St Lawrence Gap, Christ Church.
Willie's Water Sports, Paradise Beach Hotel, St Michael.

Sailing & Surfing

Willie's Water Sports, St James.
Watersports Centre, Hilton Hotel, St Michael.
Club Mistral, Christ Church.

Deep Sea Fishing

Blue Jay Charters, St James.
Barracuda Too, Christ Church.

Further Reading

History & Politics

Historic Houses of Barbados by Warren Alleyne. Bridgetown: Barbados National Trust.
Afro-Caribbean Women & Resistance to Slavery in Barbados by Hilary Beckles. London Karnak House, 1988.
Black Rebellion in Barbados: The Struggle Against Slavery, 1627-1838 by Hilary Beckles. Carib Research & Publications, 1987.
The Church in Barbados in the 17th Century by P.F. Campbell. Barbados Museum and Historical Society, 1982.
Women and Politics in Barbados, 1948-1981 by Neville C. Duncan. Institute of Social and Economic Research, University of the West Indies, 1983.
Plantation Slavery in Barbados by Jerome S. Handler. Harvard University Press, 1976.
Barbados: A History from Amerindians to Independence by F.A. Hoyos. London: Macmillan Caribbean.
Grantley Adams and the Social Revolution by F.A. Hoyos. London: Macmillan Caribbean.
Emancipation, Sugar and Federalism by Claude Levy. Gainesville University Press, 1980.
A True and Exact History of the Island of Barbados (1647) by Richard Ligon. London, Frank Cass & Co. Ltd., 1970.
History of Barbados: From the First Discovery of the Island in the Year 1605, Till the Accession of Lord Seaforth (1801) by John Poyen. London: Bibio Dist., 1971.
A History of Barbados. Ronald Tree. New York: Beekman; London: Fletcher and Son, 1972.
The Civilised Island of Barbados, A Social History 1750-1860 by K. Watson. Caribbean Graphics.

Natural History

The Geology and Mineral Resource Assessment of the Island of Barbados by Leslie H. Barker. Barbados Government Print Office, 1981.
Natural History of Barbados (1756) by Griffith Hughes. Ayer Co. Publishers, 1971.

Photography

A Barbados Journey by Roger LaBrucherie. Imágenes Press, 1979.
Images of Barbados by Roger LaBrucherie. California: Imágenes Press, 1979.

Sport

Sir Garfield Sobers by G. Bell. Nelson Caribbean.
West Indies Cricket Annual by Tony Cozier, (ed.). Barbados: Caribbean Communications, (published yearly).

Fiction & Poetry

Mother Poem by Edward Braithwaite. Oxford: New York: Oxford University Press, 1977.
Sun Poem; Braithwaite by Edward Braithwaite. Oxford; New York: Oxford University Press, 1982.
How Music Came to the Ainchan People by Timothy Callender. St Michael, Barbados, 1979.
Christopher by Geoffrey Drayton. London: Secker & Warburg, Collins, 1961.
Spoils of Eden by Robert Fowler. New York, Dodd Mead, 1985.
Man from the People by Lionel Hutchinson. London, Collins, 1969.
Black Madonna Poems by Tony Kellman. Bridgetown: 1975.
Saw The House in Half by Oliver Jackman. Washington, D.C. Howard University Press, 1974.
East Wind in Paradise by Carl Jackson. London, New Beacon Books Ltd., 1981.
The Emigrants by George Lamming. London: Allison & Busby, 1980.
In the Castle of My Skin by George Lamming. London, Schocken, 1983.
The Pleasure of Exile by George Lamming. London, Allison & Busby: Schocken, 1984.
The Pig-Sticking Season by Jonathan Small. Jamaica Poems, 1985, 1966.

General

Barbadian Society; Past and Present by Jean H. Callender. Cave Hill: Main Library, University of the West Indies (Barbados), 1981.

Barbadian Society, Past and Present by Jean H. Callender. Cave Hill: Main Library, University of the West Indies (Barbados), 1981.

Notes for a Glossary of Words and Phrases of Barbadian Dialect by Frank A. Collymore. Bridgetown 1955.

Quality of Life in Barbados by Graham Dann. Macmillan Caribbean, 1984.

Colonial Madness: Mental Health in the Barbadian Social Order by Lawrence E. Fisher. New Jersey: Rutgers University Press, 1985.

Facing the Challenge of Emancipation: A Study of the Ministry of William Hart Coleridge, First Bishop of Barbados, 1824–1842 by Sehon Goodridge. Bridgetown: Cedar Press, 1981.

Barbados, Our Island Home by F.A. Hoyos. London: Macmillan Caribbean.

Historic Churches of Barbados by Barbara Hill (ed. Henry Fraser), Bridgetown: Art Heritage Publishers, 1984.

East Wind in Paradise by Carl Jackson. London: New Beacon Books, 1981.

Barbados and America by David Kent. Arlington, Va.: CM Kent, 1980.

Barbados: A Smiling Island by Bruce G. Lynch. Brown Books, 1975.

Folk Songs of Barbados by Trevor Marshall. Barbados: Cedar Press, 1981.

The Economy of Barbados, 1946-1980 by DeLisle Worrell. Bridgetown: Central bank of Barbados, 1982.

Other Insight Guides

Among Apa Publications' main series of nearly 200 Insight Guides, destinations in this region include *Bahamas, Bermuda, Cuba, Jamaica, Puerto Rico,* and *Trinidad and Tobago.*

Discover the birthplace of calypso, steel drums and complex, cosmopolitan culture in *Insight Guide: Trinidad and Tobago.*

Insight Guide: Puerto Rico takes the adventurous visitor through the colourful streets of San Juan, into the richly populated waters of the Caribbean.

Insight Pocket Guides

Also available are companion volumes *Insight Pocket Guides: Jamaica, Bahamas and Puerto Rico.* These books feature the author's personal recommendations and are especially suitable for visitors with limited time to spare. A practical and easy-to-use pullout map smooths the way through the islands and sights.

Insight Pocket Guide: Bahamas shows visitors the best of the beaches and the most fertile seas along this archipelago of 700 islands.

Insight Compact Guides

Insight Compact Guides are handy mini encyclopedias which are both fact-packed and intensely practical, with text, pictures and maps all carefully cross-referenced. Titles in this series include Bahamas, Barbados, Dominican Republic and Jamaica.

Index

A
B
C
D
E
F
G
H

J
a
b
c
d
e
f
g
h
i

k
l

313

The World of Insight Guides

400 books in three complementary series cover every major destination in every continent.

Insight Guides

Alaska
Alsace
Amazon Wildlife
American Southwest
Amsterdam
Argentina
Atlanta
Athens
Australia
Austria
Bahamas
Bali
Baltic States
Bangkok
Barbados
Barcelona
Bay of Naples
Beijing
Belgium
Belize
Berlin
Bermuda
Boston
Brazil
Brittany
Brussels
Budapest
Buenos Aires
Burgundy
Burma (Myanmar)
Cairo
Calcutta
California
Canada
Caribbean
Catalonia
Channel Islands
Chicago
Chile
China
Cologne
Continental Europe
Corsica
Costa Rica
Crete
Crossing America
Cuba
Cyprus
Czech & Slovak Republics
Delhi, Jaipur, Agra
Denmark
Dresden
Dublin
Düsseldorf
East African Wildlife
East Asia
Eastern Europe
Ecuador
Edinburgh
Egypt
Finland
Florence
Florida
France
Frankfurt
French Riviera
Gambia & Senegal
Germany
Glasgow
Gran Canaria
Great Barrier Reef
Great Britain
Greece
Greek Islands
Hamburg
Hawaii
Hong Kong
Hungary
Iceland
India
India's Western Himalaya
Indian Wildlife
Indonesia
Ireland
Israel
Istanbul
Italy
Jamaica
Japan
Java
Jerusalem
Jordan
Kathmandu
Kenya
Korea
Lisbon
Loire Valley
London
Los Angeles
Madeira
Madrid
Malaysia
Mallorca & Ibiza
Malta
Marine Life in the South China Sea
Melbourne
Mexico
Mexico City
Miami
Montreal
Morocco
Moscow
Munich
Namibia
Native America
Nepal
Netherlands
New England
New Orleans
New York City
New York State
New Zealand
Nile
Normandy
Northern California
Northern Spain
Norway
Oman & the UAE
Oxford
Old South
Pacific Northwest
Pakistán
Paris
Peru
Philadelphia
Philippines
Poland
Portugal
Prague
Provence
Puerto Rico
Rajasthan
Rhine
Rio de Janeiro
Rockies
Rome
Russia
St Petersburg
San Francisco
Sardinia
Scotland
Seattle
Sicily
Singapore
South Africa
South America
South Asia
South India
South Tyrol
Southeast Asia
Southeast Asia Wildlife
Southern California
Southern Spain
Spain
Sri Lanka
Sweden
Switzerland
Sydney
Taiwan
Tenerife
Texas
Thailand
Tokyo
Trinidad & Tobago
Tunisia
Turkey
Turkish Coast
Tuscany
Umbria
US National Parks East
US National Parks West
Vancouver
Venezuela
Venice
Vienna
Vietnam
Wales
Washington DC
Waterways of Europe
Wild West
Yemen

Insight Pocket Guides

Aegean Islands★
Algarve★
Alsace
Amsterdam★
Athens★
Atlanta★
Bahamas★
Baja Peninsula★
Bali★
Bali Bird Walks
Bangkok★
Barbados★
Barcelona★
Bavaria★
Beijing★
Berlin★
Bermuda★
Bhutan★
Boston★
British Columbia★
Brittany★
Brussels★
Budapest & Surroundings★
Canton★
Chiang Mai★
Chicago★
Corsica★
Costa Blanca★
Costa Brava★
Costa del Sol/Marbella★
Costa Rica★
Crete★
Denmark★
Fiji★
Florence★
Florida★
Florida Keys★
French Riviera★
Gran Canaria★
Hawaii★
Hong Kong★
Hungary
Ibiza★
Ireland★
Ireland's Southwest★
Israel★
Istanbul★
Jakarta★
Jamaica★
Kathmandu Bikes & Hikes★
Kenya★
Kuala Lumpur★
Lisbon★
Loire Valley★
London★
Macau★
Madrid★
Malacca
Maldives
Mallorca★
Malta★
Mexico City★
Miami★
Milan★
Montreal★
Morocco★
Moscow
Munich★
Nepal★
New Delhi
New Orleans★
New York City★
New Zealand★
Northern California★
Oslo/Bergen★
Paris★
Penang★
Phuket★
Prague★
Provence★
Puerto Rico★
Quebec★
Rhodes★
Rome★
Sabah★
St Petersburg★
San Francisco★
Sardinia
Scotland★
Seville★
Seychelles★
Sicily★
Sikkim
Singapore★
Southeast England
Southern California★
Southern Spain★
Sri Lanka★
Sydney★
Tenerife★
Thailand★
Tibet★
Toronto★
Tunisia★
Turkish Coast★
Tuscany★
Venice★
Vienna★
Vietnam★
Yogyakarta
Yucatan Peninsula★

★ = Insight Pocket Guides with Pull out Maps

Insight Compact Guides

Algarve
Amsterdam
Bahamas
Bali
Bangkok
Barbados
Barcelona
Beijing
Belgium
Berlin
Brittany
Brussels
Budapest
Burgundy
Copenhagen
Costa Brava
Costa Rica
Crete
Cyprus
Czech Republic
Denmark
Dominican Republic
Dublin
Egypt
Finland
Florence
Gran Canaria
Greece
Holland
Hong Kong
Ireland
Israel
Italian Lakes
Italian Riviera
Jamaica
Jerusalem
Lisbon
Madeira
Mallorca
Malta
Milan
Moscow
Munich
Normandy
Norway
Paris
Poland
Portugal
Prague
Provence
Rhodes
Rome
St Petersburg
Salzburg
Singapore
Switzerland
Sydney
Tenerife
Thailand
Turkey
Turkish Coast
Tuscany

UK regional titles:
Bath & Surroundings
Cambridge & East Anglia
Cornwall
Cotswolds
Devon & Exmoor
Edinburgh
Lake District
London
New Forest
North York Moors
Northumbria
Oxford
Peak District
Scotland
Scottish Highlands
Shakespeare Country
Snowdonia
South Downs
York
Yorkshire Dales

USA regional titles:
Boston
Cape Cod
Chicago
Florida
Florida Keys
Hawaii: Maui
Hawaii: Oahu
Las Vegas
Los Angeles
Martha's Vineyard & Nantucket
New York
San Francisco
Washington D.C.
Venice
Vienna
West of Ireland